SPEAKING CANADIAN ENGLISH

OTHER BOOKS BY MARK M. ORKIN

Speaking Canadian French

Legal Ethics

The Law of Costs

SPEAKING CANADIAN ENGLISH

*An Informal Account
of the English Language
in Canada*

by
MARK M. ORKIN

GENERAL PUBLISHING COMPANY LIMITED
TORONTO

ISBN 0-7736-0014-0

Printed by W. & G. Baird Ltd in Northern Ireland

TO IRENE

They have been at a great feast of languages, and stolen the scraps.

LOVE'S LABOUR'S LOST

PREFACE

IN OFFERING THIS SECOND PART OF A STUDY OF CANADA'S TWO official languages, I am mindful of Samuel Johnson's observation that "no dictionary of a living tongue can ever be perfect." While the present work is not intended as a dictionary, the same reservation must still be made: the story of a living language is never done. The most one can hope for is to surmise how it began, try to describe what it is and predict what it may become.

As before, I am indebted to the precursors, both ancient and modern, whose work in the field of Canadian linguistics forms the armature of this book. The post-war scholars were no doubt correct in asserting that a definitive history of Canadian English could not yet be written: the data necessary to support such a study did not then exist. Indeed, it begins to seem as though such a work would always be premature and might already be too late, for the homogenizing of North American English is far advanced. *Faute de mieux*, what I have tried to do is set down in a non-technical way an account of the origins and development of the English language as it is actually spoken in Canada. Since such a report must finally be subjective, every reader is invited to check the validity of its conclusions against his own experience. And since the last word on Canadian English will, one sincerely hopes, never be spoken, I shall be grateful for comment and amplification.

CONTENTS

LIST OF ABBREVIATIONS

Am. American

Br. British

Can. Canadian

COD The Concise Oxford Dictionary

DA A Dictionary of Americanisms on Historical Principles

DAE Dictionary of American English

DC A Dictionary of Canadianisms

J.C.L.A. The Journal of the Canadian Linguistic Association (from the fall of 1961 published as *The Canadian Journal of Linguistics*)

NED The New English Dictionary (*The Oxford English Dictionary*)

SOED The Shorter Oxford English Dictionary

CHAPTER ONE

INTRODUCTION

I myself talk Ontario English; I don't admire it, but it's all I can do; anything is better than affectation.

STEPHEN LEACOCK

INTRODUCTION

ON FIRST ENCOUNTER, THE MOST UNUSUAL THING ABOUT THE language of English-speaking Canadians is that many speakers, when they are not merely being diffident, seem hardly aware of its existence. Whether this be considered a vice—a symptom of national myopia—or a virtue, depends upon one's point of view. Eric Partridge, an inveterate student of the English languages, appears to look on it with some approval. He writes:

> In Canada [the linguistic nationalist movement] is strong, not vocal, for it is hardly conscious: Canadians have a very distinctive variety of English, far more different from that spoken in Britain than is the English spoken by Australians; yet Canadians—so imperceptibly, so constantly has the process operated—'just get on with the job'; having this very different English, they therefore do not feel the need to have it at all.[1]

This lack of concern which most English-speaking Canadians show towards their daily speech contrasts sharply with the interest of a great many French-speaking Canadians in their own distinctive variety of French, which first attracted attention well before the end of the seventeenth century and has continued to inspire study and discussion ever since. A recent bibliography of

[1] *British and American English Since 1900*, London, 1951, p. 64.

3

writings on Canadian French from its beginnings to the present day by Gaston Dulong embraced more than a thousand entries;[1] the first extended compilation, that of Geddes and Rivard in 1906, numbered almost six hundred references.[2] On the other hand, a list of writings on Canadian English, had it been drawn up at the beginning of the century, would have contained no more than a handful of references, most of them fragmentary. By 1965, W. S. Avis was able to glean only 165 titles, 124 of them published since the end of the second world war.[3]

There are, of course, good reasons for this contrast, not the least important being the fact that while English has long been the dominant language of Canada, French is the language of a minority only, with the result that the study of Canadian French has often been as much a matter of ethnic and political self-assertion as it has been of linguistic research.[4] On the other hand, most English-speaking Canadians, secure in the belief that they are the recipients in full measure of the linguistic and political

[1] *Bibliographie linguistique du Canada français*, Québec, Paris, 1966.

[2] James Geddes, Jr., and Adjutor Rivard, *Bibliographie du parler français au Canada*, Paris, Québec, 1906.

[3] *A Bibliography of Writings on Canadian English (1857–1965)*, Toronto. 1965, The nineteenth century items of consequence are A. C. Geikie, "Canadian English," *The Canadian Journal*, 1857, pp. 344–355; W. D. Lighthall, "Canadian English," *The Week* (Toronto), August 16, 1889, pp. 581–583; A. F. Chamberlain, "Dialect Research in Canada," *Dialect Notes*, 1890, pp. 45–56; George Patterson, "Notes on the Dialect of the People of Newfoundland," *Journal of American Folklore*, 1895–1897, Vol. 8, pp. 27–40, Vol. 9, pp. 19–37, Vol. 10, pp. 203–213.

[4] The decennial census of 1961 shows the following classification of population by official language and mother tongue. Mother tongue here means "the language the person first learned in childhood and still understands."

Province	Total	Official language				Mother tongue		
		English only	French only	English and French	Neither English nor French	English	French	Other
Newfoundland . .	457,853	450,945	522	5,299	1,087	451,530	3,150	3,173
Prince Edward Is.	104,629	95,296	1,219	7,938	176	95,564	7,958	1,107
Nova Scotia. . . .	737,007	684,805	5,938	44,987	1,277	680,233	39,568	17,206
New Brunswick . .	597,936	370,922	112,054	113,495	1,465	378,633	210,530	8,773
Quebec	5,259,211	608,635	3,254,850	1,338,878	56,848	697,402	4,269,689	292,120
Ontario	6,236,092	5,548,766	95,236	493,270	98,820	4,834,623	425,302	976,167
Manitoba	921,686	825,955	7,954	68,368	19,409	584,526	60,899	276,261
Saskatchewan . . .	925,181	865,821	3,853	42,074	13,433	638,156	36,163	250,862
Alberta	1,331,944	1,253,824	5,534	56,920	15,666	962,319	42,276	327,349
British Columbia .	1,629,082	1,552,560	2,559	57,504	16,459	1,318,498	26,179	284,405
Yukon	14,628	13,679	38	825	86	10,869	443	3,316
Northwest Terr. . .	22,998	13,554	109	1,614	7,721	8,181	994	13,823
Canada	18,238,247	12,284,762	3,489,866	2,231,172	232,447	10,660,534	5,123,151	2,454,562

traditions of England, have never felt the same need for reassurance as their French-speaking compatriots. This belief, however, and the neglect of Canadian English which it helped to foster, are not easily justified, since from early times the speech of English Canada has in fact differed appreciably from British English, and particularly from the dialect of southern England, which, under the name of Received Standard English, has been accepted by most Englishmen and some others as "the best English." Indeed, Canadian English is probably farther from the parent stock than Indian, Australian or South African English, and in some ways as different as American English, with which it has more in common than any other member of the English-speaking family.

The greatest barrier to the investigation of Canadian English has always been a lack of scientific information. Until very recently, language study in Canada was a trackless waste into which none but a few brave pioneers had ventured and much of which even today remains unexplored. In 1890, Alexander F. Chamberlain complained, and with justice, that "towards the investigation, scientifically, of the spoken English of the Dominion little indeed has been done." [1] Almost sixty years later, Morton W. Bloomfield pessimistically echoed Chamberlain's sentiment, adding that not enough preliminary work had been done on the subject to make a full study of Canadian English possible.[2] M. H. Scargill was saying virtually the same thing in 1957. "A definitive history of the English language in Canada," he observed, "is yet to be written, and few scholars would attempt to write it at present. The vast amount of preliminary work necessary for such a history has not been done." [3]

Of all the reasons for this long neglect of the study of Canadian English, the foremost has undoubtedly been indifference. The average Canadian of today has progressed little beyond those Americans about whom it was written more than a century ago:

[1] "Dialect Research in Canada," *Dialect Notes*, 1890, p. 45.
[2] " Canadian English and Its Relation to 18th Century American Speech," *Journal of English and Germanic Philology*, 1948, pp. 59–67.
[3] "Sources of Canadian English," *Journal of English and Germanic Philology*, 1957, pp. 610–614.

"Many . . . even of the most learned class are not altogether conscious of any national peculiarities of speech; they may have a vague suspicion of their existence, but possess no accurate knowledge of their nature." [1] This attitude is well demonstrated by Canadian schools and universities which offer courses in many of the important living languages and some of the dead ones; yet the study of Canadian English as such nowhere appears on a school curriculum. "Our French Canadian colleagues have a culture and a language of their own," writes Scargill, "and they study them. Our many Slavic communities are advanced in the study of their own language in Canada. It is the English-speaking Canadians who lag behind, who do not consider their language worthy of study, who do not seem to know or care if they have a culture and a language to give expression to it." [2]

Before the middle of the nineteenth century, it scarcely seems to have occurred to anyone that the English language spoken in Canada might be deserving of attention or comment. Indeed, if Canada had any importance at all, it was not because of her cultural or intellectual attainments. John Lambert, whose *Travels Through Canada and the United States of North America, in the Years 1806, 1807 and 1808* was published in London in 1810, observed that the true state of Canada "seemed to be as little known to the people of England as the deserts of Siberia." Into these hyperborean regions there had ventured, it is true, a few men who brought back with them words until then unknown in England. One of the earliest was the geographer, Richard Hakluyt, who in 1584 wrote: "The Esquimawes of the Grande Bay, and amonge them of Canada, Saguynay, and Hochelaga . . . are subjecte to sharpe and nippinge winters, albeit their somers be hotter moche then oures." [3] To other travellers of the seventeenth and eighteenth

---

[1] Charles Astor Bristed, "The English Language in America," in *Cambridge Essays*, London, 1855. Bristed was an American, a grandson of John Jacob Astor and one of the earliest defenders of American English as a subject worthy of serious consideration.

[2] "Canadian English and Canadian Culture in Alberta," *Journal of the Canadian Linguistic Association*, March 1955, pp. 26–29.

[3] This citation and the dates and spelling of the next five words are taken from *A Dictionary of Canadianisms on Historical Principles*, Toronto, 1967. See also C. J. Lovell, "A Sampling of Materials for a Dictionary of Canadian English on Historical Principles," *J.C.L.A.*, 1958, pp. 7–33.

centuries, we owe *Barren Ground* (1691) for the tundras stretching east and west of Hudson Bay, *pemmican* in the spelling *pimmegan* (1743), *bluff* (1792), to signify a clump of trees, *muskeg*, spelled *muskake* (1775), and *baked-apple* (1775), the fruit of the cloudberry plant (*rubus chamaemorus*), also called *bakeapple*.

With the opening of the nineteenth century, a little light was shed on this darkness by a procession of visitors to the Canadas, who, in the fashion of travellers everywhere, hastened to set down their impressions in print.[1] The few travel books written by Americans or Continental Europeans saw the frontier scene with some detachment, as A. R. M. Lower has noted,[2] and lacked the supercilious tone of many of the English works, which were largely a catalogue of grievances and criticisms. If one may fairly judge from the latter, the early Canadians were an illiterate, money-grubbing, evil-smelling lot from the very beginning, English and French alike, and they did little, if anything, at least during the nineteenth century, to mend their untaught, unmannerly ways. Canada itself was looked upon as a sort of makeshift England, as unenlightened as it was remote, and wholly lacking in the *agréments* of the original.

The British traveller, when he thought about it at all, expected to find his own brand of English spoken in the Canadas, and was distressed by the prevalence of American words and speech habits. If these did not provoke the hostility and intolerance, sometimes amounting to downright vilification, which British observers have often reserved for Americanisms encountered on their native heath, they were at least greeted with a distinct sniff of disapproval.[3] As early as 1821, John Howison, in *Sketches of Upper Canada, Domestic, Local and Characteristic*, published at Edinburgh, had remarked of the settlers that "their object is to have a great

[1] A good introduction to these sightseers may be found in Gerald M. Craig, *Early Travellers in the Canadas, 1791–1867*, Toronto, 1955.

[2] *Canadians in the Making*, Toronto, 1958, p. 202.

[3] The major alarums and excursions in the long feud between England and America in matters of language, which began as early as 1735 and still continues, were traced with grim relish by H. L. Mencken in *The American Language*, New York, 4th ed., 1936, pp. 3–89. A one-volume edition of this monumental work appeared in 1963, edited and with new material by Raven I. McDavid, Jr., with the assistance of David W. Maurer.

deal of land under *improvement,* as they call it";[1] and an anonymous writer of the 1830's wrote disparagingly of "the mis-adoption of *would* for *should* by the Canadians in the American manner," and the use of *clear out* in the sense of go away.[2]

In 1839, Anna Jameson, an English expatriate and author of *Winter Studies or Summer Rambles in Canada,* also made use of the now familiar aside, "At Hamilton I hired a light *wagon,* as they call it."[3] In the same vein, the Honourable Amelia M. Murray wrote of her Canadian sojourn in *Letters from the United States, Cuba and Canada* (1856): "These farms are divided into what are called lots; each lot is one hundred acres."[4] One may note in passing that most of the words which these early travellers brought home with them were in fact of irreproachable British origin, although fallen into disuse in the land of their birth. Thus, *improvement* in the sense quoted is traced by the *Shorter Oxford English Dictionary* to 1473 and identified as obsolete except in United States dialect; *wagon* (or waggon) in this sense is traced by the same source to 1615 with the notation "now only colonial and U.S.";[5] and *lot* as here used to 1450 "now chiefly U.S." The *DC* traces its first Canadian use to 1750.

These scattered references would indicate that the earliest observers of Canadian English looked upon it as little more than an impure version of their mother tongue; nor was there any doubt in some minds about the nature and source of the impurities. "It is really melancholy," wrote Dr. Thomas Rolph, still another visiting Englishman, of his travels through Upper Canada in 1832–1833, "to traverse the province and go into many of the common schools; you will find a herd of children instructed by

[1] According to the *DC*, the term *under improvement* to denote land cleared of brush and ready for farming was in use as early as 1799.

[2] [Henry Cook Todd] *Notes upon Canada and the United States from 1832 to 1840,* Toronto, 2nd ed. 1840, pp. 8, 17. Mencken, *The American Language, Supplement 1,* New York, 1945, p. 53, recalls that *to clear out* was originally a nautical term, the *Dictionary of American English* tracing its first use in a non-nautical sense to 1792. The *DC* gives no Canadian citation.

[3] Craig, *Early Travellers,* p. 64.

[4] Craig, *Early Travellers,* p. 127.

[5] Almost any four-wheeled, horse-drawn vehicle may be called a *wagon* in North America; in England, the term is used only for a strong vehicle used in the transport of heavy goods.

some anti-British adventurer, instilling into the young and tender minds sentiments hostile to the parent state . . . and American spelling books, dictionaries and grammar, teaching them an anti-British dialect and idiom." [1]

Such was the view and thesis of the Reverend A. Constable Geikie, when, in a paper read before the Canadian Institute at Toronto in the year 1857, he used the expression "Canadian English" to characterize "a corrupt dialect growing up amongst our population, and gradually finding access to our periodical literature, until it threatens to produce a language as unlike our noble mother tongue as the negro patua, or the Chinese pidgeon English." [2] The "lawless and vulgar innovations" of this new speech Geikie divided into two groups, both of them in his opinion wholly bad. The first were what we would now call Americanisms: "words which are neither English in character, nor needed to supply any deficiency in the language; and even where peculiar circumstances may make such a coinage, or such perversion of the words from their primary significance pardonable, the circumstances are continually disregarded, and they are applied in cases where no such need exists, to the exclusion of the proper phrase, and to the injury of the language." These offenders, he pointed out in language which still finds its echo today in letters to the editor, "are imported by travellers, daily circulated by American newspapers, and eagerly incorporated into the language of our provincial press." Some of Geikie's examples of American encroachments were *guess* for think;[3] *betterments* for improvements to new land;[4] *lot* as a division of land with its congener *town lot; boss*, "the euphemism for the unpalatable word master;" [5] and

---

[1] J. G. Hodgins, *Documentary History of Education in Upper Canada*, Toronto, 1895, Vol. III, p. 3., quoted in H. F. Angus, *Canada and Her Great Neighbour*, Toronto, 1938, p. 88.

[2] "Canadian English," *The Canadian Journal*, 1857, pp. 344–355.

[3] *Guess*, in this sense, is called "Middle English only" by the *SOED*. It has been repeatedly castigated as an Americanism at least since 1814: H. L. Mencken, *The American Language*, 1936, pp. 22 *et seq.*

[4] The *DA* traces this use back to the Vermont State Papers of 1785.

[5] From the Dutch *baas*—master. If Geikie was reporting correctly, *boss* must have been a recent arrival in Canada. Henry Cook Todd in *Notes upon Canada and the United States from 1832 to 1840*, observed that in Canada servants "do not use the term *boss*, but in speaking of their employers designate them as mister and mistress" (p. 78). Washington Irving used *boss* in 1809. In the form *bass*, the *DA* dates it back to 1653.

store, "the invariable term for a shop." [1] It may be noted in passing that, apart from *betterments*, these words were still current in Canadian speech more than a hundred years later.

Worse than these, however, in Geikie's opinion, were the "new words . . . coined for ourselves by a process similar to that which calls them into being in the neighbouring States." If by this Geikie meant to imply Canadianisms, then many of his examples were wide of the mark, being in fact American borrowings. In this class, he included *donation* for a gift, which is *donated* at a *donation-meeting; loan* for lend;[2] *first-class* in the sense of able or great; *located* for situated; *considerable* for a good deal, and *considerable much* for very well; *rendition* applied alike to the delivery of a jury's verdict or the performance of a piece of music;[3] the use of *hung* for hanged as applied to felons; *posted-up* for well-informed;[4] and *fix* in the sense of mend. Geikie's particular scorn was saved for the lowly monosyllable *bug*, which is, although of English parentage, he remarked, universally avoided in the motherland. Yet there are those, he wrote, who would apply "this nauseous title to the beautiful firefly which makes our fields so glorious on a warm summer night. Canadians call it the 'lightning-bug'! Here, we have, not simply an abuse of language but a breach of good taste, which it might be thought no person of refinement could ever perpetrate." *Bug* has, of course, long been a standard term in England for the bed-bug (*cimex lectularius*), being one of those words like *bum* (a hobo in North America, but

[1] The *SOED* calls *store* "chiefly U.S. and colonial" and traces it to 1740. The plural designation "the stores" has been used in England since about 1852 to describe what North Americans would call a department store. In the sense of a retail shop, *store* is traced to 1764 by the *DC*.

[2] *Donation* in this sense is as old as 1577 according to the *SOED*. "Donate," writes H. W. Horwill in *A Dictionary of Modern American Usage*, Oxford, 1935, "is a word which in England is eschewed by good writers as a pretentious and magniloquent vulgarism. In America, on the other hand, it has acquired a place in the vocabulary of quite reputable terms." "The verb [*loan*] has been expelled from idiomatic southern English by *lend*," writes H. W. Fowler, "but was formerly current, and survives in U.S. and locally in U.K."

[3] The earliest example of the latter sense cited by the *SOED* is 1858, and by the *DA*, 1877.

[4] The *SOED* calls this "orig. U.S. colloq." and dates it 1847. It was good enough for Thackeray who wrote, "To . . . keep myself 'posted up' . . . with the literature of the day."

in England, the backside) whose usage differs often in a startling way on opposite sides of the Atlantic.[1]

Geikie regarded such departures from his concept of pure English with deepest disapproval, declaring that "our newspaper and other writers should abstain from the attempt to add new force to the English tongue by improving the language of Shakespeare, Bacon, Dryden and Addison." This determination to maintain in Canada the well of English undefiled harks back to certain English critics of the young American language of a century earlier, typified by Samuel Johnson's astringent review of an American book: "This treatise is written with such elegance as the subject admits, tho' not without some mixture of the American dialect, a tract of corruption to which every language widely diffused must always be exposed." [2]

The fact that Geikie, like Johnson before him, was trying to hold back the tide should not deny him credit for having single-handedly discovered Canadian English, even though he was against it. One may reject his thesis and disprove his lexicography, yet he deserves recognition as the first person to give any extended consideration to the state of the English language in Canada.

Despite Geikie's disapproval, a recognizable Canadian speech was beginning to be heard in the land, and it was not the English of England. According to two anonymous observers writing in 1862: "As every one knows, the tone of voice is very different between Americans and Englishmen, but it is also different between Canadians and Englishmen, the Canadians to a slight degree participating in the universal twang prevalent in the Northern States. From one's mode of speech one is soon discovered to be lately from England, whether travelling north or south of the St. Lawrence, and the occasional variations in the wording of a phrase often make known to another person the country of one's birth." [3]

---

[1] The *cockroach* (*blatta orientalis*), whose name is derived from the Spanish *cucaracha*, is in England commonly called *black-beetle*.

[2] *The Literary Magazine*, 1756. Johnson's review is used by Mencken as the starting point of his diatribe against English critics in *The American Language*, p. 4.

[3] *The United States and Canada as Seen by Two Brothers in 1858 and 1861*, London, 1862, quoted by Craig, *Early Travellers*, p. 251.

Not until 1889 was the cause taken up again by W. D. Lighthall in a magazine article which, although it made use of the same title, contained no mention of Geikie's paper. Quite clearly, Geikie's views still prevailed, however, and Lighthall lost no time in contradicting them. For the first time one may hear an authentic Canadian voice speaking without preconceptions about the actual state of Canadian English:

It would surprise the average British Canadian to hear it suggested that the language of his people presents any very distinctive features, so widespread are certain half-conscious notions that, excepting a few French, the language of the home-born people of our country is some very British and very un-American and practically uniform dialect, and that, although English, Scotch and Irish immigrants have individually imported their several variations, these never long remain without melting into that uniform dialect.

These general impressions, which were not long ago proclaimed unchallenged in the Dominion Parliament by a leading member, are not correct. Neither do our home-born people speak a uniform dialect at all; nor is a very British dialect general; nor is our speech even practically free from Americanisms; nor is the time near when some, at least, of the variants will disappear. It can be shown that there is a possibility of the English language itself withdrawing from more than half the area of the original Province; that what remains will be long diversified by traces of dialectic division; and that our daily speech is far more like that current in the United States than we suspect.[1]

A few observers had previously noted the profusion of races thronging the early Canadas, still marked with the speech and manners of their countries of origin and showing little inclination to coalesce. Thus, recalling the "greater uniformity of speech throughout the United States" which he laid chiefly to the use

[1] "Canadian English," *The Week* (Toronto) August 16, 1889, pp. 581-583. William Douw Lighthall was born at Hamilton, Ontario, in 1857 and educated at McGill University. A lawyer by profession, he also wrote verse and historical fiction. He was president of The Royal Society of Canada, 1917-1918, and survived until 1954.

of school books with written accents, a visiting clergyman, Isaac
Fidler, had observed in 1832: "In Canada we find all the dialects
of England in full force. There is not the same system of teaching
as in the States, nor the same extent of travelling. Yet I think it
quite probable that the Canadians will eventually lose the different
dialects, in the same manner as is felt in America, and perhaps by
similar means." [1]

More than a decade later the same phenomenon was noted by
John Robert Godley, one of the more sympathetic observers of
the nineteenth-century Canadian scene: "Everybody is a foreigner
here; and 'home' in their mouths invariably means another
country . . . one man addresses you in a rich Cork brogue, the
next in broad Scotch, and a third in undeniable Yorkshire: the
Yankee may be known by his broad-brimmed hat, lank figure
and nasal drawl; then you have the French Canadian, chattering
patois . . . the German . . . and the Italian . . . as easily distinguishable as at home." [2]

Lighthall, writing twenty-two years after Confederation, remarked on the resemblance of Canadian speech to that of the
United States. On the east coast, he recalled, had settled the
"Acadian Loyalists," largely from the New England states, whose
distinctive dialect, called in the Maritime Provinces *Bluenose*,
covered "nearly the whole of New Brunswick and the greater part
of Nova Scotia, outside of Halifax, where British garrisons have
strongly influenced the lower and society classes." By way of
authority, Lighthall invoked Thomas Chandler Haliburton (1796–
1865), born at Windsor, Nova Scotia, and author of *The Clockmaker, or The Sayings and Doings of Samuel Slick of Slickville* (1836).
According to Haliburton, "the accent of Bluenose is provincial,
inclining more to the Yankee than to English, his utterance rapid
and his conversation liberally garnished with dry humour."
Lighthall quotes as an example a passage from Haliburton's *The
Old Judge; or Life in a Colony* (1849):

"So you never see a pickinick, sir?"
"No, not here."

[1] *Observations on Professions, Literature, Manners, and Emigration, in the United States
and Canada, Made during a Residence There in 1832*, London, 1833, p. 339.
[2] *Letters from America*, London, 1844, quoted by Craig, *Early Travellers*, pp. 143–144.

"What, are you an entire stranger in these parts?"
"Yes."
"Lawful heart, you don't say so. So be I. I live to the
Millponds at Yarmouth where I am to home."
"Then perhaps you never see a 'bee,' sir?"
"No."
"Nor a 'raising'?" "No." "Nor a 'quilting'?" "No."
"Nor a 'husking'?" "No." "Nor a 'berrying'?" "No."
"Scissors and pins! Why you hain't seen nothing of our ways
yet . . . but here's John; he's generally allowed to be the
greatest hand at a 'role' in these clearings—the critter's so
strong. No it ain't John, neither! Creation! how vexed
he would be."

"This," adds Lighthall, "is obviously almost pure Yankee. It
must be left to local students to discover any differences."
Excepted from the Bluenose country were Cape Breton and
Pictou county, almost wholly settled by the descendants of Highlanders who arrived in the years following 1773, as well as by
disbanded Highland regiments, along with a few thousand
"Associated Loyalists" and a few "Acadian French." Lighthall
reported the characteristics of what he called Acadian Scotch as
follows:

(1) The s is often pronounced with the soft instead of the
hard sound, as in 'reserve,' pronounced somewhat as if
written 're-serve.' (2) The u is often pronounced as if y
preceded it, as in 'Jerusalem' which you will hear pronounced
'Jeryusalem' or as if h preceded, as in 'pursue' pronounced
somewhat as if written 'purshue.' (3) A common and most
characteristic turn of speech consists in the use of 'whatever,'
sometimes in the sense of 'at any rate,' as in the following
sentences: 'The crop is very good whatever.' 'Money may be
plentiful, but the times are bad, whatever.' (4) So, too, there
is a peculiar use of the word 'altogether' as meaning much
the same as 'very' or 'extremely;' 'He is a good preacher
altogether,' i.e., an eminently good preacher. (5) Among
the people of Highland descent we find many peculiarities
owing to the use of negatives in Gaelic idioms, which are

foreign to our English tongue, such as 'It is a long time since I did not see you.' (6) Among those whose knowledge of English is limited there is a great confusion in the use of pronouns. So marked and so common is this that it has given rise to the popular saying that a Highlander calls everything 'she' except his wife, who is always 'he.' The effect is sometimes ludicrous. (7) Again there is sometimes a singular transposition of prepositions. Thus a friend of mine inquired of a stranger whence he came. The answer was 'From Cape Breton over.' (8) Another expression often heard here among housewives is apt to strike a stranger oddly. Bread when heavy is said to be 'sad.'

Moving farther west, Lighthall found a dialect which he called Chateauguay Scotch dominating the English-speaking portions of three Quebec counties, Huntingdon, Chateauguay and Beauharnois, all lying south of the St. Lawrence River. As late as the 1880's, this dialect, although much weakened by Americanisms and school English, still showed definite characteristics which Lighthall catalogued in some detail:

The use of 'them' for adjective 'those'—almost universal in Canadian country districts; the mention of thick liquids, such as soup or porridge, in the plural, i.e., 'do you like them thick or thin?;' 'fur to' for infinitive 'to;' 'just like' nearly always used for 'like;' 'the blame is not all on the side of him;' 'The terrible bad condition of the roads;' 'to help replenish his pocket;' 'or neither did he indicate;' 'six foot of;' 'six load of;' 'porridge' in contrast to the neighbouring American 'mush,' 'oatmeal' or 'suppawn' (Dutch); 'daft,' 'dour,' 'fou,' 'canny,' 'poorly' (ill); 'ing-ins' (onions); 'gayrl' (girl); 'weemen' (women); 'near' (stingy); 'dighted' (silly).

In Ontario, Lighthall observed a Loyalist English markedly different from that of the Maritime Provinces, a difference which he attributed to three factors: more immigration, a better diffusion of education, and an original Loyalist population drawn from New York and the middle colonies, whereas Acadia had been settled from Massachusetts and the Eastern States. Among later influences, he noted that "in our large towns bodies of Irish immigrants have affected the pronunciation and phrases of the lower classes, while a similar effect is being produced upon the society class by English new comers." [1]

Lighthall was among the first to cast a linguistic eye westward. "What the effect of the *Prairie* and *Rocky Mountain country* may be," he wrote, "is still shrouded till we can make out its elements of immigration. The 'ranch,' [2] the 'blizzard,' [3] 'the Forks of the Red Deer' River,[4] 'tepee,' are already ours from across that border. 'Métis' [5] (half-breed), 'Nichi' (Indian),[6] and, I think 'coulée' [7] are peculiar, I believe, to our own West." In the same year, John McLean, a Methodist missionary writing out of "nine years spent among the Blood Indians of the Canadian North-West,"[8] reported a number of American expressions from beyond the Great Lakes: *broncho, canyon, cayuse, chapps, corral, lariat, mavrock* ("a calf which

[1] A. R. M. Lower in *Canadians in the Making*, Toronto, 1958, recalls that the Irish dominated Ontario for much of the nineteenth century; in 1851, there were 176,000 Irish in Upper Canada as against 82,000 English and 75,000 Scots.

[2] *Ranch* in the sense of a cattle farm or estate is no older than 1831 according to the *DA*, although it was used in 1808 to signify "a hut or house in the country." It derives from the Spanish-American *rancho*, a small farm.

[3] The *SOED* chivalrously says that *blizzard* is "orig. U.S.," dating it back to 1829, but the *DA* with equal generosity concedes that neither the word nor its most prevailing sense ("a violent storm of fine driving snow accompanied by intense cold") can be conclusively shown to have originated in America. The earliest Canadian citation in the *DC* is 1866.

[4] *Forks* is at least as old as 1645 according to the *DA*, and still going strong.

[5] The best that both the *SOED* and the *DA* can do for *métis* is 1839, but the *DC* traces it back to 1816. The *métis* or *metis* were of mixed Indian and white blood, their name being cognate with the Spanish-American *mestizo*, deriving ultimately from the late Latin *misticius* (L. *mixtus*), "mixed." The earliest French dialect form appears as *matives*, later *métifs*. The *métis* called themselves *gens libres*, "free people." By their neighbours, they were known under a variety of names including *Bois Brûlés* and *Metiss*, also *Métis of the Red River* and *Red River people* from the fact that large numbers of them settled in that region after 1818. They were also called the *People of the North* (Joseph Nicollet, *Report Intended to Illustrate a Map of the Hydrographical Basin of the Upper Mississippi River*, Washington, 1843, p. 49). Their name is not to be confused with the place name *Métis sur Mer*, Quebec, also known as *Métis* or *Mitis*, which is derived from the Micmac *mitisk*, meaning birch or aspen.

[6] *Nitchie*—a friend, in Indian parlance, especially when used of another Indian—is called obsolete by the *DC*, which traces it back to 1768-1782. However, C. J. Lovell, "A Sampling of Materials . . . etc.", cited above, garnered six Canadian quotations ranging from 1865 to 1956. The spellings include *nidge, neejee,* and *nee-chee*.

[7] The *DC* traces *coulee* ("the dry bed of a stream") to 1804, antedating by three years the *DA*'s earliest citation.

[8] *The Indians, Their Manners and Customs*, Toronto, 1889, pp. 197-201.

has lost its mother"),[1] *quirt* and *sombrero*, along with a smattering of French borrowings like *lodge* and *shanty*.

In the year following publication of Lighthall's article, Alexander F. Chamberlain, a young Englishman who had received his education in Canada, contributed a study entitled "Dialect Research in Canada" to the American periodical *Dialect Notes*.[2] Chamberlain's paper, while characterizing the work of Geikie and Lighthall as "rather general comments and sketches than attempts at scientific delineation," was in fact largely a re-working of their material. He agreed with Lighthall that several dialects of English were spoken in the Dominion, and that Ontario English in particular abounded in Americanisms, some going back to the original Loyalist settlers and others of more recent importation. He also indicated the need to study English dialect words brought over by immigrants and listed a number of examples heard in and around Peterborough during the '80s, among them *mollycoddle*, a fool,[3] *smike* as in "We haven't had a *smike* of rain down here all summer," and "Put your feet in your slippers. I don't like to see you *squaddling* about like that."

Chamberlain also collected some native Canadian terms which had sprung from the activities of political parties, among them *Orangist*, *Rielite*, *restrictionist* (an "advocate of protective tariff"), *political union* ("a less offensive term than annexation" to describe the absorption of Canada by the United States) and *sawoff*. In Manitoba, Chamberlain found areas where, because of immigration from Europe, "neither French nor English is the dominant tongue," while farther west was a peculiar dialect resembling that of the hunting and cattle-raising districts of the United States. He was also among the first to call attention to the English spoken

[1] Originally *maverick*, from Samuel A. Maverick, "a Texas cattle owner who neglected to brand the calves of a small herd he once owned" (*DA*, 1867), the word had by 1881 come to mean "a calf that is following no cow, and is unbranded." In the sense of "one who will not affiliate with a regular political party," the word is traced by the *DA* to 1886.

[2] 1890, p. 45. Chamberlain subsequently lived in the United States teaching at Clark until his death in 1914. He contributed a number of papers to various scientific journals on Indian words in American English and Canadian French.

[3] The *SOED* gives the meaning "one who coddles himself or is coddled; an effeminate man." *Molly*, a pet name for Mary, originally meant a milksop.

in the region of Hudson Bay, where colonists about Port Nelson were still using words and meanings which Henry Ellis had noted in 1748,[1] among them *frost-smoke*, "a thick black vapor, arising in winter," *quick-hatch*, the wolverine, and *juniper* as applied to the fir or larch.

Chamberlain deplored the fact that there had been little scientific investigation of the spoken English of Canada, but apart from six or seven fragmentary studies by as many hands over the next fifty years nothing else of consequence was attempted before the end of the second world war. Until then, the record of Canadian English study was a poor thing compared with the ferment of interest in the American language, which had been the subject of research and debate ever since the Revolutionary Wars,[2] or even with Australian or Austral English, which, first observed as early as 1826, has continued to inspire general studies.[3] In 1954, however, a group of scholars founded the Canadian Linguistic Association to promote "the scientific study . . . of the written and spoken language of Canada," and through its biannual *Journal* and annual meetings, the Association has provided a focal point for research on this and many other matters.[4] The most important fruits of this collaboration have been a series of dictionaries for use in Canadian schools, culminating in *A*

[1] Henry Ellis was Governor of Nova Scotia, 1761–1763. A hydrographer by profession, his *A Voyage to Hudson's Bay* appeared in 1748.

[2] A good account of the early writings may be found in M. M. Mathews, *The Beginnings of American English*, Chicago, 1931. The standard work is George Philip Krapp, *The English Language in America*, 2 vols., New York, 1925, which has been somewhat overshadowed by the more entertaining work of H. L. Mencken in *The American Language*, 4th ed., New York, 1936, and its two Supplements published in 1945 and 1948. Very useful recent studies are Margaret Nicholson, *A Dictionary of American-English Usage*, New York, 1958, based on H. W. Fowler's *Modern English Usage;* and Albert H. Marckwardt, *American English*, New York, 1958.

[3] *A Dictionary of Australasian Words*, containing more than seven hundred new words and new meanings of old words, new phrases, etc., which have entered the English language from Australia, Tasmania and New Zealand, was published as a supplement to the 1898 edition of Webster's *International Dictionary*. The earliest standard work is *Austral English* by Edward E. Morris, London, 1898, and the latest, Sidney J. Baker, *The Australian Language*, Sydney, 1945; and see J. A. W. Bennett, "English as It Is Spoken in New Zealand," *American Speech*, 1943, pp. 81–95.

[4] The president of the Association is Dr. Walter S. Avis, Royal Military College, Kingston, Ontario.

Dictionary of Canadianisms on Historical Principles.[1] No less important, however, was the fact that for the first time a scientific investigation of Canadian English was being conducted by many hands to establish not only historical background but current usage, without which no understanding of the English language in Canada would be possible.

---

[1] Toronto, 1967. Produced by the Lexicographical Centre for Canadian English, University of Victoria, in British Columbia, its avowed purpose was to provide "a historical record of words and expressions characteristic of the various spheres of Canadian life during the almost four centuries that English has been used in Canada." The editors defined a Canadianism as ". . . a word, expression or meaning which is natural to Canada or which is distinctly characteristic of Canadian usage though not necessarily exclusive to Canada; *Winnipeg couch* falls into the first category, *chesterfield* ('sofa') into the second." One of the interesting revelations of the *DC* has been the number of words for which the earliest Canadian citation antedates the earliest citation in the *DA* or the *DAE*. To some degree, this had been anticipated by the compilers of the *DAE* under Sir William Craigie, who gathered in a number of Canadian gleanings along with the great volume of American material, no distinction being made between the two sources. In presenting the *DC*, Walter S. Avis, the Editor-in-Chief, did not claim that a term common to both sides of the border should be called a Canadianism merely on the ground of priority of appearance in Canada. He offered a typically Canadian compromise: ". . . the problem of identifying many terms as specifically 'American' or 'Canadian' is virtually impossible of solution. . . . In view of the difficulty and, perhaps, pointlessness of trying to identify many words in common use on this continent as being 'American' or 'Canadian', lexicographers compiling dictionaries of the English used in North America might be well advised to adopt the label *North Americanism*."

CHAPTER TWO

HALLMARKS

Canada is a political expression. This must be borne in mind when we speak of Canadian literature.

GOLDWIN SMITH

HALLMARKS

1

DURING MOST OF ITS HISTORY, CANADIAN ENGLISH CONTINUED TO exhibit those characteristics which Lighthall had perceived in 1889: a marked and growing resemblance to American speech, a lack of uniformity and, particularly in the written language, a falling below "the standard of England's great literature." Lighthall's analysis, made long before there had been any scientific investigation of Canadian English, was a prescient one. He saw clearly that, despite the many legal, political and sentimental ties with England, and despite a marked national antipathy of long standing to the United States, the emergent Canadian language resembled American English far more than British English, and he correctly predicted that Canadian and American English would continue to grow even closer together.

The extent to which Americanisms had penetrated Canadian speech during the first half of the nineteenth century still remains to be investigated, but it was undoubtedly considerable. Among the terms which Geikie[1] denounced with some heat as being far too common in Canada were the following:

buggy	*on board*
caucus	*chisel*
dicker	*pants*
down town	*fixings*

[1] "Canadian English," *The Canadian Journal*, 1857, pp. 344–355.

limbs (legs)	*loafer*
location	*stump orator*
log-rolling	*make tracks*
notions	*trade*, v.

He also objected strongly to the widespread use of such "American" preterites as *chode, dolve, feeled, freezed* or *friz, guv, holp, riz* and *swole*. Yet many of these terms were so inseparably a part of Canadian English that by 1889 Lighthall was asking: "What Canadian, on reading a list of Americanisms like, say, that in 'Appleton's Cyclopaedia' will not feel surprise at his familiarity with the greater number?" [1] It is true, Lighthall noted, that "I guess," "I reckon" and "I calc'late" were seldom heard outside "Bluenosedom," as he dubbed the Maritime Provinces, and "real nice" and "wall now" not at all, while "orate," "placate" and "to suicide" had never taken root; yet the American influence was to be heard on every side.

Among American expressions which Lighthall observed in Canada were:

balance (remainder)	*horse-cars*
bluffing it off	*knickerbockers*
cars	*mean* (unkind)
check (railway)	*reliable*
clever (skilful)	*a rushing business*
dock (wharf)	*sidewalk*
dry-goods	*stoop* (threshold)
dry-goods clerk	*street-cars*
fall (autumn)	*ticket office*
hitch (a horse)	

He also noted such expressions as *Is that so? What's that?* (Br., *What do you say?*) and *He lives on State Street* (Br., *in State Street*). "There is no help for it," Lighthall concluded stoically, "we must admit that in this we have been annexed."

In the following year, A. F. Chamberlain noted that "owing to the frequency of contact and commercial intercourse with the United States, the English of the Province of Ontario abounds in

---

[1] "Canadian English," *The Week* (Toronto), August 16, 1889, pp. 581–583.

so-called Americanisms," some of which, he was careful to point out, were "due to the original settlers, and are not recent importations." [1] To Lighthall's word-list, he added as being current in Ontario during the decade 1880–1890:

boom	*punt*
buck-saw	*river-driver*
coal-oil	*saw-buck*
drive (logs)	*saw-horse*
gallynipper	*saw-log*
great big	*scow*
mud-scow	*smart*
pike-pole	*so-long*

By the first quarter of the present century, it was becoming generally recognized that Canadian English resembled American speech more than it did British. As Sir Robert A. Falconer, then president of the University of Toronto, observed in 1925: "All commentators agree that there is a distinctive Canadian speech throughout the Dominion although all have not agreed upon what it was. Whatever it may be, it has far closer affinities with the American language than with the speech of England." [2]

This is not to say that Canadian and American English are identical, although many writers have inclined more and more to equate them.[3] Thus in 1934, one observer, reporting on the general speech of Canadians living between Toronto and Kingston, described it as being "superficially indistinguishable from that of their neighbours on the other side of Lake Ontario." [4] The

[1] "Dialect Research in Canada," *Dialect Notes*, 1890, p. 45.

[2] *The United States as a Neighbour*, Cambridge, 1925, p. 203. Born at Charlottetown, Prince Edward Island, Falconer was president of the University of Toronto from 1907 to 1932.

[3] Rupert Brooke, who visited Canada briefly in 1913, observed: "It is the one distinction between the Canadian and American languages that Canadians tend to say 'bunch' but Americans 'crowd'." (*The Prose of Rupert Brooke*, ed. Christopher Hassall, London, 1956, p. 29).

[4] Evelyn R. Ahrend, "Ontario Speech," *American Speech*, 1934, pp. 136–139. The comparison of Canadian and American speech has provided a good exercise in simile. Thus Palmer, Martin and Blandford in their *Dictionary of English Pronunciation with American Variants* (Cambridge, 1926, p. xxvii) grouped the two dialects together as "facets of the same gem," an assumption for which Raven I. McDavid, Jr., took them sharply to task in his abridgement of *The American Language*, New York, 1963, pp. 468–470.

same view was expressed in more learned fashion a few years later by Martin Joos, who prefaced a detailed phonological study of Canadian speech with the observation that Ontario English differs from the neighbouring General American speech (for example, that of rural New York or Wisconsin) in only two items of any phonological consequence.[1] Such observations have not been confined to Ontario speech, for the conclusion that Canadian English as a whole must be regarded as no more than a variant of General American, and a not particularly striking one at that, was reached by Morley Ayearst in a brief comment in 1939.[2] Professor M. W. Bloomfield, the first of the post-war commentators, expressed the furthst limit of this view in forthright tones: "Canadian English, as has been recognized by some observers, is to all intents and purposes General American with a few modified sounds usually paralleled in American sub-dialects and with some vocabulary variation."[3]

The tendency to treat Canadian and American English as virtually the same has not wanted for more recent followers. "Canada," wrote Professor Mario Pei, "while forming a part of the British Empire, belongs linguistically to the American division of English."[4] Even Henry Alexander, the doyen of Canadian linguists, reported to the Royal Commission on National Development in the Arts, Letters and Sciences that "the speech of most Canadians belongs to a type of English that appears fairly consistently throughout the central portion of the North American continent."[5] In the same vein, Walter S. Avis observed in 1954

[1] "A Phonological Dilemma in Canadian English," *Language*, 1942, pp. 141–144. The two items are that the diphthongs *ow* and *ai* (as in *out* and *ride*) occur each with two variants, and *pod* and *pawed* are homophones. Raven I. McDavid, Jr., in his abridged edition of *The American Language* (New York, 1963, p. 470) notes that although both these features occur elsewhere in North America, it is only in Ontario and Western Canada that they occur together. Curiously, neither has yet been found in any dialect of the British Isles.

[2] "A Note on Canadian Speech," *American Speech*, October, 1939, pp. 231–233.

[3] "Canadian English and Its Relation to Eighteenth Century American Speech," *Journal of English and Germanic Philology*, 1948, pp. 59–67.

[4] *The Story of English*, Philadelphia, 1952. Professor Pei continued to equate Canadian and American English in *Language for Everybody*, New York, 1956.

[5] "The English Language in Canada," in *Royal Commission Studies, A Selection of Essays Prepared for the Royal Commission on National Development in the Arts, Letters and Sciences*, Ottawa, 1951, p. 13.

that "our present knowledge of Canadian English suggests that, by and large, Canada is an extension of the northern speech area of the United States." [1] More recently, M. H. Scargill has asserted that Canadian English does not differ from the other varieties of English in pronunciation, grammar or spelling, although he lays claim to some independence in vocabulary.[2] But even that claim has been called in question on the ground that almost half the terms which Scargill cited as distinctively Canadian—words like *outage* and *rampike*—"hardly seem central to everyday Canadian life." [3]

Although the weight of such informed opinion should not be lightly disregarded, more than a few Canadians will remain unconvinced that Canadian and American English are identical. The stock joke that a Canadian is a person who is mistaken for an American in Britain and for an Englishman in the United States appears wrong on both counts. A Canadian speaker when he is being himself undoubtedly sounds more like an American than he does an Englishman. Yet many a Canadian feels that the speech of Americans is as distinguishable from his own as that of Englishmen, and he is not flattered at being mistaken for either of them. Much of this view may be attributed to nationalism. In 1934, Evelyn Ahrend perceived that many Canadians "recognize that their speech is distinctive and are inclined to regard American speech habits disparagingly. Although occasional Britishisms are encountered... Canadians are no more fond of Southern British speech than they are of American." [4]

Although Canadian English has been called "a blend of British and American English," [5] one may postulate that the English language spoken in Canada exhibits enough differences in vocabulary, syntax and pronunciation to distinguish it from both American and British English. It has much in common with both these

[1] "Speech Differences Along the Ontario-United States Border: I, Vocabulary," *J.C.L.A.*, 1954, pp. 13–18.
[2] "Canadians Speak Canadian," *Saturday Night*, Dec. 8, 1956, pp. 16–18.
[3] Christopher Dean, "Is There a Literary Canadian English?" *American Speech*, 1963, pp. 278–282. The *DC* does not contain *outage*, but defines *rampike* as "a tall, dead tree, especially one that is blackened and branchless from being caught in a forest fire."
[4] "Ontario Speech," *American Speech*, 1934, pp. 136–139.
[5] Christopher Dean, "Is There a Literary Canadian English?" cited above.

English dialects, but it appears to be something more than a mixture of the two; and in this resides its claim to a distinctive name and more extended consideration than it has generally received. Canadian English, according to Avis, "is neither American nor British, but a complex different in many respects from both," and he goes on to qualify his earlier identification of Canada as an extension of the northern speech area of the United States by adding:

> A detailed survey of Canadian speech habits would probably reveal that a number of isoglosses run parallel to the political boundary, too few, perhaps, to set Canada completely apart from the northern variety of American (i.e., North American) English, but certainly enough to establish a speech area in many ways distinct from the principal area. The sum of these isoglosses, representing lexical, phonological, grammatical, syntactical and semantical differences would be equivalent to what is distinctly Canadian about the English language in North America. Needless to say, many of these linguistic features would be shared with English speakers elsewhere, for example in Great Britain and in non-northern speech areas of the United States.[1]

2

Many writers in the past have held the view that the English language spoken in the United States differs from the English of Great Britain in being almost wholly without dialectal variations. H. L. Mencken once boasted: "In place of the discordant local dialects of all the other major countries, including England, we have a general *Volkssprache* for the whole nation, and if it is conditioned at all it is only by minor differences in pronunciation and vocabulary, and by the linguistic struggles of various groups

---

[1] "Speech Differences Along the Ontario-United States Border: III, Pronunciation," *J.C.L.A.*, October, 1956, p. 55.

of newcomers. No other country can show such linguistic solidarity, nor any approach to it—not even Canada, for there a large minority of the population resists speaking English altogether." [1]

It has usually been considered, as Mencken's closing words indicate, that a similar standardization of language prevails throughout Canada, French speakers always excepted, but this is being disproved by *The Linguistic Atlas of the United States and Canada*, in the light of which all theories about North American speech must now be read. *The Atlas*, launched and carried on indefatigably since 1930 by Dr. Hans Kurath and his group of scholars, is the only systematic large-scale study of regional speech in the English-speaking world,[2] and although this great work is still far from complete, enough has been published to make clear that Mencken and others overstated the case for linguistic solidarity. The fact is that dialects are changing very slowly, despite the influence of radio, television, the movies and big cities. North American English turns out to be far from uniform, with considerable variation among communities and even among members of the same community.[3] So far as Canada is concerned, the *Linguistic Atlas* still remains to be written.[4] Yet the limited amount of field work already done, chiefly in the Maritime Provinces, indicates that far more variety exists in Canadian English than was formerly believed. Longer periods of exposure to education and the spread of mass communication have not yet succeeded in reducing the dialects of the early settlers to a common denominator.

These dialects were from the beginning one of the most noteworthy aspects of Canadian speech. We have already seen how,

---

[1] *The American Language*, 4th ed., New York, 1936, p. 90.

[2] R. I. McDavid, Jr., "Linguistic Geography in Canada: An Introduction," *J.C.L.A.*, 1954, pp. 3–8. *The Atlas* and its lasting value are assessed by Dr. McDavid who refutes its critics in "The Second Round in Dialectology of North American English," *J.C.L.A.*, 1960, pp. 108–114.

[3] Henry Alexander, "Linguistic Geography," *Queen's Quarterly*, 1940, pp. 38–47.

[4] For a progress report on the *Linguistic Atlas* in Canada down to 1954, see R. I. McDavid, Jr.: "Linguistic Geography in Canada: An Introduction," *J.C.L.A.*, October, 1954, pp. 3–8. This résumé may be brought up to date by consulting the annual reports on the *Atlas* appearing in *The Publications of the American Dialect Society* as well as the *Journal* of the Canadian Linguistic Association published bi-annually since 1954.

as early as 1832, Isaac Fidler found many of the dialects of England flourishing in Canada, and in 1844, John Robert Godley recalling his travels in Upper Canada described "the exceedingly heterogeneous and exotic character of its population," which included Irish, Scots, Yorkshire, Yankee, French, German and Italian elements, to which a later observer added Dutch and Pennsylvania German.[1] Although all commentators foresaw a growing uniformity, the levelling out of the dialects was long delayed, in large part by the mass immigration preceding the first world war when the opening of the West to settlers from Europe duplicated conditions which Godley had found in Upper Canada more than half a century earlier. F. E. L. Priestley has pointed out impressionistically that a traveller crossing the continent as recently as 1920 "would have noted characteristic speech only as far west as the Great Lakes; he would have recognized in the Highland districts of Cape Breton Island and the Nova Scotia mainland the familiar pronunciation, intonation, and turn of phrase of the Gael speaking English as a second language; elsewhere in the Maritimes he would have observed a largely uniform style of speech, not harsh but unmistakable in its vowels and consonants . . . ; in Ontario he would have found a somewhat harsher and flatter speech, closer in pronunciation to American, but, in the fact, close only to the speech of upper New York (and not identical with it); by listening closely, he would have detected differences from American in intonation and sentence pitch, and perhaps lesser differences in vocabulary." West of Winnipeg our traveller would have encountered a bewildering variety of tongues in towns "where English, if spoken at all, had to work its way through a thick accent, which might be Ukrainian, German, Esthonian, Finnish, Norwegian, Swedish or Czech." In fine, "the only mark of Canadian English west of Winnipeg was its heterogeneity."[2]

This lack of uniformity is by no means confined to pronunciation, as may be illustrated by the wide variety of terms used in different parts of the continent to denote the same things. Thus a

[1] A. F. Chamberlain, "Dialect Research in Canada," *Dialect Notes*, 1890, p. 45.
[2] In Eric Partridge, *British and American English Since 1900*, London, 1951, pp. 74–75.

New Englander might describe a *seesaw* as a *teeter, teeter-board, teenter, tinter, teetle, tilt, tilter* or *tilter board*, not to mention a *dandle, dandle-board* or *tippety-bounce*. In Nova Scotia, in addition to most of the New England terms one can also hear *tippin board* and *sawman*.[1] On the other hand, the term most favoured in Ontario, *teeter-totter*, is rarely used in either Nova Scotia or New England.[2]

A word which has received a generous share of attention from linguists is *shivaree*, derived from the French *charivari* and used to describe the ribald and sometimes riotous celebration staged by friends of a newly-married couple. The *DC* traces it back to 1827, and both the word and its many variants are still said to be common to all of Canada and much of the United States excepting the eastern seaboard and parts of the South.[3] Depending on the district, it may also be called a *callathumpin, celebration, rouser, saluting, serenade, tin-panning* and *tin-pan shower*. To these, the *DA* adds *belling* in Western Pennsylvania, *horning* in Rhode Island and *skimmelton* in the Hudson Valley. With the exception of the last three, most of these terms may also be heard in Nova Scotia, although the practice itself is said to be dying out.[4]

Still another expression which illustrates the wide variation to be found in North American speech is *angleworm*, its most common New England synonyms being *angledog, angler, dirtworm, eelworm, muckworm, nightcrawler, nightprowler, nightwalker* and *rainworm*. None of these terms would ever be used by an Ontario angler except, rarely, *nightcrawler*, the word in most common use being *dew-worm* or just plain *worm*.[5]

Much of this linguistic variety is attributable to the survival

[1] Henry Alexander, *The Story of Our Language*, Toronto, 1940, pp. 223-224; H. Kurath, "New England Words for the Seesaw," *American Speech*, April, 1933, pp. 14-18.

[2] *American Speech*, December, 1949, p. 251.

[3] The literature on *shivaree* is extensive. See Henry Alexander, *The Story of Our Language*, p. 224; M. H. Hanley, "Serenade in New England," *American Speech*, April, 1933, pp. 24-26; R. I. McDavid, Jr., "Shivaree: An Example of Cultural Diffusion," *American Speech*, 1949, pp. 49-55. The *DC* gives the latest Canadian citation as 1962.

[4] Henry Alexander, *The Story of Our Language*, cited above.

[5] W. S. Avis, "Speech Differences Along the Ontario-United States Border: I, Vocabulary," *J.C.L.A.*, October, 1954, pp. 13-18. Less than 3 per cent of the speakers questioned by Avis used *nightcrawler*.

of older English forms of pronunciation and vocabulary, a phenomenon well illustrated throughout the Maritimes, where Professor Henry Alexander in carrying out his investigations for the *Linguistic Atlas* reported the frequent occurrence around 1940 of *deef* for deaf, *fortnit* for fortnight, and *weskit* for waistcoat.[1] In Nova Scotia, cuffs are often called *wristbands*, pronounced *rizbans*, the form Mrs. still appears as *mistress*, particularly when the speaker's background is Scottish and the upper part of the house is sometimes referred to as the *chamber*. Many everyday objects in other areas may be described in a variety of ways. Thus along the "Middle Border" from Fort William, Ontario, to Estevan, Saskatchewan, the common American term *setting hen* appears as *hatching hen*, or *hatcher;* and *piggery* or *pig-stable* are the usual words for *pig-pen* or *pigsty*.[2] In rural Alberta, M. H. Scargill found that horses and cattle are said to graze variously in the *meadow*, the *pasture* or the *lease;* chickens may be kept in a *chicken-coop*, *henhouse* or *chicken-yard*, and pigs in a *colony-house*, *pig-pen*, *hog-pen* or just plain *sty*.[3] The person who looks after them might be a *hired man*, *flunky*, *chore-boy* or *labourer*, who starts his day at *sunrise*, *daybreak*, *dawn* or, on occasion, *sun up*. Many rural terms common elsewhere are unknown in Alberta; the "bookish" *gee* and *haw*, observes Scargill, are rarely used when giving directions to a horse, and instead of *summer fallow*, Alberta farmers prefer to talk about *idle land*, *breaking* or *back setting*. The same lack of uniformity is found in the cities where the noon meal may be either *lunch* or *dinner*, an Alberta housewife may either *fix* the table, *set* the table, or *lay* the table, while the fat from roasting meat may be called, in descending order of frequency, *grease*, *lard*, *dripping*, *fat*, *tallow*, *suet* or *gristle*.

The sheer size of Canada has given rise to an extensive vocabulary of topographical terms. In 1886, W. F. Ganong listed a number of unusual words in use by the people of New Brunswick, among them *aboideau*, a dike or dam, *barachois*, a lagoon at the

---

[1] "Linguistic Geography," *Queen's Quarterly*, 1940, pp. 38–47.

[2] H. B. Allen, "Canadian American Speech Differences Along the Middle Border," *J.C.L.A.*, 1959, pp. 17–24. Fort William is now Thunder Bay.

[3] "A Pilot Study of Alberta Speech: Vocabulary," *J.C.L.A.*, October, 1954, pp. 21–22.

mouth of a river, *bedoo* or *pudoo*, a branch without outlet of a stream, *bogan*, a marshy cove, *horseback*, a narrow gravel ridge, *intervale*, the alluvial flats beside a river, *tickle*, a narrow passage between island and shore, and *thrum* or *thrum-cap*, a detached mass of rock near a high shore.[1]

To these, C. J. Lovell has added a number of terms not all exclusively Canadian but interesting for their variety, among them *alkali flat, Barren Grounds, buffalo wallow, caribou bog, coteau, divide, draw, droke, esker, gumbo, hoodoo, knap, mamelle, muskeg, oak opening, pocalogan, poplar bluff, prairie* and its many congeners, *sandhill, sault* and *tamarack swamp*. Canadian weather has also spawned and borrowed a great diversity of terms, among those listed by Lovell being *anchor ice, barber, black blizzard, blizzardous, breakup, dry farming, duster, frazil, freezeup, frost boil, glitter, gullywasher, Manitoba wave, road ban, robin storm, silver thaw, slob, smelt storm, snow shed* and *squaw winter.*[2]

3

A third characteristic of Canadian English, which is to some extent bound up with the first two, is that in the beginning it tended to fall short of the high standards which characterize the best written English. For this there was good reason. The English-speaking peoples who settled Canada—Loyalists from the United States, Scotsmen, Englishmen and later Irishmen—although they counted some educated and cultured men among them, were in great measure of limited education and attainments, and the language which they spoke reflected their humble origins. It is true that many of the early travellers vastly overstated Canadian shortcomings. "The British or American settlers in the back townships," John Lambert observed sourly in the first decade of the

---

[1] "A Monograph of the Place-Nomenclature of the Province of New Brunswick," *Royal Society of Canada, Proceedings and Transactions*, 1896, 2nd ser. Vol. II, pp. 125–289.
[2] "Whys and Hows of Collecting for the Dictionary of Canadian English—I, Scope and Source Material," *J.C.L.A.*, October, 1955, pp. 5–8.

nineteenth century, "teach their own children the common rudi-
ments of education; but the Canadians are themselves uneducated,
and ignorant even of the smallest degree of learning; therefore
they have it not in their power to supply the want of a school in
their own family, and thus do they propagate from age to age the
ignorance of their ancestors." [1] Lambert noted that the general
deficiency in education among the great body of the people had
been the subject of much newspaper comment, and he felt that this
was largely caused "by their own parsimonious frugality" in refusing
to spend a sufficient amount on the education of their children.

This attitude was carried to an impossible extreme by John M.
Duncan, a young Glaswegian with a firm no-nonsense, no-popery
outlook who visited Montreal in 1818–1819. "We cannot expect,"
he remarked airily of the English-speaking community, "that the
demand for books here can be at all equal to that of home, or even
the United States; among the great majority of the Canadians
none but a few of the females are able to read." [2] Such generally
was the view which visitors took of the Canadas. As late as 1856,
Isabella (Bird) Bishop, yet another English expatriate *in partibus
infidelium*, wrote sadly:

> At present few people, comparatively speaking, are more
> than half educated. The knowledge of this fact lowers the
> tone of the press, and circumscribes both authors and
> speakers, as any allusions to history or general literature
> would be very imperfectly, if at all, understood . . . Canada
> as yet possesses no literature of her own, and the literary man
> is surrounded by difficulties. Independently of the heavy
> task of addressing himself to uneducated minds, unable to
> appreciate depth of thought and beauty of language, it is
> not likely that, where the absorbing passion is the acquisition
> of wealth, much encouragement would be given to the
> struggles of native talent. [3]

[1] *Travels Through Canada and the United States of North America, in the Years 1806,
1807 and 1808*, 3rd ed., London, 1816, cited by Gerald M. Craig, *Early Travellers in the
Canadas, 1791–1867*, Toronto, 1953, p. 32.

[2] *Travels Through Part of the United States and Canada in 1818 and 1819*, Glasgow, 1823,
cited by Craig, pp. 57–58.

[3] *The English Woman in America*, London, 1856, cited by Craig, pp. 216–217.

If here and there amid this chorus of gloom a friendly voice was raised on behalf of Canada, it rarely came from the mother country. Thus Michael Smith, a Baptist minister from Pennsylvania, managed to form quite a favourable impression of Ontario, and his travel notes under the title *A Geographical View of the Province of Upper Canada, and Promiscuous Remarks upon the Government* (1813) were widely read in the United States. "The greater part of the inhabitants of Canada," he wrote, "are not well-educated, for as they were poor when they came to the Province, and the country being but thinly settled for a number of years, they had but little chance for the benefit of schools, but, since the country has become more settled, and the inhabitants rich, or in a good way of living, which is almost universally the case, they pay considerable attention to learning." [1]

It seems safe to conclude that the picture was generally overdrawn. Sir William Craigie, commenting on the sarcastic retort to critics of American English that the first English colonists "unhappily could bring over no English better than Shakespeare's," has pointed out that those who settle a new colony never carry with them the whole of their mother tongue, but only "the stock of words regularly employed in speaking of the affairs of everyday life." [2] This will be expanded according to "the literary tastes and abilities of those who write in the new surroundings," and until they have developed a literature comparable to that of the mother country, they will "have neither reason nor scope to avail themselves of the full vocabulary which has already been created, or is in the process of creation, among their kinsmen at home."

The development of an adequate Canadian literature has been slow. It is true that as long ago as 1836, with the publication of Thomas Chandler Haliburton's *The Clockmaker; or, The Sayings and Doings of Samuel Slick of Slickville*, a native Canadian author

---

[1] Cited by Craig, p. 39.
[2] "The Study of English," *Society for Pure English, Tract No. XXVII*, 1927, pp. 199–200.

gained international repute,[1] but very few literary works of the nineteenth century have survived, among them *Wacousta* (1832) by John Richardson and William Kirby's *The Golden Dog* (1877). The humble origins of the early settlers, the slow growth of educational facilities, the lack of big cities and their attendant cultural advantages, all these concurred to retard the development of a national literature and a sharing to the full in the evolution of the English language.[2]

Edward H. Dewart put the case for early Canadian letters in his *Selections from the Canadian Poets* (1864): "Our colonial position, whatever may be its political advantages, is not favourable to the growth of an indigenous literature. Not only are our mental wants supplied by the brain of the Mother Country, under circumstances that utterly preclude competition; but the majority of persons of taste and education in Canada are emigrants from the Old Country, whose tenderest affections cling around the land they have left." It was a view shared by many observers of the Canadian literary scene,[3] and we have little reason to doubt its substantial accuracy, although even as Dewart wrote the colonial tutelage was coming to an end. With Charles G. D. Roberts, whose first book *Orion and Other Poems* appeared in 1880, and the school of writers which followed Confederation, the voice of a new nation began to be heard. And if the first words were reminiscent of English models, its later utterances breathed a sturdier spirit of independence. The fact remains that Canada in the nineteenth century was still largely a frontier society, and Dewart's "persons of taste and education" found little to sustain

---

[1] *The Clockmaker* is largely a collection of dialect stories of the American frontier, Sam Slick himself being an itinerant New Englander. The book throws some light on Canadian English of the colonial period. See Elna Bengtsson, *The Language and Vocabulary of Sam Slick*, Uppsala, 1956; W. S. Avis, *"Darn* in the Clockmaker," *American Speech*, 1951, pp. 302–303.

[2] In *Canadians in the Making* (1958), Professor A. R. M. Lower recalls that in the year 1871, although Canada boasted a population of 3,500,000 people, only some 400,000 or 12 per cent were to be found in the cities and towns; indeed only twenty places in the whole country had a population of more than 5,000.

[3] Thus Sir John G. Bourinot in *The Intellectual Development of the Canadian People*, 1881, p. 116: "Striking originality can hardly be developed to any great extent in a dependency which naturally, and perhaps wisely in some cases, looks for all its traditions and habits of thought to a parent state."

them in the wilderness. The same lack of cultural interests which had roused Samuel Butler in 1875 to cry out "O God! O Montreal!" moved Archibald Lampman to a darker despair: "How utterly destitute of all light and charm are the intellectual conditions of our people and the institutions of our public life! How barren! How barbarous!" [1]

The cultural evolution of Canada still remains to be adequately surveyed, as does the development of her standards of written and spoken language. Eric Partridge, a New Zealander by birth, in drawing the distinction between the speech and writing of Commonwealth countries and that of England has noted that "the alembicated, the etiolate, the highly elaborate are seldom present in the writings and almost entirely absent from the speech of the Dominions." [2] A less abstruse view was taken by Christopher Dean in examining the written language as it exists today in Canada at the literary level.[3] His analysis of some 154 pages of modern Canadian short stories revealed that although 52 words and constructions would strike a British reader as non-British, 40 of them were common in American usage, 10 were "undetermined" and only 2 were Canadian. Dean's conclusion—"that there is no distinctive type of Canadian literary English which would be recognized by everyone"—seems unexceptionable despite the limited field of his survey, as does his surmise that Canadian writing strikes American readers by its Britishisms. What is needed is a qualitative analysis of Canadian writing to establish the extent to which Canadian letters have fulfilled Sir William Craigie's thesis and belied the gloomy verdict of earlier British observers.

[1] The Toronto *Globe*, February 27, 1892.

[2] *British and American English Since 1900*, London, 1951, p. 69.

[3] "Is There a Distinctive Literary Canadian English?" *American Speech*, 1963, pp. 278–282.

CHAPTER THREE

THE ORIGINS OF CANADIAN ENGLISH

Language is a city, to the building of which every human being brought a stone.

EMERSON

THE ORIGINS OF CANADIAN ENGLISH

IF CANADIAN ENGLISH IS BOTH LIKE AND UNLIKE GENERAL
American, it also resembles and differs from British English, in
particular the dialect of southern England called Received
Standard English. There has been a good deal of discussion about
why this should be so, most of it with little basis in fact, for it was
not until recently that an appreciable body of information about
Canadian English began to accumulate. This lack of scientific
evidence did not, however, discourage observers from speculating
about the evolution of Canadian English, and it has not always
been easy to weigh their theories "because it is difficult to disprove
by documented evidence what they propose without such
evidence." [1]

1

Theories about the origin of Canadian English correspond to
different stages in our development as a nation. One view, which

[1] M. H. Scargill, "Sources of Canadian English," *Journal of English and Germanic
Philology*, 1957, pp. 610–614. For a helpful introduction to the subject coupled with a
plea for common sense and tolerance, see Pierre Daviault, "The Evolution of the
English and French Languages in Canada," *Transactions of the Royal Society of Canada*,
Ser. 3, 1959, pp. 63–72. And see M. H. Scargill, "The Growth of Canadian English,"
in *Literary History of Canada*, ed. by C. F. Klink, Toronto, 1965, pp. 251–259.

goes back to colonial days, was that Canadian English was purely and simply British English. Although this theory is scarcely tenable today in its original form because Canadian speech is obviously very much like American, a modified version is still widely current at popular levels, namely that over the years the pristine British English of Canada has become contaminated by the hated Yankee tongue. The views of this inhibiting school were shared by early British travellers and expatriates, no less than by some native-born Canadians who either sent their sons to England to be educated or entrusted them to a few private schools staffed for the most part by English masters. A similar attitude prevailed for a long time among Canadian educators, thanks in part to the pro-British reforms of Egerton Ryerson, so that a large part of the Canadian school system was consciously and deliberately oriented toward England and away from the United States. The efforts of Ryerson and others with similar views have significantly affected the English language spoken in Canada, "for the practice of 'teaching British' has a long history in this country." [1]

It is of course true that the literature of England forms part of the common heritage of every English-speaking country and as such may rightly claim a prominent place in school studies. That part of Canadian education, however, which concerns itself with syntax, grammar and spelling has for a hundred years and more been based almost exclusively on British models. The "official" orthography taught in Canadian schools is and always has been the British standard of spelling, and the "official" dictionaries are British, the various Oxford and kindred lexicons and not Webster being in most cases the ranking authorities. Nor until very recently has there ever been any attempt to relate the Oxford dictionaries to current Canadian usage, a condition which was partly remedied by the appearance in 1962 of *The Canadian Dictionary*. This work was prepared at the Lexicographic Research Centre of the University of Montreal under the editorship in chief of Jean-Paul Vinay and an impressive board of Canadian linguists. Its avowed aim is, in Dr. Vinay's words, to provide

---

[1] W. S. Avis, "Canadian English Merits a Dictionary," *Culture*, 1957, p. 247.

"direct guidance on the terminology and style which are peculiar to the French and English of Canada." It was followed by the *Dictionary of Canadian English* series published at Toronto, the effect of which on Canadian education has yet to be assessed.[1]

Perhaps by dint of this concerted attempt to keep Canadian schooling British, the old belief that Canadian English is British English has been accepted without question by many scholars. As eminent a linguist as Arthur G. Kennedy discussed Canadian English under the heading "The British Empire Today," with no hint in the twelve lines allotted to the subject in a book of some 618 pages that Canadian is anything but British English, with a smattering of Indian, Canadian French, Scots and Irish; of American or home-grown influence, we hear not a word. According to Professor Kennedy:

> In Canada, however, the British became more permanently established, with the winning of the land from the French at the end of the French and Indian War, in 1763; and today in places like the City of Victoria, Canadian life and culture are essentially British in spite of a strong coloring given by the American Indian and Canadian-French population.[2] The outstanding peculiarity of the Canadian linguistic situation is that in some parts, such as Quebec, French has survived and is spoken as commonly as English. This bilingual situation, with the strong immigration of Scotch and Irish, has given to the Canadian culture a coloring quite different from that of any other part of the British Empire.

Other authorities are equally misleading. In the first edition of *A History of the English Language* (1935), Albert C. Baugh dealt

---

[1] The *Dictionary of Canadian English* series comprises *The Beginning Dictionary*, Toronto, 1962, *The Intermediate Dictionary*, Toronto, 1963, and *The Senior Dictionary*, Toronto, 1967.

[2] *Current English*, Boston, 1935, p. 150. In fact, the French influence in British Columbia is negligible. According to the census of 1961, more than 59 per cent of the population is of British ancestry, compared with only 4 per cent of French origin. The French in British Columbia are outnumbered by Scandinavians ($6\frac{1}{2}$ per cent) and Germans (7 per cent). The linguistic influence of "American Indian" is even less evident.

briefly with Canadian English in a chapter entitled "Nineteenth Century British English," although he invoked no authority more recent than Geikie:

> Canadian English, as would be expected, has much in common with that of the United States while retaining a number of features of English pronunciation and vocabulary. Thus one finds *lift* for *elevator, perambulator* for *baby-carriage*, etc. The influence of the United States has been very strong. A writer in the *Canadian Journal* in 1857 complains of the new words adopted from us, 'imported by travellers, daily circulated by American newspapers and eagerly incorporated into the language of our provincial press.' Needless to say, he considers the influence wholly bad, and his words are still echoed by Canadians who deplore the wide circulation of American books and magazines in Canada and in recent years the further influence of the moving picture and the radio. On the whole, however, one must consider that Canadian English has diverged from that of England in much the same way that the English of the United States has developed special qualities, because the conditions under which the language has evolved in the two countries are very similar.[1]

It will be noted that Baugh speaks of Canadian English as *retaining* certain features of English pronunciation and vocabulary, which would seem to imply that it was originally British English modified by the very strong influence of the United States. Yet Baugh gives no examples of "retained" English pronunciation, and his two instances of "retained" English vocabulary, *lift* and *perambulator*, are not and never have been standard Canadian usage. In his second edition (1957), Baugh came to modify this position somewhat and wrote of Canadian English as "retaining a few features of English pronunciation and spelling." In keeping with this change, he dropped the references to *lift* and *perambulator*, and substituted no new examples. Instead, Baugh remarked on

---

[1] *A History of the English Language*, New York, 1935, pp. 397–398.

the influence of the early settlers from the United States[1] and added a new conclusion, supported however by no new evidence, that "nevertheless the English of Canada can only be described as a variety of American English."

The theory that Canadian English is British English would seem best rebutted by the fact that Canadian English has many more affinities with General American than with Standard English, although some observers refused to be put down by this fact. In order to account for the apparent failure of language to follow the flag, they have developed the theory that somewhere along the way the pure British *Ursprache* of Canada became affected or, in the popular view, contaminated by American words, pronunciation and speech forms passing across the international border. This is by some considered to be the only or at any rate the only significant influence on Canadian speech. As H. W. Horwill wrote in *American Variations*: "The language spoken and written in the United States today presents many striking differences from that current at home. This distinction is much more strongly marked than the difference between the English of the mother country and that of the overseas Dominions and colonies—with the exception, of course, of Canada, whose speech has been strongly affected by the contact with her neighbour." [2]

The contamination theory of the origin of Canadian English, attractive though it may be to some on patriotic grounds, has not been supported by any weight of evidence. As both Lighthall and Chamberlain realized in the last century, it is not easy to say which American idioms are the product of normal social and commercial intercourse with the United States and which were brought in by the first American settlers and thus have as valid a claim to be part of the original English speech of Canada as any British English expressions. The contamination theory has, however, hardened into folklore and probably cannot now be convincingly refuted. At the popular level, the pollution of Canadian

---

[1] Citing Morton W. Bloomfield's paper "Canadian English and Its Relation to Eighteenth Century American Speech," *Journal of English and Germanic Philology*, 1948, pp. 59–67, which had appeared midway between the first and second editions of Baugh's book.

[2] *Society for Pure English, Tract, No. XLV*, 1936, p. 175.

English by American has long provided a favourite subject for newspaper controversy. One such battle was described at length and with relish by H. L. Mencken, who related how, in January, 1937, C. Egerton Lowe, an Englishman, launched a one-man crusade in Toronto against the insidious infiltration of Yankee speech. The Detroit *Free Press* rose to the challenge, and presently other zealots joined in with a running denunciation of Mencken's *The American Language* and the American vulgar tongue that was still going on briskly several years later.[1]

The very Senate of Canada proved not to be immune to infection, and the Ottawa *Journal* solemnly editorialized: "With the disappearance of Gladstonian haberdashery and frock-coats, ponderosity of language could no longer be properly sustained, and now antiquarians can trace but the faintest vestiges in the Senate chamber. The stimulus of Burke's orations and classical English speech has given place to the stimulus of Hollywood and the airwaves."[2]

Even Mencken himself, enlightened observer though he sometimes was, fell partial victim to this theory, although as an American of the whole blood he could scarcely entertain the notion that his mother tongue might be a contaminating influence. Accordingly, his version of the fallacy was that American English by reason of its innate virtues drove the original British English out of Canada, presumably by the operation of a kind of linguistic Gresham's Law in reverse. Expounding without dissent the alleged belief of the average American in the superiority of his

[1] *The American Language*, Supplement I, New York, 1945, p. 71. The "Letters to the Editor" columns of most Canadian daily newspapers continue to echo such sentiments; witness the following blast which appeared in the Toronto *Globe and Mail* of September 25, 1959, the *casus belli* being the pronunciation of a CBC announcer: "The man had the effrontery to pronounce 'Reveille' as 'REvelly'! That is an American bugle call, never used in any civilized army. In Canada and in other parts of the Commonwealth, it is, as every good soldier knows, 'ReVELly.' This is not the first time Canadians have been exposed to ignorant radio people's mayhem on the English language. Is the CBC out to wreck the Commonwealth or is it just too ignorant to know better? How long must we tolerate such insults to our mother tongue?"

[2] "Parliament Goes to Hollywood," April 7, 1934. In another editorial entitled "Mr. Hoover at the Microphone" (August 13, 1932), the *Journal* critized the President's pronunciation of such words as *constitution, revenue* and *tumultuous*, expressing the hope that "Americanese" would not be "spread by radio . . . in Canada."

native tongue, Mencken wrote: "He believes, and on very plausible grounds, that American is better on all counts [than Standard English]—clearer, more rational, and above all, more charming. And he holds not illogically that there is no reason under the sun why a dialect spoken almost uniformly by nearly 125,000,000 people should yield anything to the dialect of a small minority in a nation of 45,000,000. He sees that wherever American and this dialect come into fair competition—as in Canada, for example, or in the Far East—American tends to prevail." [1]

Elsewhere, commenting on one result of this fair competition, Mencken noted: "In Canada, despite the social influence of English usage, the flat *a* has conquered, and along the Canadian-New England border it is actually regarded as a Canadianism, especially in such words as *calm* and *aunt*." [2] This kind of theorizing is, of course, as unsatisfactory as it is unscientific. Mencken would apparently have us believe that at one time Standard English was spoken in Canada and that American speech came into competition with it and conquered, one example being the victory of the "flat *a*" over the "broad *a*." But Mencken tendered no evidence that Standard English was ever current in Canada, nor did he explain when and where American and Standard English came "into fair competition." As M. W. Bloomfield and others have pointed out, Mencken betrays here his ignorance of the source of Canadian English, "for the 'flat *a*' in most cases never had a rival *a* to conquer." [3]

No advocate of the British English theory has ever identified the dialect which is alleged to have been the original English speech of Canada. Was Received Standard the English tongue that Geikie found in Canada and whose virtues he wished to safeguard? Or was it Northern English with which both Canadian and American have much more in common? We will probably never be able to reconstruct the original English speech of Canada, but if we except Nova Scotia and Newfoundland it was

[1] *The American Language*, New York, 1936, pp. 608–609.
[2] The same, p. 338.
[3] Morton W. Bloomfield, "Canadian English and Its Relation to Eighteenth Century American Speech," *J.E.G.P.*, 1948, pp. 59–67.

certainly not British English, using that term in the sense of English imported directly from the British Isles. For the greater part of English-speaking Canada east of the Great Lakes was not in the first instance settled by Englishmen at all, but by Americans. The United Empire Loyalists were our Founding Fathers, and the language which they brought with them was that of the inhabitants of eighteenth-century New York and Pennsylvania, many of whose distinctive words may to this day be found embedded in our daily speech.

2

Although both the British English and the contamination theories were not entirely renounced, the political climate which had fostered them was changing. The decline of the Family Compact, the advent of Confederation and the growing spirit of independence which followed it made men less inclined to think of England as their only spiritual and cultural home. Increasingly, American speech came to be recognized not as an interloper but as one of the original elements of Canadian English. At first, this view found modest enough expression. Of the English of Nova Scotia, Chamberlain remarked that "it bears marked affinities to the dialect of the New England States, whence very many of the early settlers came." Farther west, he noted, "the early settlers of Ontario were principally loyalists and *émigrés* from the state of New York and from Pennsylvania, and much that characterized the English speech of those states is still traceable in their descendants." [1] As time went on, however, the view developed that Canadian is *like* American English chiefly because it *is* American English, and its origins are to be found in the eighteenth-century speech brought to Canada by the United Empire Loyalists who fled the thirteen colonies following the Revolutionary War. "The Loyalists had moulded Canada," announced Morton W.

[1] "Dialect Research in Canada," *Dialect Notes*, 1890, pp. 43–56.

Bloomfield, "created its ruling caste and set its social standards among which was its language." [1]

The importance of the Loyalists in eighteenth and nineteenth-century Canada has long been accepted, although Loyalist influence is usually looked on as political, one of its main contributions being an obstinate anti-American pro-British bias. No less important, however, were other influences—cultural, educational and, one cannot doubt, linguistic. Although the Loyalists were from every walk of life,[2] in Bloomfield's view they had one thing in common: ". . . they were conservatives who had suffered for their loyalties. Hence to the normal conservatism of emigrating linguistic groups there was added in this case a strong political and psychological conservatism. This frame of mind was to have its effect upon Canadian English and Canadian life." [3]

The Loyalists established schools and universities wherever they came to rest and may be credited with founding a good part of the educational systems of Ontario and the Maritime Provinces.[4] Along with their kind of municipal government, the American settlers introduced to Upper Canada "the equalitarian grade school," either borrowing their text books from the United States or following American models. It is true that the later reforms of Ryerson, himself a second-generation Loyalist, helped strengthen the prestige of British English, particularly among the upper classes, but "it seems clear that the American idiom was

[1] "Canadian English and Its Relation to Eighteenth Century American Speech," *J.E.G.P.*, 1948, pp. 59–67. In the United States, those who adhered to the British cause during the War of Independence were called *Loyalists* or *Tories*. In Canada the words *United Empire* were added by Lord Dorchester, better known as Sir Guy Carleton, who proposed in 1789 that all Loyalists "who had adhered to the unity of the Empire, and joined the Royal Standard in America before the Treaty of Separation in the year 1783" were "to be distinguished by the letters U.E. affixed to their names, alluding to their great principle, the unity of the Empire." (*Encyclopedia Canadiana*, Ottawa, 1958, vol. 10, p. 184.)

[2] See Falconer, *The United States as a Neighbour*, Cambridge, 1925, for some account of Loyalist personages. Their political influence is discussed by A. G. Bradley in *The United Empire Loyalists, Founders of British Canada*, London, 1932.

[3] Morton W. Bloomfield, "Canadian English and Its Relation to Eighteenth Century American Speech," cited above.

[4] This aspect of Loyalist activities has yet to be adequately studied. See *Report of the Historiographer of the Education Department of the Province of Ontario for the Year 1908*, "*What We Owe to the United Empire Loyalists in the Matter of Education*," Toronto, 1909.

ensconced in Ontario when the great stream of British immigrants began to flow into the country during the later stages of development." [1]

The Loyalist theory of Canadian English has not gone unchallenged. M. H. Scargill of the University of Victoria points out that it rests on certain assumptions which are not necessarily true and, in any event, not applicable to Canadian English everywhere. In Scargill's view, the theory assumes that one type of English, General American, is spoken throughout Canada; that this derives from a well-developed set of Loyalist speech habits; that Loyalist speech was markedly different from the eighteenth-century English spoken in the Maritimes; that British soldiers and settlers between 1713 and 1776 contributed nothing to the early history of the English language in Canada; that the later influence of British officers, clergy and teachers was equally without effect on standards of speech; and that the English language in Canada has developed nothing on its own. [2]

It is difficult to adjudicate such claims in the abstract, and one can perhaps understand how Canadian English has evolved only by examining the people who first spoke it. An imaginary line drawn at the time of the American Revolution (which, more surely than the fall of Quebec in 1759, marks the opening phase of modern Canada) would show an English-speaking population of about 25,000 whose composition can be analysed with reasonable accuracy. In the far east, Newfoundland, which did not become part of Canada until 1949, was the first English-speaking colony in North America. Following the landing of Sir Humphrey Gilbert in 1583 under letters patent from Elizabeth I, the island was colonized almost wholly by settlers from Ireland and the southwest counties of England. By 1763, when Labrador was added to the governorship of Newfoundland by the Treaty of Paris, the population comprised some 8,000 souls whose distinctive brand of English has been relatively unaffected by prevailing North American

[1] Walter S. Avis, "Canadian English Merits a Dictionary," *Culture*, 1957, pp. 245–256.
[2] "Sources of Canadian English," *Journal of English and Germanic Philology*, 1957, pp. 610–614.

speechways. In turn, it has had little influence on the language of the rest of English-speaking Canada.

Nova Scotia, which some have sought to identify with the Markland of early Norse voyagers, had first been settled in 1604 by the French who named the peninsula Acadie. After having been bandied back and forth six times between France and England, it was finally ceded to Great Britain by the Peace of Utrecht in 1713 as "Acadia or Nova Scotia," the latter name having been conferred by a patent of James I in 1621. Colonization proceeded slowly and with difficulty, owing to the greater attraction of the American colonies, and as late as 1784 Nova Scotia was "a nominal British province without any British settlement." [1] When Halifax was founded in 1749, a call for volunteer settlers made in London, Holland and Germany brought many from Britain, a thousand from the American colonies and about 1,500 Germans and Swiss who settled at Lunenburg. In the meantime, the native Acadians had occupied most of the desirable land along the Bay of Fundy, thus hindering future British expansion, and were expelled in 1755 on the now familiar ground that their loyalty was suspect. To replace them, Governor Lawrence of Nova Scotia issued a proclamation to the American colonies which was so well answered that by 1775 it is estimated that there was "a total population, excluding Indians, of about 18,000 of whom at least two-thirds and possible three-quarters were New Englanders." [2] Since this total included the non-exported remnant of the French Acadians and about 2,000 Germans and Swiss, the number of British English colonists in Nova Scotia could not have been more than about 3,000.

Two groups stood out clearly in the maritime colony: the British garrison, clergy and governing class, centred chiefly at

---

[1] J. B. Brebner and M. L. Hanson, *The Mingling of the Canadian and American Peoples*, New Haven, 1940, p. 37; A. G. Bradley, *The United Empire Loyalists, Founders of British Canada*, London, 1932, p. 119.

[2] For an account of the colonization of Nova Scotia, see William Douglass, *A Summary Historical and Political of the First Planting, Progressive Improvements and the Present State of the British Settlements in North America*, London, 1755, Vol. I, p. 330. A. G. Bradley, *The United Empire Loyalists, Founders of British Canada*, London, 1932, puts the total population of Nova Scotia at 14,000 in 1782, "including some very troublesome Micmac Indians."

Halifax; and the Scots, both English-speaking Lowlanders and Gaelic-speaking Highlanders, who had settled for the most part in Pictou and Antigonish counties, Cape Breton Island and Prince Edward Island. One of the most notable features of early Canadian life was "the pervasive Caledonian influence," thanks to which English Canada of the first half of the ninteenth century was "mainly American and Scottish by origin, although Loyalist politically." [1] The early Scottish migrations to British North America rank second only in importance to those from the United States. Soon after the Rebellion of 1745, a small stream of emigrants had set sail for Nova Scotia and, after 1759, for Quebec, where the first Scottish element was provided by the disbanding of the Fraser Highlanders and the Black Watch after the fall of New France. Suspended during the war with the American colonies, "after 1783 emigration became more general, its spirit pervading every class till, unable to live as he had lived and unwilling to become a mechanical drudge like the despised Lowlander, the Highlander listened to the tale of the fortunate lands and betook himself to a country of reputed freedom and plenty." [2] By 1803, the total emigration from the Highlands was about 12,000, and the movement continued well into the nineteenth century, populating large areas of the Maritimes as well as both Upper and Lower Canada.

At the time of the Treaty of Paris in 1763, Quebec, with a French population of perhaps 60,000, contained only a few hundred English-speaking persons. By 1766, there were no more than 600 of them, chiefly merchants and fur traders; in the year 1774, they were estimated at about two or three thousand, and it is impossible to distinguish between those who were natives of Great Britain and those who had come from "the old colonies," i.e., the United States. [3] The territory south of the St. Lawrence River, now known as the Eastern Townships, had been reserved for future settlement and was virtually uninhabited. As for the

---

[1] F. E. L. Priestley in Eric Partridge, *British and American English Since 1900*, London, 1951, pp. 72–79.

[2] Helen I. Cowan, *British Emigration to British North America; The First Hundred Years*, Toronto, 1961.

[3] J. B. Brebner and M. L. Hanson, *The Mingling of the Canadian and American Peoples*, pp. 41–42.

rest of the country, primeval forest stretched west of Montreal and along the northern shores of Lakes Ontario and Erie, broken only by a handful of trading posts which had been established by the French at strategic points: Fort Frontenac, where Kingston now stands, Toronto (called by the French Fort Rouillé), Fort Niagara, Detroit, Michilimackinac at the entrance to Lake Michigan, Sault Ste. Marie and a fortified place where now stands Thunder Bay. Otherwise, the country was virgin wilderness forming part of the old province of Quebec with a predominantly French type of government at Quebec City. There were probably not more than a few hundred English-speaking persons in all of what is now Ontario.

Into these territories—a Nova Scotia which still included New Brunswick and Prince Edward Island, and Quebec, which comprised the rest of the known country east of the Lakehead—there poured during the years 1783 and 1784 a flood of Loyalists whose numbers have never been exactly counted. Not less than 35,000 entered Nova Scotia, and although many moved on to what was to become Upper Canada, "the alternative goal of the exiles," the population of the province may well have doubled in two years. Brebner and Hanson, probably the most accurate of the many authorities, offer this estimate: Nova Scotia, 20,000; New Brunswick (separated from Nova Scotia in 1784), 14,000; Prince Edward Island, 600; Cape Breton, 400.

Quebec received a smaller but by no means negligible number. Brebner and Hanson, after a careful analysis of the evidence, conclude that 6,800 Loyalists were in the old Province of Quebec, then all of Canada, in 1785. This number, which is sometimes put as high as 10,000, settled chiefly in what became in 1791 Upper Canada, the Ontario of today, to be followed by an equal number of later Loyalists. Some doubtless came directly from the dissident States, others moved on from Nova Scotia and New Brunswick as the interior of the country became more populous.

The counting of Loyalists is a difficult and uncertain business, but a figure of 40,000 would be close to the mark, and this was greatly increased by the current of migration from the United States, which continued to flow for almost thirty years after the peace of 1783. "In the beginning," say Brebner and Hanson,

c

"the predominant factor was no doubt sentiment towards the British Crown, but with the passing years the advantages and opportunities of settlement in Canada became more important, then eventually predominant. . . . The migration of the Loyalists gradually shaded off into a migration of pioneer farmers whose only motive was the traditional American search for better lands and a perfect home." [1]

Even Quebec felt their influence, and although Loyalists had not at first been encouraged to settle in the Eastern Townships, after 1792 this policy was reversed and by 1807 approximately 15,000 Americans had moved north to settle below the St. Lawrence River. By 1812, the total population of the Eastern Townships was estimated at 20,000, "derived almost entirely from American stock which, with the exception of the Loyalists from New York, had been drawn from New England." [2] Isaac Weld, one of the early travellers, reported of Sorel in the 1790's: "This is the only town on the St. Lawrence, between Montreal and Quebec, wherein English is the predominant language. The inhabitants consist principally of Loyalists from the United States, who took refuge in Canada." [3] One of the best-known migratory New Englanders was Philemon Wright, a native of Woburn, Massachussetts, who founded the town of Hull, Quebec, in 1800, settling there with his family and a small colony of artisans and farmers brought from New England. There was also a sprinkling of Germans, Mennonites and Dunkers from the eastern counties of Pennsylvania who settled in large numbers in the Niagara Peninsula, in the counties of Welland and Waterloo, and at Markham, north of Toronto.

In time, the continuing drift of Americans began to worry many Canadians who feared this republican invasion, and a strong prejudice became evident against the growing American population. The writer of an authorized gazetteer of Upper Canada in

---

[1] *The Mingling of the Canadian and American Peoples*, p. 66.
[2] The same, p. 74. A. G. Bradley in *The United Empire Loyalists, Founders of British Canada*, p. 170, says that by 1800 there were 160,000 persons in Lower Canada of whom one-sixth were English-speaking, "the majority being American farmers from the Border States with a proportion of old Loyalists."
[3] *Travels Through the States of North America, and the Provinces of Upper and Lower Canada, During the Year 1795, 1796 and 1797*, London, 1799.

1812 analysed the population of the province, which then numbered about 100,000, as being four-fifths American and one-fifth British.[1] Following the War of 1812, the British government set out to colonize the province as a means of counteracting this powerful concentration of Americans, and a flow of emigration from Great Britain began which continued throughout the century, ending the nagging fears of American encroachment. By the time of Confederation, half of Canada's population of 3,500,000 was of British descent.

The effect of early American emigration to Canada—to call it "Loyalist" only would be misleading—must have been considerable. "It is a well-known fact," Thomas C. Trueblood has observed, "that first emigrants from the mother country will set the pace for the prevailing speech of the new country. . . . Take, for example, Australia. The first settlers there were from the lower ranks of society, many of them convicts chiefly from the cockney class who were deported from England to New South Wales and Tasmania long before the better class of Englishman began to go there. So these people set the pace for the cockney accent of the country." [2] A similar example may be provided by Canada, the more so since it was not until at least 1815 that Britain, relieved of the enormous burden of the Napoleonic wars, seriously began to look to the Canadas as an outlet for her surplus population. By that time, some thirty years after the first Loyalist influx, Canada was "mainly a colony of Americans, created by Americans, living by choice under British rule." [3] Later generations have been inclined to gloss over the American part in the formation of Canada, sometimes to conceal actions which today appear wholly uncommendable, as when eight or ten thousand native Acadians were driven out and replaced for the most part by New Englanders, a procedure familiar in the twentieth century as "transfer of populations." The real story of the Acadians has

---

[1] Michael Smith, *A Geographical View of the Province of Upper Canada, and Promiscuous Remarks upon the Government*, Hartford, 1813; Brebner and Hanson, *The Mingling of the Canadian and American Peoples*, p. 90.

[2] "Spoken English," *Quarterly Journal of Speech*, 1933, pp. 513–521.

[3] A. G. Bradley, *The United Empire Loyalists, Founders of British Canada*, p. 269.

been romanticized out of existence, but this population shift in Nova Scotia long before the Loyalists arrived left an indelible imprint upon Maritime English. Similarly, their strong adherence to the British cause obscured the fact that the Loyalists were Americans, and their distinctive speechways can still be traced by linguistic geographers from Nova Scotia to the Great Lakes.

M. H. Scargill has expressed doubt whether any such thing as "American English" existed for the Loyalists to bring with them.[1] But it is a fact that long before the end of the eighteenth century, a distinctive American speech had begun to emerge. According to Allen Walker Read, contemporary Englishmen were well aware that the English language spoken in America had developed a character of its own, although some of them had little notion of its distinctive traits.[2] They were, Read notes, struck by its uniformity and absence of dialects, by its unaccented, even monotonous pronunciation, and by its vigorous vocabulary, qualities which, one may surmise, would have been imported into Canada by the pre-revolutionary New Englanders who settled in Nova Scotia, no less than by the Loyalists and "late Loyalists" who came mostly from New York and Pennsylvania. It remains to be seen how extensive were the differences between Loyalist speech and eighteenth-century British English. Professor Scargill thought them slight, and his diggings in pre-Loyalist Nova Scotia have uncovered a vein of colonial English which much resembles both British and American usage of the period.[3] Most of his examples are of spelling: *tarmes* (terms), *keept* (kept), *midle* (meddle), *togither*, *perticular*, *oppertunity*, *barrill*, *deligates*, *deputys*, *mentain*, *strick* (strict), *askt*, *sworen* (sworn), together with a few grammatical constructions: *His Excellency mouth*, *reflections that was cast* and *was you*.

The exact flavour of early Canadian English is impossible to determine at this distance in time, but it would have been pre-

---

[1] "Canadians Speak Canadian," *Saturday Night*, December 8, 1956, pp. 16–18.

[2] "British Recognition of American Speech in the Eighteenth Century," *Dialect Notes*, 1933, pp. 313–334.

[3] "Eighteenth Century English in Nova Scotia," *J.C.L.A.*, 1956, p. 3. The source studied was the Original Minutes of His Majesty's Council at Annapolis, 1720–1739.

ponderantly eighteenth-century American with a leaven of British English of the period insofar as the two may have differed, touched in certain regions with a sprinkling of Scots, German and Acadian French. The experts are not in agreement about the effect of later emigration from Great Britain. In Scargill's view, the later and more extensive pioneer settlements may have destroyed the influence of Loyalist speech, and there is no doubt that they deeply changed the nature of the original British North American colonies. On the other hand, F. E. L. Priestley feels that the massive British immigration after Waterloo did not change the prevailing linguistic character of Canada because many of these British immigrants were in fact of Irish and Scottish origin and tended to form colonies in restricted areas, "whereas the English dispersed and presumably took on a protective colouring." Priestley surmises that because of their association with the old colonial regime Englishmen were suspect and their distinctive accent taboo. A. R. M. Lower has pointed out that, compared with both Scots and Irishmen, the middle and lower-class Englishman as a racial group is almost without features and untraceable. "Irish and Scottish settlements may be found all over eastern Canada," he writes, "and in some districts an Irish or Scottish accent is still discernible (notably the Ottawa Valley), but nowhere in the country, except curiously enough among the Lunenburg Germans, are there traces of English accent, and practically nowhere are there to be found 'English' settlements recognized as such." [1]

Perhaps the weakest point in the Loyalist theory is its disregard of other and later influences. Bloomfield does go so far as to concede that "the continuing influence of the United States has also been a factor that cannot be ignored, although Canada's sense of inferiority and pride has generally kept it as slight as possible." [2] But he would allow little weight to other influences and remains

[1] *Canadians in the Making*, Toronto, 1958, p. 196. Describing how quietly the Scots consolidated themselves and rose in the social scale, Lower recalls the endless list of "Macs" in our political annals, beginning with the great Sir John A., an immigrant of 1820, and "the blessed lot of those lucky enough to be born with the name of McKenzie."

[2] "Canadian English and Its Relation to Eighteenth Century American Speech," *J.E.G.P.*, 1948, pp. 59–67.

firm in his conclusion that "Canadian English is basically eighteenth-century American English modified by Southern Standard English and the English taught by Scots school teachers." This dogmatism is not, however, justified by a preponderance of evidence, for no one can say with certainty that those characteristics of Canadian speech which may also be found below the border came in the first instance from the United States. Some of them may be traced separately to British English sources; thus it has been suggested that such Canadian pronunciations as the vowel sound of *hot*, the low front vowel in *grass*, and the pronunciation of *tomato* to rhyme with *potato*, may well have come in originally from England and later been strengthened by their presence in the United States.[1]

The pronounced "American" cast of much of the English spoken in Western Canada is attributable to the fact that the English-speaking West was settled almost entirely from Eastern Canada and the United States. Farmers from Upper Canada and Lord Selkirk's Red River Scots opened up Manitoba in the 1870's with the help of land-hungry Americans from across the line, and a generation later Saskatchewan and Alberta were settled, in part from Ontario but mostly from the American West where "the frontier was fast disappearing and . . . the supply of cheap land was less than the still active demand."[2] Thus by the turn of the century, some 6,000 Mormons had settled in Manitoba; and by 1915, a million Americans were living in Southern Alberta and Saskatchewan. Fewer Americans were drawn to British Columbia because the type of farmland was not to their liking. As a result, their place was largely taken by immigrants from Great Britain, although American influence was always strong here as elsewhere because the north-south lines of communication have been more active than those running east and west, particularly before Canada was spanned by the transcontinental railways. Some American invasions were purely local and temporary, as when at

---

[1] M. H. Scargill, "Sources of Canadian English," *J.E.G.P.*, 1957, pp. 610–614.

[2] W. S. Avis, "Canadian English Merits a Dictionary," *Culture*, 1957, pp. 245–256. See M. L. Hanson, "A Résumé of the History of Canadian and American Population Relations," *Conference on Canadian-American Affairs*, Boston, 1937.

the time of the Civil War about 15,000 "skedaddlers" crossed the border, many of them surreptitiously. Upon President Johnson's issuing an amnesty proclamation in 1865 most of them returned home, leaving few traces of their residence except for an occasional place name like *Skedaddle Ridge* near Mapleton, New Brunswick.[1]

---

[1] Brebner and Hanson, *The Mingling of the Canadian and American Peoples*, p. 158. Samuel Phillips Day in *English America, or Pictures of Canadian Places and People*, London, 1864, Vol. I, p. 257, quoted a local journal as describing how the trains arrived laden with young and middle-aged men from all parts of the West, who were "flying to Canada like cravens to escape the draught." Robin W. Winks, *Canada and the United States: The Civil War Years*, Baltimore, 1960, p. 206, recalls that there was a *Skedaddlers' Reach* on Campobello Island.

CHAPTER FOUR

ITS INGREDIENTS

The present Earl of Marchmont . . . told me, with great good humour, that the master of a shop in London, where he was not known, said to him, "I suppose, Sir, you are an American." "Why so, Sir?" (said his Lordship) "Because, Sir!" (replied the shopkeeper) "you speak neither English nor Scotch, but something different from both, which I conclude is the language of America."

SAMUEL JOHNSON

ITS INGREDIENTS

I Canadianisms, Americanisms and Britishisms[1]

"THERE ARE," ERIC PARTRIDGE HAS OBSERVED, "AND ALWAYS
will be variations in the vocabulary of each Dominion as compared
with that of Britain. That is only natural. Natural, because
inevitable. Different fauna and flora; an aboriginal race with its
customs, implements, weapons, clothes; different geographical
and topographical features; climatic differences; in short, new
conditions, new needs, new activities; these require a special
vocabulary, and that special vocabulary becomes part of the
everyday, as well as of the cultural, life of the Dominion. Finally,
the more basic and the more picturesque words and phrases work
their way into the general vocabulary of British English and,
indeed, constitute a major reason for our speaking *British English*
as opposed to *English*." [2]

The North American invasion of English speech began at least
as early as 1565 with *maize*, to be followed by an ever-increasing
flood of new and sometimes outlandish words. Long before the
Revolutionary Wars, the differences between American and
British English had become considerable, and a great controversy
arose about their respective virtues and vices.[3] "The Americans,"

---

[1] For an account of the French element in Canadian English, see the author's
Speaking Canadian French, Toronto, 1967.

[2] *British and American English Since 1900*, London, 1951.

[3] For an appreciation of the differences, see Allen Walker Read, "British Recognition of American Speech in the Eighteenth Century," *Dialect Notes*, 1933, p. 313.

writes M. M. Mathews, "were quick to claim that the language used by them was vastly superior to that employed in England and the English lost no time in taking the opposite view of the matter. These two views have ever since been maintained with varying degrees of vigor by their adherents." [1] Thus Mencken quotes one Francis Moore, who in 1744 raised the earliest alarm against the defilement of English by the American colonists in his description of the newly-founded village of Savannah: "It stands upon the flat of a Hill; the Bank of the River (which they in barbarous English call a *bluff*) is steep, and about forty-five foot perpendicular."

A few years later, Samuel Johnson added his considerable weight to the English end of the rope, and, as Mencken demonstrated with almost ghoulish satisfaction, the tug of war has continued without respite for some two hundred years.[2] Americans for their part have never ceased to resent British slurs upon their language, and to echo Noah Webster's call to arms contained in *Dissertations on the English Language*, (Boston, 1789):

As an independent nation, [Webster proclaimed] . . . our honour requires us to have a system of our own, in language as well as government. Great Britain, whose children we are, and whose language we speak, should no longer be *our* standard; for the taste of her writers is already corrupted, and her language on the decline. . . . Numerous local causes, such as a new country, new associations of people, new combinations of ideas in arts and sciences, and some intercourse with tribes wholly unknown in Europe, will introduce new words into the American tongue. These causes will produce, in a course of time, a language in North America as different from the future language of England as the modern Dutch, Danish and Swedish are from the German, or from one another.

Brave words, although robbed of some of their effect by the title

---

[1] *The Beginnings of American English*, Chicago, 1931, p. 9.
[2] See *The American Language*, New York, 1936, pp. 3 *et seq.*, for a diverting account of the skirmishes between American and British English. The subject is less discursively considered in two essays by Henry Alexander, "Is There an American Language?" *Queen's Quarterly*, 1926, pp. 191–202, and "American English," *Queen's Quarterly*, 1937, pp. 169–175.

of Webster's major work, *An American Dictionary of the English Language* (1828). The fact of the matter is, of course, that the dialects of English used in England and the United States are so alike and their similarities so outweigh their differences that there is really very little to choose between them. Certainly the differences between an Alabama speaker and, say, a Michigan speaker are at least as great as the differences between speakers of Standard English and General American.

The absence of any such linguistic warfare between England and the countries of the Empire—later Commonwealth—may be attributed to a number of causes. There was, to begin with, a lack of information about the varieties of English spoken throughout the old Empire. Most Englishmen, if they thought about it at all, would have taken for granted that Dominions English, as Eric Partridge inadequately calls it, was so like the language of the Mother Country—albeit of a thinner, poorer, and far less refined sort—as to call for no special consideration. There was little appreciation of the English spoken in the Australian outback or the clearings of Upper Canada, and to the extent that these deviated from the British standard they were visited with little more than mild disapproval. Englishmen have never felt called upon to display towards the overseas possessions which remained loyal the same keen resentment that was inspired by the rebellious American colonies, an animus which extended even to the minutiae of pronunciation and spelling. For their part, the Dominions, lacking in their early days the political emancipation of the United States and without a literature comparable to that of the homeland, tended to ignore or disparage the growing distinctiveness of their respective varieties of English. Notwithstanding such reticence, however, Canada has developed, over the two hundred years of her existence as a predominantly English-speaking nation, a distinctive vocabulary which merits serious consideration.

Some idea of the resources of Canadian English may be gathered from C. J. Lovell's elaborate classification of Canadian vocabulary[1] under no fewer than sixteen headings: —>

---

[1] "Whys and Hows of Collecting for the Dictionary of Canadian English: I, Scope and Source Material," *J.C.L.A.*, October, 1955, pp. 3–8. Some of Lovell's examples are not, of course, distinctively Canadian.

(1) Direct adoptions from native American languages, such as *comatik, namaycush, pemmican, shaganappi, tuladi;*

(2) Loan-words from Canadian French, frequently with Indian antecedents, such as *babiche, caribou, cariole, gaspereau, seigniory, tarreau;*

(3) Spanish-American terms introduced from the South-western United States, such as *broncho, corral, coyote, placer, stampede;*

(4) Borrowings from other languages, such as *Doukhobor, frankfurt, hamburger, kegler, kibitzer;*

(5) Words from the above classes used in combination with English, such as *dude ranch, mackinaw boat, prairie steppe, sockeye salmon, toboggan slide, wiener roast;*

(6) Words originated in Canada, embracing such outright coinages as Banting's *insulin* [see, however, p. 69] and Gesner's *kerosene,* but more often adapted from existing words, such as *chesterbed, liveyer, longlinerman, mountie, Socred, splake;*

(7) Geographical names, such as *Acadia, Eastern Townships, French Shore, Rupert's Land, Saskatchewan;*

(8) Figurative expressions pertaining to the foregoing, such as *Athens of Canada, Digby chicken, Garden of the Dominion, Land of the Little Sticks, Loyalist City, Maritimes, Sunrise Province;*

(9) Names descriptive of the peoples of various places or regions, such as *Assiniboian, Bluenose, Herring Choker, Maritimer, Quebec(k)er, Vancouverian, Yukoner;*

(10) Abbreviations of the names of provinces, territories, etc., and of various institutions, such as *Assa., Man., Manit., M.L.A., Nfld., R.C.M.P., Sask., U.C., Y.T.;*

(11) Everyday words formed into combinations unfamiliar abroad, such as *apartment block, bush pilot, fishing admiral, New Canadian, staking rush;*

(12) Words replacing synonyms more often used in England, such as *elevator* (lift), *gasoline* (petrol), *movies* (cinema), *sidewalk* (pavement), *truck* (lorry);

(13) Terms representing different things than in British English, such as *black cat* (marten), *crocus* (prairie anemone), *north country, maid of honor, robin;*

(14) Words which have developed additional meanings unknown in England, such as *concession, frontier, reeve, unionist* ('an advocate of Confederation'), *warden;*
(15) Words shifted from one part of speech to another, such as *allowable*, n. (from allowable oil production), *beveraged*, v. ('having a beverage licence'), *duplex*, v. (convert a single family residence into a duplex apartment), *gravel*, n. (gravel road), *hydro*, n. (word element, but in Canadian usage this represents a shortening of hydro-electric), *storms*, n. pl. (storm windows);
(16) Apparent survivals from various Scottish and English dialects such as *bultow, drake, glitter, knap, rampike, turr, var.*

The first Canadian vocabulary was that of the frontier, and it was probably extensive, although like frontier French it vanished before the inroads of civilization. With the close of the eighteenth century an increasing number of Canadianisms began to appear. As the frontier receded and the land opened up before a flood of American Loyalist and British settlers, new words had to be found to describe objects and institutions which were either new to European experience or appreciably different from things existing elsewhere. One example was *plains provisions*, a Red River colony term for buffalo meat.[1] Others were the *French coast* (1842) or *Treaty Shore* of Newfoundland; *separate school* (1835), not to be found in any English or American dictionary;[2] *Red River cart* (1858); *York boat* (1864); *union station* (1865); the *McIntosh* (1910) or *McIntosh Red* (1878), a superior eating apple first found in Dundas County, Ontario, by John McIntosh in 1811; *Land of the Little Sticks* (1896), "a region of stunted trees at the southern edge of the Barren Lands;" and a number of political terms such as *M.P.P.* (1836); *acclamation* (1844), an election without opposition; and *endorsation* (1869), approval or ratification.

As time went on, observers began to form some appreciation of

---

[1] Robert M. Hamilton, *Canadian Quotations and Phrases*, Toronto, 1952, p. 20, where the term is identified as "early nineteenth century." The *DC* calls it *"Obs."*

[2] C. J. Lovell defines it as "a sectarian school, operated outside a local public school system, supported by ratepayers of a minority faith, who elect their own trustees." In Ontario, separate schools are Roman Catholic schools; in Quebec, they are Protestant schools.

these new terms, although the rudimentary state of Canadian linguistics led to much confusion between Canadianisms and Americanisms. Thus W. D. Lighthall, writing in 1889,[1] compiled a list of "Universal Canadianisms," by which he meant "terms peculiar to the whole of the country," but in fact these were largely expressions common also to the United States, such as *sleigh, bob-sleigh* or *bob; American,* for an inhabitant of the United States; and a variety of terms for the international boundary, including *the line, the boundary line* and *the lines.* The *DA* traces *sleigh* back to 1696, the early spelling *slee* indicating its Dutch origin; in 1703, it was written *slay,*[2] and by 1799 had assumed the form we know today. *Bob-sleigh* and *bob* are traced by the same source to 1853 and 1856 respectively, and *American,* in the sense given, to 1782 and possibly to 1697 in the *Magnalia Christi Americana* (1702) of Cotton Mather. *The line* was used in the United States as early as 1809 to designate the boundary with Canada. The *DC* traces its first Canadian use to 1812.

The early Canadianisms which have remained are deeply embedded in our history: *metis* (1816),[3] a half-breed of white and Indian ancestry; *The Company* (1697), an ellipsis for the Hudson's Bay Company;[4] *whiskey jack* (1743), the blue jay, a corruption of the Cree *wisketjan; muskeg* (1775); *pemmican* (1743); *seigniory* (1703); *saskatoon* (1800); *Canuck* (1849); *nitchie* (1768–82); *timber limit* (1854); *end of steel* (1909)—these are all reminiscent of the early days of white settlement. They have been followed by a succession of newer Canadianisms, some of them evoked by more modern phenomena: *remittance man* (1896) and its congeners *remittance grabber* and *remittance farmer; mountie* (1914); *hydro* (1916); *bush pilot* (1936); *chuck wagon* (1923); *blue line* (1931); *faceoff* (1896); *grid road* (1957) and *cat train* (1946).

[1] "Canadian English," *The Week* (Toronto) August 16, 1889, pp. 581–583. A similar confusion is to be found in John Sandilands, *Western Canadian Dictionary and Phrasebook,* Winnipeg, 1912 ("Explaining the Plain English for the Special Benefit of Newcomers, the Meaning of the Most Common Canadianisms, Colloquialisms and Slang, added to which is a Selection of Items of General Information Helpful to the Newcomer.")

[2] In this form its first Canadian use was 1764, according to the *DC.*

[3] The dating of these terms is taken from the *DC.*

[4] Its original form was "The Governor and Company of Adventurers of England Trading into Hudson's Bay."

Although the number of Canadianisms turns out to be more extensive than one might have expected—the *Dictionary of Canadianisms on Historical Principles* (1967) runs to some 879 double-columned pages—the truth seems to be that Canadians are not prolific coiners of words, being content for the most part to borrow American and British English expressions, inventing new words sparsely and reluctantly as befits a reputedly laconic people. Those Canadianisms which relate to objects originally or exclusively found or developed in Canada are often manufactured in the crudest way from the names of the finder or developer, as *McIntosh Red, Fife wheat, Durham boat, McGill fence;* or of the place with which they are closely associated, as *York boat, Red River cart, Kamloops trout;* or by coining such neologisms as *Socred, mountie, Newfie, splake.*

Insulin was a more imaginative effort, although it is almost certainly not a Canadianism; Sir Frederick Banting's original name was *isletin* after the islets of Langerhans which produced it.[1] Somewhat more originality is shown in the names of various peoples, as *Herring Choker* and *Spud Islander,* and in a number of regional expressions. Thus from the Maritimes come *bogan, fish flake, rampike, tilt;* from Ontario, *firereels, pogey, pool train;* from the Prairie Provinces, *bombardier, grid road, pothole trout, wheat factory;* and from British Columbia, *longstocking, salt chuck, steelhead.* The most fertile field of all has been that of animal and plant names, whence may be gleaned a rich harvest, among them, for birds, *fool hen, venison hawk;* for animals, *burdash, chipmunk, harp, muskox;* for fish, *goldeye, keta, kokanee, muspike;* for plants, *avalanche lily, chokecherry, deadman's daisy, epinette, fiddlehead* or *fiddleneck, moosemisse, snow apple* and *soopolallie.*[2]

In general, however, Canadian English lacks much of the verbal fantasy and sheer uninhibited gusto of American English, which if

---

[1] C. J. Lovell in "A Sampling of Materials for a Dictionary of Canadian English based on Historical Principles," p. 24, remarks that the name *insulin* had been used during the ten years prior to Banting's discovery by a number of investigators including De Meyer of Belgium and Schafer of Edinburgh.

[2] W. S. Avis, "Canadian English Needs a Dictionary," *Culture,* 1957, pp. 245–256. And see Pierre Berton, "A Glossary of Distinctive Canadian Terms," *Toronto Daily Star,* October 23, 1962; "Explaining and Expanding Our Own Canadian Glossary," *Toronto Daily Star,* October 31, 1962.

one considers the letter *b* alone has improvised *bellboy*, to *blaze a trail*, *barbershop*, *barroom*, *beeline*, *bleachers*, *blue laws*, to *bluff*, *bobsled*, *bogus*, to *boom*, *boondoggle*, *boost*, *brainy* and *bully;* not to mention, if one digs into the vernacular, *ballyhoo*, *baloney*, *bamboozle*, *bandwagon*, *bargain-counter*, *bark up the wrong tree*, *barrel-house*, *bathtub gin*, to *bellyache*, *bonehead*, *boob*, *bop*, *breadbasket*, *bulldoze*, *burp*, and so on and on. An American can describe the state of being drunk or call a man a fool in fifty different ways without ever repeating himself. As Mr. Dooley once observed: "When we Americans are through with the English language, it will look as if it has been run over by a musical comedy." By contrast, Canadian word coinages are often pedestrian, although not without occasional sparks of wit as in *Bennett buggy* and *remittance man*.[1]

In their daily vocabulary, Canadians thread an uncertain and apparently arbitrary path between British and American usage. Why, for example, should Canadians prefer the American *airplane*, *aluminum*, *specialty* to the British *aeroplane*, *aluminium* and *speciality*, while at the same time favouring the British *innings*, over the American *inning*? Why use *billboard*, *editorial*, *gas* and *muffler* instead of *hoarding*, *leader*, *petrol* and *silencer*, while saying *blinds*, *porridge* and *tap* for *shades*, *oatmeal* and *faucet*? "The English language in Canada," remarked Henry Alexander, "is clearly an amalgam of North American English and British English, with a strong leaning toward the American pattern."[2] And he went on to point out that when British English and American English use different words to denote a certain object, Canadian English usually, though not always, lines up with American English. As we have already noted, the reasons why this is so are still being warmly debated by the experts. Regardless, however, of whether one

---

[1] The *Bennett buggy* was a horse-drawn, motorless automobile used during the Depression by prairie farmers who could not afford to maintain a gasoline-propelled vehicle. Its name derives from R. B. Bennett, Prime Minister of Canada from 1930 to 1935. A contemporary and parallel American coinage was *Hooverville*, defined by the *DA* as "a village of cheap makeshift houses." *Remittance man* was also a western term, denoting "an immigrant, commonly regarded as a ne'er-do-well son of the British aristocracy, who subsisted upon periodical remittances from his family" (C. J. Lovell, "A Sampling of Materials for a Dictionary of Canadian English based on Historical Principles," *J.C.L.A.*, 1958, p. 30. Lovell's citations for *remittance man* range from 1906 ¹⁹⁵⁷ proof of the staying power of the custom).

here a Canadian Language?" *CBC Times*, February 27, 1955, pp. 2-3.

accepts either the Loyalist or British English theories of the origin of Canadian speech, the fact remains that the influence of American on Canadian English vocabulary, although it could never be accurately measured, has been enormous.

Mencken, an indefatigable cataloguer, once listed some hundreds of instances where speakers in England and the United States would use different words to describe the same thing. An examination of Mencken's word-list reveals that only rarely does widespread Canadian usage clearly follow the British model; we usually say *luggage* instead of the American *baggage* (although we prefer *baggage-car* and *baggage-check*); *made-to-measure* instead of *custom-made* clothes; *porridge* and not *oatmeal* (boiled); *drains* and not *sewerage* in a house; *staircase* and not *stairway; tie* and not *necktie; tinsmith* and not *tinner; wash-basin* and not *wash-bowl;* and *waste-paper basket* and not *waste basket* (although the shorter term is making progress in Canada).

As for several dozen of Mencken's specimens, the British and American terms flourish side by side in Canada, although they are not always synonymous. Thus Canadians drive a *motor-car* (usually contracted to *car*) but also an *automobile;* we live in either a *flat* or an *apartment* (although Canadian usage requires that the latter be self-contained and the former not); we do both *odd jobs* and *chores;* make use of *clothes-pegs* as well as *clothes-pins,* carry out both *rubbish* and *junk;* receive either a *parcel* or *package* from the hands of a *postman* or *letter-carrier;* pour our drink from either a *jug* or *pitcher;* wear both *overshoes* and *galoshes;* hold up our trousers with both *braces* and *suspenders;* eat *undercut* or *filet* as well as *tenderloin;* and *sirloin* no less than *porterhouse;* retire to either *lavatory* or *toilet;* play with both a *pack* and a *deck* of cards; and get away from it all by taking either a *holiday* or a *vacation.*

Mencken's word-lists are already becoming archaic, and current Canadian usage sometimes follows neither of his sets of doublets; instead it has adopted different terms which in many instances are probably also current American. Thus, instead of *dust-bin* (Br.) or *ash-can* (Am.), Canadians prefer *garbage-can* or *garbage-pail;* instead of *dust-cart* (Br.) or *ash-cart* (Am.), we have *garbage-wagon* or (since the advent of the internal combustion engine) *garbage truck;* instead of *dustman* (Br.) or *ashman* (Am.), the practitioner of this vocation is generally referred to as the *garbage-man*, while *rubbish* (Br.) and *junk* (Am.), although both are in widespread use, are less common in Canada than *garbage*.[1] Likewise, *combinations* (Br.) and *union-suit* (Am.) may have some currency among the older generation along with the custom of wearing them, but the common term, often used derisively, is *long underwear*, although the Americanism *long johns* is making headway in Canada.

Sometimes the distinctive Canadian term is a hybrid, as when instead of *fowl-run* (Br.) or *chicken-yard* (Am.) we prefer *chicken-run*. It is interesting to note that in many cases the American and hence the Canadian term is shorter and more concise than the English, as *chain-store—multiple-shop; cheese-cloth—butter muslin; drug-store—chemist's shop; garters—sock-suspenders* and so on. When both the English and the American terms are current in Canada, the longer English word is sometimes preferred among fastidious speakers as the more genteel or socially acceptable mode of expression; thus *toilet* (Am.) and *lavatory* (Br.) are both used, although with different social connotations, by many Canadian speakers. As a rule, however, the choice is innocent of ulterior motives. During 1931, a fairly spirited debate was waged in the Montreal press over the appropriate term to indicate an increase in wages.[2] Apparently some Montrealers of that era preferred the English *rise* to the American *raise*, although nowadays the expression *a rise in pay* has no currency whatever in central Canada, except perhaps among transplanted Englishmen.

The strong leaning of Canadian English toward the American pattern was demonstrated by Donald E. Hamilton in a study of Montreal English carried out during 1957 and 1958.[3] An earlier observer, who identified herself as a newcomer from "the States," had reported in 1929 that the English spoken in Montreal was more British than American,[4] and she offered the following word-list with the comment that an American who comes to live in

---

[1] Americans commonly distinguish between *trash*, which goes in an ash-can or ash-barrel, and *garbage* which goes in a garbage-pail. *Junk* is old stuff of doubtful value sold to the *junkman*, while *rubbish* is an affected or literary term.

[2] Helen C. Munroe, " 'Raise' or 'Rise'?" *American Speech*, 1931, pp. 407–410.

[3] "Notes on Montreal English," *J.C.L.A.*, 1958, pp. 70–79.

[4] Helen C. Munroe, "Montreal English," *American Speech*, 1929, p. 21.

Montreal learns to substitute the first of each pair of words for the second:

pram	baby carriage
boot	shoe
tin	can
basement	cellar
biscuit	cracker
sweet	dessert
level crossing	grade crossing
flat	floor (storey)
gallery	porch
pickerel	pike
serviette	napkin
sleigh	sled
tram	street-car
tramway	street-car lines
braces	suspenders
garden	yard
zed	zee[1]

To these, she added a number of phrases, the Montreal preference being in each case the first:

different to	different from or different than
putting on side	putting on airs
long holidays	summer vacation
bath himself	bathe himself

This observer was soon corrected by W. S. W. McLay, who pointed out that "in both Toronto and Montreal the ordinary speech of even cultivated Canadians approximates in the matter of words to that of the United States rather than to that of England, except of course for Old Country people living in Canada or those who have visited England and wish to display the fact by their speech." [2] McLay noted that in Toronto, "which rather

[1] See John Lardner, "Languages Here and There," *The New Yorker*, September 26, 1959, pp. 171–174.
[2] "A Note on Canadian English," *American Speech*, 1930, pp. 328–329.

boasts of more English speech than the English of England," the usual words are *baby carriage* and not *pram*, *street-car* and not *tram*, *dessert* and not *sweet;* moreover that *pickerel* and *pike* are different kinds of fish, and *boot* and *shoe* are not synonyms, a boot in Canada being something that comes up above the ankle. *Zed*, he conceded, "has always been the Canadian pronunciation of the name of the letter."

D. E. Hamilton, writing some thirty years later, found nothing irreconcilable about these two views, and suggested that the first opinion was based on observations of usage "in the higher levels of Montreal society where even today the patterns of usage are apt to bear a closer resemblance to British English than to American." Hamilton did not himself attempt to distinguish between different social levels, but conducted his survey among "educated Montrealers, regardless of their social position." His conclusion was that Montreal English bears a closer resemblance to General American than to British English, more so indeed than Ontario English, whose close affinity to American speech had previously been pointed out.[1] In the list which follows, the words standing in the first column are in most cases used by a majority of the Montreal speakers tested, and are also the usual General American term. The second column contains the British English equivalent, although it must be borne in mind that with the vast interchange of printed and spoken material among the three countries the lines of division between respective usages are no longer as clear as they were thirty years ago when Mencken was writing his last edition of *The American Language*.[2]

Montreal English (American)	*British English*
apartment	flat
back-yard	back garden
bathrobe or kimono	dressing-gown

[1] W. S. Avis, "Speech Differences Along the Ontario-United States Border: Pronunciation," *J.C.L.A.*, October, 1956, pp. 41–59.

[2] The dangers of comparison lie in wait for even the most careful researcher. Thus the fifth (abridged) edition of *The American Language* (New York, 1963, p. 204) notes that "the English and Canadians reduce *permanent* to *perm*, as they do *refrigerator* to *fridge*." *Fridge* may indeed be heard in the land, but *perm* is not and never has been general Canadian usage.

boundary	frontier
candy	sweets
flash-light	torch
glue	mucilage
hall	hallway, passage
janitor	caretaker
kerosene	coal oil
living-room	parlor, sitting-room
pants	trousers
roomer	lodger
sidewalk	pavement
sugar-bowl	sugar-basin
sweater	pullover
taxes	rates
undershirt	vest
wrench	spanner

It is interesting to note that not all Montreal speakers favoured the American term over the British equivalent, nor did they favour all American terms to the same degree. Thus, more than 90 per cent of the Montrealers tested preferred *back-yard, candy, flash-light, sidewalk, street-car, sugar-bowl, taxes, undershirt* and *wrench*, to the British English equivalents. More than 75 per cent preferred *apartment, boundary, clothes-pin, glue, hall, janitor, living-room, pants* and *roomer*. With the remainder of the items on Hamilton's list, usage was more evenly divided. While 58 per cent of his Montreal speakers preferred *suspenders* to *braces*, a scant 50 per cent preferred *kerosene* to *coal oil*, and only 44 per cent preferred *bathrobe*, although almost as many showed a preference for *dressing-gown*, the remainder preferring *kimono*, an American variant.

Dialect studies such as these are always local, and one would not be justified in concluding that this pattern necessarily repeats itself in other parts of Canada. Four words from the Montreal list can, however, be compared with a similar test conducted along the Ontario-United States border several years earlier.[1] The comparison is interesting because in three cases Ontario usage

[1] W. S. Avis, "Speech Differences Along the Ontario-United States Border: Vocabulary," *J.C.L.A.*, October, 1954, pp. 13–18.

corresponds to British, while Montreal usage prefers the American term. Thus where 71 per cent of Montrealers preferred *napkin*, 79 per cent of Ontarioans chose *serviette*; 58 per cent of Montreal speakers said *suspenders* as against 81 per cent of Ontario speakers who preferred *braces;* and 50 per cent of Montrealers preferred to say *kerosene*, whereas an overwhelming 86 per cent of Ontario speakers said *coal oil*. A fourth word, *can*, was preferred by a majority of both groups over the British *tin*, although by 74 per cent of Montrealers as against only 57 per cent of Ontarioans.

This is not to say that Montreal speakers are pro-American and Ontario speakers pro-British in their choice of vocabulary, for both researchers, working with somewhat different word-lists, came to substantially the same conclusion: namely, that as between Canada and the neighbouring United States, "the total number of speech differences is relatively small in comparison with the linguistic features held in common." Moreover, Montreal speakers decidedly preferred a number of British alternatives:

Montreal English (British)	American English
biscuit	cookie
blinds	shades
cupboard	closet
holidays	vacation
odd jobs	chores
postman	letter carrier[1]
tap	faucet

A similar preference among Ontario speakers for certain British forms may be observed, but, as in Montreal, the number of such words is very small among all but first-generation British English speakers.

It remains to be seen whether these local studies will be confirmed elsewhere in Canada. Harold B. Allen of the University of Minnesota on the basis of a very limited investigation goes some way toward corroborating similar findings along "the middle

---

[1] Most Americans would say *mailman*.

border," i.e., from Fort William, Ontario, to Estevan, Saskatchewan.[1] As might be expected, he concluded that "American speech apparently has had greater influence north of the border than Canadian English has had south of the border," although he found "nearly fifty lexical, semantic, and phonological forms that are either peculiarly or largely Canadian in this transborder region," of which the most important lexical items are the following:

"Middle border" Canadian	*Midwest American*
asphalt road	blacktop
blinds	shades
boulevard[2]	berm, boulevard
chesterfield	sofa
coil, haycoil	cock, haycock
corn rick	corn crib
counterpane	bedspread
dibs	marbles, migs
draw (a load)	haul
elastic band	rubber band
feather	(corn) silk
hatching hen, hatcher	setting hen
hayland	meadow
neigh	whinner
quoits[3]	horseshoes
sheaf	bundle
stook	shock
tap	faucet
tea party	coffee party
veranda	porch

Mention should also be made of the interrogative *eh?*, pronounced to rhyme with "hay" and used when calling for the

[1] "Canadian-American Speech Differences Along the Middle Border," *J.C.L.A.*, 1959, pp. 17–24. The Canadian territory here surveyed is adjacent to Minnesota, Iowa, North and South Dakota and Nebraska, and the material comprised five field records made in the course of compiling data for the *Linguistic Atlas*. The Canadian communities in question were Fort Knox and Fort Frances, Ontario, Sprague and Killarney, Manitoba, and Estevan, Saskatchewan.

[2] In Ontario, this is commonly called the *median*.

[3] The eastern Canadian term is *horseshoes*.

repetition of something not heard or understood clearly. This, says Allen, "is so exclusively a Canadian feature that immigragration officials use it as an identifying clue." By contrast, however, relatively few American terms are not also to be found north of the border in this area. Some common American words which failed to make the crossing are *coffee clutch, kaffee klatsch* or *coffee party; davenport; hoghouse; mush* for a sort of cornmeal porridge; *pavement* for concrete highway; and the animal call, *Come, bossie!*

There has never been other than an imaginary boundary between Canada and the United States, as studies in linguistic geography clearly demonstrate. For example, a basic regional similarity exists between the speech of New York State, Ontario and Michigan because eastern Ontario was originally settled by Loyalists from New York and western New England, while Michigan in its turn drew much of its early population from Ontario and New York State. The migration of Pennsylvania Loyalists is demonstrated by the presence around Welland, Ontario, of a number of Pennsylvania words still in current use: *weatherboards* for clapboard; *overhead*, a barn loft; and *thick milk* for sour milk.[1]

Nor is the movement of words between Canada and the United States always from an area of greater to one of lesser density. R. I. McDavid, Jr., has traced such probable American borrowings from Canada as *stook* and *coal oil*, showing how they are found "predominantly in communities near the border, where it is reasonable to suspect Canadian influence."[2] The number of such words is understandably small: among them are *whippletree*, and *darning needle*, the dragon fly, neither of which is mentioned in the *DA*. A few common Canadian words may also be noted which have never succeeded in crossing the border: *county town; warden* for the principal officer of a county; and *reeve*, the chief township official; *chesterfield* for what in the United States is commonly called a davenport or sofa, and *coil*, "a small pile of hay raked up in a field."

---

[1] R. I. McDavid, Jr., "Why Do We Talk That Way?" *CBC Times*, February 11–17, 1951, pp. 2, 8.

[2] "Midland and Canadian Words in Upstate New York," *American Speech*, 1951, pp. 248–256.

The use of *store* for the English shop is an Americanism much commented upon and deplored from earliest times by English travellers. The word is traced in the United States to 1721 by the *DAE* and according to Pickering, writing in 1816, was then current in Canada. It is still the standard Canadian term to describe a retail establishment, although *shop* may often be found where some attempt at elegance is sought, a pretension which reaches the height of folly in *shoppe*. *Shop* is, however, good Canadian usage in such combinations as *barber shop* and *bake-shop*, although we have with our usual inconsistency borrowed from the United States *book-store*, traced by the *DAE* to 1763, *grocery-store*, traced to 1774, and *drug-store*, traced by the same source to 1819.

Certain walks of life are clothed almost entirely in American terminology. Thus a Canadian starting off on a trip by *railroad*[1] (Br. *railway*) will go to a *ticket-office* (*booking office*) where he may buy either a *one-way ticket* (*single ticket*) or a *round trip ticket* (*return-trip ticket*) from a *ticket agent* (*booking clerk*). As train time approaches, he will probably take a *taxi* (*cab*), which he may either engage at a *taxi-stand* (*cab-rank*) or hail as it is *cruising* (*crawling*). Our traveller proceeds to the *union station* (*joint station*), where he *checks his baggage* (*registers his luggage*) in the *check room* (*left-luggage room*) until the train which was delayed in the *roundhouse* (*running shed*) arrives at the station. When the *conductor* (*guard*) calls "*All aboard!*" ("*Take your seats, please!*"), our Canadian *gets on* (*in*) the train and walks down the *aisles* (*corridors*) from *car to car* (*carriage to carriage*) until he reaches the *chair-car* or *parlour-car* (*pullman car* or *saloon carriage*), where he sits down and composes himself in patience for the journey.

In due course, he proceeds to the *dining-car* or *diner* (*restaurant car*). While he is eating, a *freight train* (*goods train*) passes, and he watches the *freight-cars* (*goods-waggons*), which are followed by severals *coal cars* or *gondolas* (*mineral-waggons*) and the *caboose* (*brake-van*). As he nears his destination, a number of *commuters* (*season-ticket holders*) get on, and then the train passes beside a

---

[1] One explanation offered for the difference between British and American railroading terms is that in England the railroads took over a vocabulary of stage-coach terms, such as *coach, booking office, guard, driver*, whereas in America the vocabulary of steamboating was drawn on; hence, *all aboard, berth, caboose*.

stretch of the *road-bed* (*permanent way*), where the *ties* (*sleepers*) and *rails* (*metals*) are being replaced by a gang of *tracklayers* (*platelayers*), following an accident in which a train was *derailed* (*left the metals*). Finally, the train arrives *on time* (*up to time*); our passenger gets *off* (*out*) and walks toward the exit, passing en route the *baggage-car* (*luggage van*) and *mail-car* (*postal van*), and nodding to the *engineer* (*engine driver*). During his journey on a Canadian train, he will have encountered no more than one or two terms borrowed from English railroading: *level crossing* rather than the American *grade crossing*, and *shunting* instead of *switching*.

Our voyager will have the same kind of experience if he goes by road, for virtually the entire vocabulary of Canadian motoring is American, the British equivalents being here shown in parentheses. Thus we speak of the *battery* (*accumulator*), *fender* (*wing*), *gear-shift* (*gear lever*), *generator* (*dynamo*), *hood* (*bonnet*), *low gear* (*first speed*), *monkey wrench* (*spanner*), *muffler* (*silencer*), *sedan* (*saloon-car*), *top* (*hood*), *windshield* (*wind-screen*), *spark-plug* (*sparking-plug*) and a *truck* (*lorry*). Our highway may be a *main road* (*arterial* or *trunk road*), and here and there the motorist will encounter a *detour* (*road diversion*) where a curve is being newly *banked* (*superelevated*) and the *shoulder* (*verge*) widened. It goes without saying that our motorist may have to stop at a *gas station* or *filling station* (*petrol pump*) for *gasoline* or *gas* (*petrol*). As with railroading, a few English terms stick in our vocabulary; we prefer the English *sump* to the American *oil-pan*, although the latter term is gaining ground, but such transatlantic borrowings are few and far between.

As might be expected, the vocabulary of our press is almost exclusively American, from the *publisher*, called in England the *proprietor*, through the *editorial* (Br. *leading article* or *leader*) to the *advertisements*, abbreviated to *ads* rather than the British *adverts*. The same tendency is shown in many other fields—finance, the arts and sciences, and trade unionism, the latter being in any case almost wholly controlled by parent unions in the United States, euphemistically called *international unions*.

In certain other domains—the political and legal, for example— our institutions are largely patterned on English models, and the words which clothe them are English rather than American. Thus, the language of Canadian parliamentary institutions is largely borrowed from Great Britain, to the extent that these are applicable to a federal state. The British North America Act, commonly referred to in written and spoken Canadian as the *B.N.A. Act*, provided for the union of the three provinces of Canada, Nova Scotia and New Brunswick into "one Dominion under the name of Canada . . . with a constitution similar in principle to that of the United Kingdom." In the B.N.A. Act are to be found many terms which have since come to form part of our parliamentary and constitutional vocabulary: *dominion, provinces* as political divisions of a federal state, *Governor-General, privy council, Lieutenant-Governor, executive council, parliament, House of Commons, Upper House, session* (of parliament), *member* (of the House of Commons), *electoral district, decennial census, disallowance, legislature, legislative assembly*, and a number of catch-phrases connected with constitutional law, such as *peace, order and good government; trade and commerce;* and *property and civil rights*. Other parliamentary terms have also been borrowed from the Mother of Parliaments, among them *Leader of the Opposition, Gentleman Usher of the Black Rod, division, back-bencher* and *Hansard* for the official report of the proceedings of parliament.

In the same way, much of our political vocabulary is English; words like *constituency* and *by-election* would not be readily understood in the United States except by students of politics and government. A few terms in our political domain are also current in American speech, being derived independently from a common British source, as *cabinet, speaker, committee;* while others are obviously American in inspiration and unknown in England, as *senate* and *senator, convention* in the sense of a political gathering convened to select a leader, and a *delegate* to such a convention. The same parliamentary and political vocabulary appears at the provincial level, with the addition of a few distinctive terms. Thus, *Premier* (pronounced "preem-yer") instead of Prime Minister (although some provinces have adopted the latter term); *Member of Provincial Parliament* abbreviated to *M.P.P.* (1826), or *Member of Legislative Assembly* reduced to *M.L.A.* (1897).[1] By contrast,

[1] The dates of first use are taken from the *DC*.

the vocabulary of our local and municipal government is predominantly American, indicating the largely New England origin of these institutions: as *mayor, controller, ward*. Moreover, an aspirant to political life is said to *run for office*, as Americans do, rather than to *stand for office* as he would in Great Britain. One exception is the word *riding*, which is unknown in the United States, to denote an electoral district or constituency. The name, although not the connotation, is borrowed from the English *riding* (from the Old Norse—"third part") defined by the *SOED* as "one of the three administrative districts into which Yorkshire is divided."

Canada has never experienced to any extent the pullulation of boards, bodies and bureaux which characterized the American scene chiefly during and after the days of the New Deal, nor have we felt impelled to abbreviate or devise nicknames for those relatively few agencies which do exist. Accordingly, Canadian public life is largely lacking in such terms as *TVA, RFC, AEC, NLRB, FCC, SEC, AAA* and the like. If hard pressed, one might work up a handful like *C.B.C., C.M.H.C., H.E.P.C., N.R.C., L.C.B.O.*, but we cannot begin to rival the rich alphabet soup of American bureaucracy. Likewise there is nothing in our political vocabulary to compare with such inspired neologisms as *boondoggle, mugwump, gobbledygook, McCarthyism* and the like. The phenomena which inspired such terms also exist in Canada; but our political jargon still largely follows the old school tie or British parliamentary standard according to which strong feelings are masked behind such well-worn circumlocutions as "the Honourable Member for So-and-so," and "I would advise the Honourable Gentleman that the answer to his question is in the negative."

Something of the same formality invests the names of the political parties. The *Liberal Party* is usually referred to as just that, or, in popular speech, the *Liberals*. On rare occasions, a political orator, usually of the same stripe, may refer jocosely to *Grits* in an attempt to evoke the memory of old battles, but the word, current a hundred years ago, is scarcely understood today, and its use can only be described as an affectation. Similarly, the *Conservative Party* is never seriously called anything else, popularly abridged to the *Conservatives*. For some years, its official title has been "The Progressive Conservative Party of Canada," but the adjective has never really caught on except in party literature, although the abbreviation *P.C.* appears in Hansard and is sometimes used to fit the exigencies of a newspaper headline. Quite often, the name *Tory* is invoked, recalling the old name of the Conservative party in England. On the other hand, *Grit*, the old Liberal party label, seems to be of wholly Canadian origin, although the *SOED* places it immediately after the American slang term for spirit or stamina, with which it has no connection. The name, traced to 1852,[1] was formerly *Clear Grit* (1850), and is attributed to one David Christie who wanted in the party only those who were "all sand and no dirt, clear grit all the way through."[2] The term, which has never acquired the slightly pejorative connotations that adhere to *Tory*, once boasted many derivatives: *Grittish*, *Grit(t)ism*, *Gritty* and *Grittiest*, "most radical of Liberals,"[3] none of which has survived to brighten the political scene.

The tendency of the two major parties to dominate Canadian politics obscures the fact that in pre-Confederation days a spate of lesser political groups competed with each other and rent the air with their battle cries. Samuel Phillips Day, writing in 1864,[4] listed no less than six distinct political faiths: *Blues*, "persons who uphold the doctrine of the temporal power of the Roman Church;" *Rouges*, "those who oppose the Church of Rome on temporal questions;" *Tories*, "a party almost extinct, but who once were the supporters of 'the Old Family Compact';" *Conservatives*, "the adherents and admirers of the J. A. Macdonald and Cartier's administration and policy;" *Hincksite Reformers*, "adherents to the policy of Baldwin, associated with that of the Grand Trunk;" *Clear-Grits*, "outré Democrats. These embrace every class of politician in Canada, so far at least as it has been possible for me to ascertain." Nor was this list exhaustive. In Lower

---

[1] C. J. Lovell, "A Sampling of Materials for a Dictionary of Canadian English," *J.C.L.A.*, 1958, pp. 16–17, 22–23. The *DC* can muster only four citations for *Grit*, three of them prior to 1907.

[2] C. J. Lovell, "A Sampling of Materials . . ." p. 16; *Encyclopedia Canadiana*, Vol. 5, p. 44.

[3] C. J. Lovell, "A Sampling of Materials . . ." p. 23.

[4] *English America: or Pictures of Canadian Places and People*, London, 1864, Vol. 1, p. 44.

Canada, *Bleu* and *Castor* were current political terms,[1] and members of the Reform Party came to be known as *anti-bureaucrates* or *patriotes*.[2]

Canadian parliamentary language is far removed from the ideal attributed to Premier Souphoulis of Greece: "The right to insult is one of Democracy's main features. I'm sure it never happens in America that journalists insult Government leaders as they do here. You can't insult in another language as you can in Greek."[3] It is true that parliamentary invective, like any other idiom, varies from century to century and from country to country. Norman W. Wilding and Philip Laundy recall in *An Encyclopaedia of Parliament* (London, 1958) that "when Lord Shaftesbury took his seat as Lord Chancellor in 1672 the Duke of York called him a rascal and a villain. (The Chancellor replied that he was obliged to His Royal Highness for not calling him a coward and a papist as well.)"

The ground-rules have changed somewhat since the days of Charles II. Thus, say Wilding and Laundy, "any epithet which reflects upon the character of a member of either House is considered disorderly," but this general principle has not been applied to the same extent throughout the Commonwealth. Perhaps only one rule is universal, that no member of parliament may accuse another of not telling the truth; although even here some latitude is tolerated. The expression *terminological inexactitude* has been permitted, possible because of its impressive length and periphrastic form, but not *a complete distortion of the facts*. Apart from the ban on calling a fellow member a liar, however, there is not always agreement as to what constitutes an unparliamentary expression. Thus, although *fool* has been permitted in the Mother of Parliaments, it is banned in South Africa. On the other hand, *rat* has been allowed in South Africa but not in Britain. Australia has specifically forbidden one member of parliament to refer to another as *a sewer rat, a jabbering nincompoop, a cad, a bounder, a miserable body-snatcher*, or *my winey friend*.[4] British parliamentary

---

[1] W. D. Lighthall, "Canadian English," *The Week* (Toronto), August 16, 1889.
[2] *Encyclopedia Canadiana*, Vol. 8, p. 229.
[3] Quoted by Mario Pei in *The Story of English*, Philadelphia, 1952.
[4] Mario Pei, *The Story of English*, Philadelphia, 1952, pp. 252–253.

usage also proscribes *cad*,[1] not to mention *blackguard, swine, traitor, stool-pigeon, pharisee, bastard* and that favourite term of communist abuse, *hooligan*.[2]

The British rules are adopted and followed in the Canadian parliamentary bible and *vade mecum, Beauchesne's Parliamentary Rules and Forms*.[3] This work relies heavily on Sir Thomas May's theopneustic text, *A Treatise on the Law, Privileges, Proceedings and Usage of Parliament*,[4] but adds little to its *index expurgatorius*. By contrast with British or Australian example, the Canadian parliamentary vocabulary can only be described as mealy-mouthed. Thus Speakers even in the bad old days banned the use of "impertinence," or saying that a member is "absolutely unfair," or that "he ceases to act as a gentleman." Things are scarcely better today, with recent rulings against such cautelous innuendos as "a menace to Parliament," "treating Parliament with contempt," and "unworthy of the position . . . of a supposedly responsible Minister." Only once, in 1953, was there a flash of something approaching genuine vituperation in "cesspool methods," but generally Ottawa lacks the objurgatory scope of other Commonwealth parliaments, notably the Legislative Assembly of Utter Pradesh, which in one year (1954) in addition to forbidding such minor indiscretions as "useless talk," "baseless," and "dogs," was called on to ban "mulish tactics," "throw him out by the neck," and "sucking the bones of the poor."[5]

---

[1] *Cad* derives from the Scots *caddie* (itself from the French *cadet*) meaning a person who goes about doing odd jobs, hence its application dating back to 1857 to the boy who carries the clubs in golf. The pejorative career of *cad* began, according to the *SOED*, at Oxford in 1831, where the term was first applied contemptuously to townspeople. Thence it acquired the broader meaning of a vulgar, ill-bred person or blackguard which it now bears.

[2] Mario Pei, *The Story of English. Hooligan*, although it was probably given its greatest pre-Soviet publicity by the American comic-strip character "Happy Hooligan," is of British parentage (*c.* 1898), apparently, says the *SOED*, from the name of "an Irish family in S.E. London conspicuous for ruffianism."

[3] Its full style is *Rules and Forms of the House of Commons of Canada, with Annotations, Comments and Precedents: A Compendium of Canadian Parliamentary Practice for the Use of Members of Parliament*, 4th ed., Toronto, 1958.

[4] 15th ed., London, 1950.

[5] These last are gleaned from *The Table*, the Journal of the Society of Clerks-at-Table in Commonwealth Parliaments, published annually at London, which contains a list of words and phrases allowed and disallowed in the legislative bodies of the Commonwealth. For a review of the subject, see Michael MacDonagh, "Unparliamentary Language," *The Nineteenth Century*, 1935, pp. 359–366.

D

The Canadian Upper House is singularly free from comminatory speech. According to the Law Clerk of the Senate, unparliamentary language is entirely unknown within its precincts, nor has any such been heard for at least thirty years.[1]

The language of both Canadian and American law is almost exclusively drawn from England. When different words exist in England and America, the tendency in Canada is to use the English term. Thus the judge's address to a jury is usually called a *charge* rather than a *summation*, and we are advised to use *recess* (verb) rather than *adjourn* when speaking of the sittings of the Court.[2] On the other hand, the person known in America as the *district attorney*, and in England as the *public prosecutor*, is in Canada called the *crown attorney*. A judge of the Supreme Court, whether of any province or of the Supreme Court of Canada, is invariably referred to as *Mr. Justice* Blank and addressed in court as *Your Lordship* or *My Lord*. A similar decorum invests other branches of the judiciary: judges of the county and district courts are referred to as *His Honour* Judge Blank and addressed as *Your Honour*, while police magistrates are known as *His Worship* Magistrate Blank, and addressed as *Your Worship*.

The field of Canadian honorifics generally is a meagre one. Hereditary honours having been abolished in Canada about 1918 and but briefly revived in 1934–1935, we are happily spared the intricacies of titles and forms of address which have spawned a considerable literature elsewhere. If one excludes the heirs to a small but uncertain number of Canadian peerages, who in any case are usually misdescribed by the press, we have only an occasional Sir or Lady left over from earlier days, and these may scarcely be said to present much of a problem. Titular and hereditary honours aside, the roundest Canadian title is *His Excellency The Right Honourable*, reserved for the Governor-General. Next in order of descent is *The Right Honourable*, which is currently attached to a few Canadians, notably present and past prime ministers and others who are members of the Imperial Privy Council, and may

[1] In answer to my private inquiry.
[2] See a letter in the Toronto *Globe and Mail*, December 7, 1957, entitled "Words and Terms for Court Proceedings" by "(The Honourable) F. D. Hogg, formerly of The Court of Appeal for Ontario."

be abbreviated to *The Rt. Hon.*, or rarely, *The Rt. Honble.* There follows the title *Honourable*, so beloved in the United States (in the spelling *Honorable*) that, notwithstanding Mencken's entertaining assault,[1] it has continued to breed and multiply in that egalitarian land. A recent tally, that of Albert H. Marckwardt in *American English* (1958), confers the title in imagination on some 2,000 functionaries of the federal judiciary and executive, and then proceeds to multiply this number by 48 (the multiplier would now be 50) to produce the truly staggering total of 102,000 possible *Honorables*, the population of a fair-sized city.

By contrast, Canada is relatively parsimonious with *Honourable*. The word is by Order in Council restricted to seven clearly defined categories of public officials: (1) Federal cabinet ministers, members of the Queen's Privy Council for Canada and all former cabinet ministers; (2) The Speaker of the House of Commons during his term of office; (3) Senators; (4) provincial Lieutenant-Governors; (5) provincial cabinet ministers and speakers of provincial legislatures during tenure of office; (6) the High Commissioners of Commonwealth countries stationed in Canada; and (7) Judges of the Supreme Court of Canada, the Exchequer Court and all provincial courts above the level of county or district courts, for a grand total of some 600 *Honourables*.

II Indian and Eskimo

Like Austral English, or what Mencken called the American language, Canadian English did not spring from native soil. The aboriginal languages—Indian and Eskimo—although they left a widely scattered legacy of place names had only a very minor influence on the main body of Canadian speech, and for the most part they remain today as they were in the beginning alien tongues which bewilder the white man with their strangeness and complexity.

[1] *The American Language*, 1936, pp. 271–276.

The first Canadianisms were borrowed from the Indian languages by early explorers and settlers to describe objects new to European experience, the language most commonly drawn on being Algonquin, one of the great linguistic stocks of North America. The largest class of words comprised the names of animals, trees, fruits and fish. Thus as early as 1683, the Minutes of the Hudson's Bay Company had recorded the acquisition of "*quickahash* (wolverine) 8 which cost £0. 10. 0." Through many spellings, the word has come down to us as *quickhatch*, derived by folk etymology from the Algonquin *kikkwahakes*, "used as the name of the animal," says the *DA*, "because it was hard to hit." Similarly, the Jesuit *Rélations* for the year 1684[1] make mention of *pekan*, a member of the weasel family sometimes called *fisher* or *black cat*, probably from the Algonquin *pékané* and not to be confused with *pecan*, a species of hickory nut which derives from the Algonquin *pakan*.

As the frontier was pushed back, a few Indian words continued to come into the language and some stayed. So *tamarack*, also from the Algonquin, was first recorded in the journals of the Lewis and Clark expedition (1805) where it is coupled with a probable Canadianism, *hackmatack* to denote several species of coniferous trees. *Hackmatack* appears in the form *tackamahacka* in Robinson and Rispin's *Journey Through Nova Scotia*, published at York in 1774.[2] To about the same period belongs *pembina* (1760), the highbush cranberry, derived from the Cree *nipin*, summer, and *minam*, whortleberry,[3] which gave its name to rivers in Manitoba and Alberta, as well as to the *pembina buggy* or *pembina cart*, blood brother to the *Red River cart*.

Contrary to popular belief, not many Indian words found their way permanently into Canadian English; such borrowings as there were related to objects previously unnamed in English. Their number was always relatively small, and most of them have

---

[1] Pascal Poirier, "Des vocables algonquins ... qui sont entrés dans la langue," *Transactions of The Royal Society of Canada*, Ser. III, 1916, p. 339.

[2] The citation is taken from the *DC* which antedates the *DA*'s earliest citation by some 18 years.

[3] *Pembina* affords yet another example of the *DC*'s earliest citation (1760) antedating that of the *DA* (1824).

long since faded away. In 1902, Alexander F. Chamberlain compiled a list of 132 words in American English derived from the Algonquin[1] of which less than two score still enjoy any currency in Canada. The history of many of these Algonquin loan-words remains obscure. Although lexicographers commonly regard them as Americanisms, it would be as accurate to call some of them Canadianisms, or at any rate North Americanisms, for the Algonquin Indians originally lived on the Gatineau River east of Ottawa, later extending their influence over much of Quebec and Ontario. Ultimately the designation came to be applied to a larger linguistic group, including the Canadian tribes, which extended from the Atlantic to the Rockies and as far south as the Ohio River and Cape Hatteras. As a result, it is not possible to ascribe an exact geographical location to many of the terms in Chamberlain's word-list, although he definitely identified as Canadian, in addition to the words noted above, *muskeg* (1775), *saskatoon* (1800), *toboggan* (1691), *wapiti* (1824) and *wendigo* (1830).[2]

Such words as made the crossing often had both form and meaning altered in the process. Thus *muskeg*, which appeared as early as 1775 in the Hudson's Bay Company records in the spelling *muskake*, meaning a swamp, was rendered variously over the years as *mashquegies* (1806) and *muskegue* (1824) before its meaning and spelling became standardized about 1860.[3] Chamberlain, and after him Mencken, suggested that a number of Indian words came into colonial English by way of Canadian French. Their passage may be indicated by spelling or pronunciation: as *carcajou*, traced by the *DC* to 1703, *caribou* (1665) and *mackinaw* (1761). To this class belongs *toboggan*, borrowed from the Canadian French *tabagan* or *tabaganne*, itself from the Micmac *tobakun*, a hand-sled.

To Chamberlain's list may be added a scattering of Chinook Jargon terms which have chiefly survived in frontier fiction: *cheechako*, a tenderfoot, traced by the *DC* to the trail of '97; *skookum*, strong, which the *DA* dates to 1847; and *potlatch* (1870),

[1] "Algonkian Words in American English," *Journal of American Folklore*, 1902, pp. 240–267.

[2] The dates of first use are taken from the *DC*.

[3] The spellings and dates of use are taken from the *DC*.

originally a festival at which gifts were distributed, and later in the expression *cultus potlatch* (*cultus* = worthless) the gift itself, usually a present or free gift.

Is *totem* to be considered a Canadianism? The word, according to the *DA* quoting Frederick Webb Hodge's *Handbook of American Indians North of Mexico* (Washington, 1907–1910), is "irregularly derived from the term *ototeman* of the Chippewa and other cognate Algonquian dialects." The *SOED* confirms this by deriving it "from *Odjibwa*, or some kindred Algonkin dialect"—*Odjibwa*, or in Canada, *Ojibwa*, being cognate with *Chippewa*, the form more commonly used in the United States. The same difficulty arises in locating the geographical source of an Ojibwa word such as *totem* that we observed in the case of many Algonquin expressions. According to the *Encyclopedia Canadiana*, the Ojibwa occupied a very large area between the Ottawa Valley and the prairies, and "although generally thought of as living north of the Great Lakes, actually they were as much at home on the south side of Lake Superior as on the north." The word would therefore have arisen in a rather vaguely defined area which, until the drawing of the international boundary, was as much Canada as the United States. The *DA*'s earliest citation is from the *Nova Francia* of Marc Lescarbot (London, 1609): "Memberton . . . carrieth hanged at his neck . . . a purse . . . within which there is I know not what as big as a small nut, which he saith to be his devil called Aoutem." In the form *totam* the *DC* traces it to 1768–1782, the spelling *totem* first appearing in 1829, and the word had a long history before being appropriated and popularized by Sir James G. Frazer in *Totemism* (1887) and *Totemism and Exogamy* (1910), and Freud in *Totem and Taboo* (Vienna, 1913). *Totem-pole*, called in England *totem-post*, a wooden post carved and painted with totem figures, is traced by the *DA* to 1880 although the practice of erecting totem-poles existed among the Indians of the Pacific coast at least as early as 1808 according to Simon Fraser's *Journals*[1] the peak of totem-pole construction occurring between 1860 and 1880.

One may also note a few pseudo-Indian terms. Thus *canoe*, despite its long association with the Canadian wilds, is in fact

---

[1] *The Letters and Journals of Simon Fraser, 1806–1808*, Toronto, 1960.

Haitian in origin, having been brought back to Europe by Columbus in the form *canoa*, its first recorded English appearance being in 1555. Originally *canoe* had reference to the dugout of the West Indies and probably came into Canada by way of the Canadian French *canot* as applied to the native birchbark canoe. Its spellings were varied: the *DC* lists *canoo* (1684) from the *Voyages* of Radisson, *cannoes* (1697) and *kinoo* (1952) from Labrador, pronounced "kin-oo." An attempt has been made to derive *barbecue* from a Canadian Indian word *barboka*, supposedly carried by the French into the Mississippi Valley.[1] But the word was probably borrowed from Haiti, the weight of opinion being that it came into American speech by way of the Spanish *barbacoa*.[2]

The term *Indian* itself had its origin in the fact that the Spanish discoverers of America, under the impression that they had reached India, called the natives whom they encountered *Indios*, i.e., "Indians." A. F. Chamberlain pointed out how deeply the word is embedded in North American speechways and his many examples include a few Canadian expressions.[3] Thus some plants received the name *Indian* "because they were new or strange or had some real or fancied connection with the aborigines," as *Indian tea*, *Indian verveine* and *Indian whort* in Labrador and Newfoundland. Canadian French also preserves memorials of the Indian in *soulier sauvage* or *botte sauvage*, moccasin, *thé sauvage*, Labrador tea, and *traine sauvage*, toboggan. Chamberlain recalled that the Indian tribes were always *Les Nations* to the early French Canadians, and the older maps show such names as *Rivière des Nations*, *Rivière des Petites Nations* and *Lac des Deux Nations*.

The term *Indian summer* is widely used in Canada and the United States to designate the period of warm pleasant weather which usually follows the first cold days of autumn. The origin of the expression is obscure, but it appears in Canada as early as 1796 in Mrs. John Graves Simcoe's *Diary*. A comparable term, *Indian winter*, was reported from Nebraska "to name a belated spell of

---

[1] J. M. Carrière, "Indian and Creole *Barboka*, American *Barbecue*," *Language*, 1957, pp. 148–150.

[2] H. L. Mencken, *The American Language*, 1936, p. 112.

[3] "Memorials of the Indian," *Journal of American Folklore*, 1902, pp. 107–116.

winter coming in the late spring." [1] While the expression has some small currency in Canada—the *DC*'s single citation is dated 1937—the same American source adds that the Canadian expression is *squaw winter* and quotes the following from the *Toronto Daily Star* of April 8, 1907: "This morning people awoke to find themselves in the midst of *squaw winter*, some three inches of soft snow having fallen during the night. The streets are full of slush now." The *DC* has, however, uncovered later citations which apply the term variously to "a mild beginning of winter" (1912) and "a spell of wintry weather occurring in early fall, especially when followed by an Indian summer" (1935, 1953). The Canadian French equivalent of Indian summer is *été des sauvages*.[2]

The name *Eskimo* is not itself of Eskimo origin, and there have been many theories about its derivation. According to one nineteenth-century scholar, it came from the French "*ceux qui maux (miaulent)*, and was expressive of the shouts of *Tey-mo*, proceeding from the fleets of kaiyaks, that surround a trading vessel in the straits of Hudson, or coasts of Labrador." Thalbitzer, a Danish ethnologist of the present century, finding a clue in the Jesuit *Rélations*, where the name appears as *Excomminquois*, suggested that it signified "a group of people that had been excluded from the church and banished by the missionaries," but this seems purely fanciful. The better view is that *Eskimo* is the English version of a Canadian French transliteration, *Esquimau*, of an Indian word which has been variously rendered as *esquimantsic*, *wiyaskimowok* or *estimeow*, meaning "eater of raw meat." In abbreviated form, it appears as *husky*, an Eskimo dog or malemute.[3] The Eskimos refer to themselves as simply *Inuit*, the people.

The number of Eskimo words which has penetrated Canadian English is even scantier than the Indian borrowings, being confined to the very limited content of Eskimo life with which the

---

[1] Mamie Meredith, "Notes on American Weather Terms," *American Speech*, 1931, p. 466.

[2] The standard French term is *été de la Saint-Martin*. See Gaston Dulong, "Le mot sauvage en franco-canadien," *J.C.L.A.*, 1961, pp. 161–163.

[3] These and other orthographical variants may be found in the *DC*. And see C. J. Lovell, "A Sampling of Materials for a Dictionary of Canadian English on Historical Principles," *J.C.L.A.*, 1958, pp. 18–21, 23–24. A similar naming is *Mohawk* ("they eat animate things").

white man was familiar: *igloo, mukluk, komatik, kayak* and the like. Although such words are not of recent usage, they have been largely overlooked by most lexicographers. Thus the *DA* gives space only to *mukluk*, originally a sealskin, then a boot of sealskin, which it traces to 1869 in the spelling "maclock," antedating the *DC*'s earliest citation by some thirty years. The *DA* ignores the well-known *kayak*, which has been current in English at least since 1757 according to the *SOED; igloo*, which the *DC* dates back to 1771; and *komatik*, an open dog sled (1824). Many Eskimo borrowings relate to articles of clothing, the best known being *parka* (1852).[1]

III Gaelic

The influence of Gaelic in Canada is no longer what it was in the days before the levelling effect of modern times began to silence the many tongues of the early settlers. W. D. Lighthall writing in 1889 reported on a number of Scottish dialects in widely separated areas, but even then, in his view, Gaelic was becoming less common, and many dialect terms, chiefly Lowland, were disappearing before the combined onslaught of school English and Americanisms.[2]

From earliest times, as J. L. Campbell has observed, "the Nova Scotian settlements were alike the most homogeneous and most isolated, and it is in these places that the Gaelic language is today still in constant use amongst a considerable portion of the population."[3] Gaelic was included in the Census for the first time in

[1] This and other dates of first noted use are taken from the *DC*, which contains a glossary of Eskimo terms.

[2] "Canadian English," *The Week* (Toronto), August 16, 1889, pp. 581–583. See Chapter 1 for an account of the early Scots dialects.

[3] J. L. Campbell, "Scottish Gaelic in Canada," *American Speech*, 1936, pp. 128–136. See also "Scottish Gaelic in Canada" by the same author, Edinburgh *Scotsman*, January 30, 1933. Gaelic is a well-defined member of the Indo-European family of languages, whose classifications are (a) Goidelic, which comprises Irish, Scottish, Gaelic and Manx; (b) Brythonic, comprising Welsh, Breton and Cornish; and (c) Gaulish. The term Gaelic is commonly used to describe the surviving Celtic languages apart from Welsh and Breton.

D*

1931, when it appeared that there were 32,000 Gaelic-speaking persons in Canada.[1] Of this number, 29,000 were native-born, 24,000 of them living in Nova Scotia, for the most part on Cape Breton Island. Nearly all were bilingual, and it is noteworthy that the number of Gaelic speakers did not decrease in the younger age groups. Campbell has pointed out that Canadian Gaelic differs from the French of Quebec or the German of Pennsylvania in that its parent tongue is in decay at home, and has been under official disapproval for nearly four hundred years. "The extreme political and economic unimportance to which the Gaelic-speaking population of Scotland has been reduced," he added "is sufficient to account for the reduction of Gaelic to a patois, dependent in Scotland as in Canada upon the English language for all its borrowings."

Campbell noted that the level of Gaelic scholarship and literary effort was somewhat lower among Canadian Gaelic speakers than in Scotland, one measure of this being the extensive borrowings of Canadian expressions and terms in both popular speech and literature. In this vein, Mencken has listed a variety of loan-words, some of them Gaelicized, as *factoraidh*, factory, *stobh*, stove, *postmhaighstir*, postmaster, *buiseal*, bushel, and *seudair*, cedar.[2] The suffix *-adh* is sometimes used for the English gerund, as *startadh*, starting, and *driveadh*, driving, and nouns are often given a Gaelic plural: *maidseachan*, matches, *sentaichean*, cents and *logaichean*, logs. There is also what Mencken calls a "softening of consonants," as *char* for car, *bheat* for beat and *pharty* for party.

Henry Alexander, who conducted a number of field-studies in the Maritimes for *The Linguistic Atlas of the United States and Canada*, reported that a goodly number of non-English speech habits could still be observed among the Gaelic-speaking residents of Nova Scotia.[3] Such speakers, he said, often had difficulty in pronouncing the "voiced" sounds *v* and *z*. There was also a general tendency to carry words over from their original Gaelic idiom, as when *loft* was used in the sense of "the upper part of a house," a

[1] According to the Census of 1961, the number of Gaelic speakers in Canada had declined to 7,533 of whom 3,702 lived in Nova Scotia.
[2] *The American Language*, New York, 1936, p. 683.
[3] *The Story of our Language*, Toronto, 1940, p. 223.

meaning which the Gaelic *lobht* has in addition to the more usual one. A few animal calls were derived from Gaelic; thus sheep were often called with a sound approximating *kiry*, *kiry*, *kiry*, or *kirsh*, *kirsh*, *kirsh*, which harks back to the Gaelic words for sheep, *caor(a)* and *caorach*.

IV Newfoundland English

Professor G. M. Story of Memorial University of Newfoundland, who has been conducting a planned study of the language and place names of the island, points out that Newfoundland dialects are almost wholly derived from those of Great Britain, especially the southwest counties and Ireland.[1] The two exceptions are an Acadian French community in the Bay St. George district and a small colony of Micmac Indians living along the south and west coasts. He adds:

> In quite general terms Newfoundland speech derives its special character from two factors, one historical and the other geographical. In the first place the very early settlement of the Island implies the 'transplanting' of English dialects of a period unusually early as Canadian communities go. Secondly, the isolation of the Island, and within it the separation of the widely-scattered fishing villages, have fostered the development of a local speech without that 'mixture' which characterizes, say, the dialect of New England, or the modifying effect of a 'standard' speech that we find in England. While these general conditions can be paralleled elsewhere, the extreme form in which they have applied in Newfoundland amounts to a major difference setting the Island linguistically apart from its neighbouring communities.

This linguistic isolation is easily understood when one realizes

---

[1] "Research in the Language and Place Names of Newfoundland," *J.C.L.A.*, 1957, pp. 47–55; "Newfoundland English Usage," *Encyclopedia Canadiana*, Ottawa, 1957.

that more than 98 per cent of the population was born in the province; out of a population of 415,074 in 1956, only 7,938 were outsiders.

The first extensive study of Newfoundland English was conducted by George Patterson, who upon his arrival in the nineties found the islanders using many English words which he had never heard before, as well as some familiar words in unfamiliar senses.[1] These peculiarities were encountered at all social and economic levels, although more commonly among uneducated speakers and writers. Patterson classified the distinctive Newfoundland vocabulary as follows:

(1) Obsolete English words, as *barm*, yeast; *brews*, 'pieces of hard biscuit soaked overnight, warmed in the morning, and then eaten with boiled codfish and butter;'[2] *child*, to denote a female child;[3] *clavy*, the shelf over a mantelpiece; *costive*, costly;[4] *dodtrel* or *dotterel*, a silly (old) person; *dout*, to extinguish; *dresh*, to go visiting; *droke*, a sloping valley between two hills; *drung*, a narrow lane; *dwoll*, a doze; *flankers*, sparks from a chimney; *flaw*, a sudden gust of wind;[5] *frore*, frozen;[6] *glutch*, to swallow; *hackle* or *cross hackle*, the cross-examination of a witness; *hat*, a bunch, heap or clump, as 'a hat of trees;' *house-place*, kitchen; *jonnick*, honest; *knap*, a knoll; *leary*, hungry or faint; *linney*, a small building;[7] *lun*, a calm; *mouch*, to play truant; *nesh*, tender and delicate; *nunch*, 'the refreshment men take with them on going to the woods;' *pook*, a haycock; *quism*, a quaint saying or conundrum; *rampike*, a dead spruce or pine tree; *slide*, a sleigh; *spancel* as a noun: 'a rope to tie a cow's hind legs;' and as

[1] "Notes on the Dialect of the People of Newfoundland," *Journal of American Folklore*, 1895, pp. 27–40; 1896, pp. 19–37; 1897, pp. 203–213.
[2] Patterson recalled the old English word *brewis* defined by Dr. Johnson as "a piece of bread soaked in boiling fat pottage made of salted meat."
[3] See *The Winter's Tale*, III, 3, "Mercy on's a barne; a very pretty barne! A boy or a childe, I wonder?"
[4] From the dialect of Norfolk, there written *costyve*.
[5] *Hamlet*, V, 1, 239: "Should patch a wall, to expel the winter's flaw."
[6] Milton: "The parching air/Burns frore and cold performs the effect of fire."
[7] Patterson compares the New England *linter* or *lenter*, possibly a corruption of *lean-to*.

a verb: 'to tie with a rope;' *strouters*, the large outer piles
of a wharf, the inner ones being called *shores;* and *yaffle*,
an armful.

(2) Familiar English words used in peculiar senses, as,
brief, applied to a disease which quickly proves fatal; *clever*,
large and handsome; *bread*, hard biscuit as opposed to soft
bread which is called *loaf; rind*, the bark of a tree; *room*,
'the whole premises of a merchant, planter or fisherman;'
spurt, a short time.

(3) Words of unknown or uncertain origin, as *bangbelly*, a
type of pudding; *callivances*, a species of white bean; *chronic*,
an old stump; *cracky*, a little dog; the *diddies*, a nightmare;
dido, a bitch; *gandy*, a pancake; *pelm*, light ashes; *shimmick*,
a term of contempt for one who attempts to deny his
Newfoundland origin; *smoochin*, hair oil; *tolt*, a solitary hill;
tuckamore, a clump of low spruce; and *willigiggin*, something
between a whisper and a giggle.

Despite the fact that the French had been fishing off the Newfoundland coast for hundreds of years, Patterson was able to find
only one word which he definitely ascribed to this source: *Jackatar*,
a corruption of *Jacques à terre*, and applied to any French Canadian
visiting the west coast of the island. Words of Indian origin were
also very rare, confirming W. F. Ganong's earlier view that "New
Brunswick and Nova Scotia where French and Indians long were
friends are rich in native names, while Newfoundland has hardly
one." [1] Patterson was able to discover only two words which he
thought might be of aboriginal origin: *babbage*, the plaiting of a
snowshoe, and *tibbage*, the small filling-in at its toe, the first of
these being obviously akin to the Canadian French *babiche*.

Patterson remarked that several of the old English words in
use in Newfoundland are also found in New England, and
wondered whether they might have been derived independently
from the common British ancestor. He concluded that most were
direct importations from England, any early intercourse between
Newfoundlanders and New England fishermen being too limited

[1] "A Monograph of the Place Nomenclature of the Province of New Brunswick,"
Royal Society of Canada, Proceedings and Transactions, 1896, vol. II, pp. 125–259.

and transient in his view to have affected the language generally. He suggested, however, that a few words may have come from that source, among them *callibogus*, a mixture of spruce beer and rum; *catamaran*, originally a raft of logs but used in Newfoundland to denote a wood sled; and *scrod*, in New England *escrod*, a broiled young codfish.

At about the same time, W. M. Tweedie was collecting examples of the dialect of New Brunswick, Nova Scotia and Newfoundland,[1] among them *auntsary*, a kind of catamaran turned up at both ends; *barber*, the vapour rising from water on a frosty day; *cagged*, said of one who has taken the pledge; *clotten house* or *tilt*, one-storey wooden house; *colcannon night* or *snap-apple night*, Hallowe'en; *conkerbill*, icicle; *crunnocks*, dry wood, as in "to spell (gather) a *gafful* (armful) of *crunnocks*;" *duckish*, dark, gloomy; *dunch*, bread not properly baked; *dwy*, a sudden squall of wind with rain or snow; *flacket*, a girl wearing loose clothing; *all of a floption*, unawares; *gly*, a squint or sidelong glance; *handsignment*, signature; *hubbles*, frozen ruts in a road; *hunkersliding*, acting unfairly; *naked* or *starknaked*, tea without milk or sugar; *nippent*, flighty; *nunny-bag*, lunch bag; *piddle*, to carry on a small business (a variant of peddle); *prog*, food; *scrammed with the cold*, very cold; *silver thaw*, a sleet storm leaving trees coated with ice; *slip one's gallows*, break a suspender button;[2] *slob*, soft snow or ice; *twinly*, tender, delicate; and *yarry*, smart or quick.

Over the years, fresh generations of observers have continued to be fascinated by Newfoundland English. In the 1920's, G. A. England likened the island to ancient Greece, with its deep bays and difficult land communications creating and preserving local differences of speech.[3] As England observed, Elizabethan and even Chaucerian words are still in general use: *bide, tarry, even so, prent* and *gobbet* to name only a few.

At first contact with the Newfoundland coast [England wrote in 1925] one finds the language of the fishing-folk,

---

[1] *Dialect Notes*, 1894, pp. 377–381.

[2] *Gallows* (pl. *gallowses*) for suspenders or braces has been used in England since 1730 according to the *SOED*. In America, the spelling and pronunciation *galluses* is more common.

[3] "Newfoundland Dialect Items," *Dialect Notes*, 1925, pp. 322–346.

who there constitute a majority of the people, in many instances almost unintelligible, especially as many of the people speak in a thick and mumbling tone. The educated classes, of course, talk good English with many Americanisms, all their relations of life and commerce being closer with the United States than with the mother-country. But even among them a tinge of dialect pronunciation usually remains. One does not have to talk long with even the best-educated of Newfoundlanders to discover his nationality. Though such Newfoundlanders will often deny that any dialects exist, the very words they use in their denials will sometimes betray them. They simply are not conscious of this fact. A Newfoundlander's way, for instance, of saying: 'Not-at-all.' with an inimitable drawl and a faint broadening toward 'ahl' reveals him, even though he may be a university man. The best-educated almost invariably mispronounce certain words, such as 'fipper' for 'flipper.' And in many a piquant and entertaining turn of speech, their race will stand revealed.

The Newfoundland dialect, as England pointed out, is a composite of English, Irish and Scottish, any approach to a standardized English having long been hindered by geographical isolation and the lack of free public schools. The language has also been uniquely affected and enriched by cod-fishing and seal-hunting, which spawned a native vocabulary of considerable interest. Out of a word-list of some 950 terms collected by England in the years 1920 and 1922, about half the expressions were concerned with fishing and sealing.[1]

Newfoundland speech is characterized, England noted, by a number of distinctive idioms. One is the frequent use of diminutives whereby a gale becomes a *breeze*, oars are *paddles*, an axe is a *hatchet*, a schooner a *skiff*, a cable a *string*, and a heavy steel hawser a *wire*. Similarly, the worst weather is only *dirt* and the

---

[1] Many of these are meticulously detailed. Thus a harp seal when newly-born is called *white jacket*, in its second year *rusty jacket*, in its third year *bedlamer* or *bellamer* (*bête de la mer*), and in its fourth year *saddleback* or *sadler*. A flipper is called a *hand*, but the word *flipper* itself is restricted to the forward flippers; *sculp* is the skin and fat of a seal, and *tow-o'-fat* a string of from three to five sculps.

best but *civil*, while a man sick in bed is merely *puckerin'* or *turned over*. There are also many distinctive pronunciations, as *marnin'* for morning; *alang* for along; and *nar, nard* or *narth* for north; *ven* for fin; and *vur* for fir. In syntax, the use of the double negative is common, as is "a fairly consistent distinction between *you* and *ye;*" the personification of inanimate objects; and the retention of old forms of the preterite, as *clomb*, or the substitution of new weak preterites for those of old strong verbs, as *beared*.[1]

England added to the earlier word-lists many terms in common use during the period 1920–1922, including: *airsome*, cold, stormy; *back east*, in Newfoundland; *bare*, out of funds, broke; *batch*, a fall of snow; *bedflies*, bedbugs, lice; *belly an' back*, odd ones (not a pair); *bleacher*, a marriageable girl; *blood of a bitch*, "a term of great reproach;" *bosthoon*, an ignorant man; *braffus*, breakfast; *bugger*, fellow, "almost a term of endearment;"[2] *chuck-a-tuck*, full; *codology*, the art or science of jollying; *dry diet*, poor food; *farmer*, a poor sailor; *fist*, to grasp, as in "then Lannigan fisted his pig by the tail;" *garagee*, free-for-all fight; *gazaroo*, boy; *hoffy*, crazy; *humgumption*, common sense; *mawzy*, close and foggy without wind; *merry-me-got*, bastard; *puckaloon*, a foot; *sharooshed*, taken aback, disappointed; *sish*, fine, slushy ice; *streel*, a slovenly woman. In Newfoundland, a person who rows alone is said to do so *crosshanded*, whence probably comes the custom of applying that term to anything done alone, for example, "I went to the dance crosshanded."[3]

Labrador because of its extreme geographical isolation has become even more of a language museum than some parts of the island of Newfoundland. Thus Mary S. Evans, who visited Labrador in 1926,[4] encountered unusual names and expressions which had been noted in George Cartwright's *Journal* a hundred

[1] G. M. Story, "Research in the Language and Place Names of Newfoundland," *J.C.L.A.*, 1957, p. 54.

[2] *Bugger* in this sense is general throughout Canada. Morley Ayearst, "A Note on Canadian Speech," *American Speech*, 1939, pp. 231–233, was quite wrong in stating that "the English meaning of *bugger* as sodomite is universal in Canada, and not its innocent usage as equivalent to fellow or chap as in the American Middle West."

[3] Harold Wilson, " 'Crosshanded' and 'Sad,' " *American Speech*, 1938, p. 236.

[4] "Terms from the Labrador Coast," *American Speech*, 1930, pp. 56–58.

and fifty years earlier.[1] As she pointed out, the isolation of the coast and the absence of foreign influence had resulted in the survival into the twentieth century of most of the seventeenth-century vocabulary brought in by early white settlers. Among the terms which she reported were *abroad*, apart; *he* used for it or this; *jig*, to fish with hook and line, and *jigger*, the hook used for this purpose; *puff-up*, the birth of a child, as in "I hear you are expecting a puff-up at your house;" *tickle*, a narrow neck of water. To this list, William Duncan Strong[2] added: *clefty*, precipitious; *lund*, quiet; *belly-catter*, ice barricade; *landwash*, beach or shore; *scrouge*, to kill; *shore crap*, shrew; *ground hurts*, a variety of blueberry growing on a low shrub, and *backy hurts*, the same on a higher shrub.[3]

A few years later, Grace Tomkinson[4] recorded the pronounced Irish flavour of Newfoundland idiom in such forms as "I'm after doing it;" "I've now come from doing it;" the widespread use of *sure*, and a rather archaic Irish vocabulary: *boneen*, a young pig; *caubeen*, a cap; *shoneen*, a double-dealer; and *plawmosh*, flattery. Scottish loan-words on the other hand were few: *crowdy*, oatmeal and milk; *piggin*, a small bucket; and *glaum*, to snatch. She also added a few words of probable French origin to Patterson's scant list: *angishore*, a weak, miserable person, from angoisseux; *vandu*, a sale, from vendu; and *goulds*, a valley with wooded sides, from goulée.[5]

What gives Newfoundland English savour for many people is its rich lode of Elizabethan and earlier words. Among Shakespearean

---

[1] Captain George Cartwright, *A Journal of Transactions and Events During a Residence of Nearly Sixteen Years on the Coast of Labrador*, Newark, 1792, ed. Charles Wendell Townsend, London, 1911.

[2] "More Labrador Survivals," *American Speech*, 1931, pp. 290–291. These words were garnered in 1927–1928. See also Elizabeth B. Greenleaf, "Newfoundland Words," *American Speech*, 1931, p. 306; B. H. Porter, "A Newfoundland Vocabulary," *American Speech*, 1963, pp. 297–301.

[3] This is not, at least primarily, a reference to the discomfort involved in picking blueberries. The fruit of various species of *vaccinium* is in England called *whortleberry* (1578) or *hurtleberry* (1460), sometimes abbreviated to *whart* (1578) or *hurt* (1542). The dates of first use are taken from the *SOED*.

[4] "Shakespeare in Newfoundland," *Dalhousie Review*, 1940, pp. 60–70.

[5] G. M. Story, "Research in the Language and Place Names of Newfoundland," p. 48, says that *goulds* is "applied variously to open meadowland and to a plant growing in such places."

terms may be noted *cam*, crooked; *draft*, rubbish; *doxey*, a sweet-heart; *ean*, a young lamb; *fadge*, to succeed; *fardel*, a bundle; *firk*, to bustle; *fust*, a mouldy loaf of bread; *sconce*, a head; and *skirr*, to hurry about. To these may be added a few Spenserian words: *younker*, youngster; *bawn*, "an expanse of foreshore where fish are spread out to dry;" and *swodge* (Spenser's *tasswage*); and even Chaucerian terms: *afeared*; *gladyer*, a joker; *empt*, empty; *more*, the root of a tree; *maugre*, in spite of; *drieth*, drought; and *footer*, an idle fellow (Chaucerian *fautoir*).[1]

As late as 1957, G. M. Story[2] was remarking on "the frequent conservatism of the untutored, isolated, popular language" which has resulted in the survival of older English dialect terms: *bavin*, a brush faggot for lighting fires; *farrell*, a book cover; *fellon*, "a sore or whitlow on the finger;" *mundel*, "porridge stick;" *oxters*, armpits; *rames*, skeleton; *sicheturms*, "small brooks that dry up in the summer." Most important of all, he found the linguistic inventiveness of the islanders to be undiminished, illustrating "that older capacity for word-creation which, in the standard language, has often seemed to be weakened by a magpie fondness for foreign derivatives." Among such creations, he lists *flirrup*, "a large lamp used on fishing-stages;" *flobber*, "a very gentle sea-lop;" *gobstick*, a stick used to remove hooks from the "gob" of a fish; *grump-heads*, posts on a wharf for tying up boats; *pucklins*, small boys; *puddick*, codfish stomach; and *scolly*, "a wide, floppy head-dress worn by fisherwomen when curing fish or working in the fields."

Much of what is distinctive of Newfoundland speech, as in any other community, derives from the characteristic occupations and preoccupations of the people. The island vocabulary, as Story remarks, is practical, even homely in character, concrete rather than abstract, centred on fishing, the weather, wild life, "and, indeed, the whole natural world as it affects the life of a fishing people." Yet Story cautions the outsider against equating conceptual thinking and intelligence, or coming to the conclusion that a Newfoundlander, because of his lack of formal education,

[1] Grace Tomkinson, "Shakespeare in Newfoundland," *Dalhousie Review*, 1940, pp. 60–70.
[2] "Research in the Language and Place Names of Newfoundland," *J.C.L.A.*, 1957, pp. 47–55.

has not an adequate vocabulary. Story suggests, by way of corrective, that such a one consider the ways in which the Islander might call him a weak-minded fool: a *gomeril*, a *joskin*, an *omadawn*, an *omaloor*, an *ownshook*, a *scoopendike* or a *scrumpshy*.

V German

Although Germans were among the very earliest non-English colonists and today form the third largest ethnic group in Canada, the effect of German upon Canadian English has been almost negligible.[1] Here and there, small pockets of German speech have become embedded in the Canadian composite and their erosion by the surrounding English dialects has provided an interesting if specialized field of study. Thus M. B. Emeneau in "The Dialect of Lunenburg, Nova Scotia" explored the German background of the English dialect spoken there.[2] Lunenburg, described in the early records as Lüneburg, was settled by a brigade of Braunschweig-Lüneberg troops left over from the American wars as a deliberate means of counteracting a stubborn residue of Catholic Acadians. There followed more Germans, Swiss and a few French Protestants, and in the resulting *mélange* German, French and English were all spoken during the early years of the settlement.

French went out of use first, but German proved more tenacious. The German colonists at Lunenburg were determined to maintain their language and Lutheran religion, and a conscious effort to Anglicize them between the years 1753 and 1777 was much resented. Finally, "the language problem was left to be solved in

[1] G. P. Krapp came to the same conclusion about the influence of German on American English: *The English Language in America*, New York, 1925, Vol. I, p. 62. German settlers began to arrive in Canada as early as 1750–1752, when some 2,000 emigrants from Brunswick, Lüneberg, Hanover and the Palatinate landed in Nova Scotia. They were followed by many more: "Pennsylvania Dutch" Loyalists and disbanded mercenaries after the War of Independence, as well as a steady stream of arrivals throughout the nineteenth and well into the twentieth century.
[2] *Language*, 1935, pp. 140–147; 1940, pp. 214–215.

time by the environmental force of an English-speaking majority."[1] Little today remains except a residue of Germanisms, of which Emeneau has collected a few specimens. In memory perhaps of the German *mitgehen* are such locutions as *will you go with? I am going with, come on with;* and from *abwaschen* directly and by analogy, *wash your face off! clean your feet off!*, although these idioms were going out of use by 1935. *Get awake* and *get asleep* were fairly frequent verbal phrases, possibly based on *wach werden,* and also *make* in the sense of to prepare a meal, and *want* for predict, as in *the paper wants rain. All* in the sense of all gone was still heard, as *my money is all;* but the *was für ein* construction, as in *what for a thing is that?* was even then becoming rare. German words were practically unknown to people under the age of forty, and Emeneau predicted that the old expressions would be forgotten in another generation. Nevertheless, a few homely terms survived in familiar speech: *lappisch* in the sense of insipid; *slurp,* to drink noisily; and *fress,* to eat greedily, the latter used chiefly in correcting a child's table manners.

Emeneau concluded that although the original German speech of the early settlers had left its mark on syntax and to some extent vocabulary, its influence was on the wane, and the language of the group had become almost completely purged of its Germanic antecedents. Substantially, the same conclusion was reached at about the same time by Henry Alexander, who found a distinct German colouring in Lunenburg County affecting pronunciation, vocabulary and syntax, although very little German was actually spoken.[2] Thus the guttural *r,* the substitution of *d* and *t* sounds for the English *th* sounds in *these* and *thick,* and a few German idioms, such as *tik of fog* for very foggy, were common. A few animal calls were also distinctive, pigs, for example, being summoned with a cry that resembled *woots, woots, woots,* or *wootch, wootch, wootch.*

Another sizable German community has long existed in Ontario. As early as 1839, Anna Jameson reported that "at Berlin [now Kitchener] the Germans have a printing-press, and publish a

---

[1] Charles E. P. Phillips, *The Development of Education in Canada,* Toronto, 1957, pp. 63–64.

[2] "Linguistic Geography," *Queen's Quarterly,* 1940, pp. 38–47; and see H. Creighton, *Folklore of Lunenburg County,* Ottawa, 1950.

newspaper in their own language, which is circulated among their countrymen throughout the whole Province." [1] As happened in Nova Scotia, Ontario German bowed before the overwhelming influence of English, and little today remains.

Much of the original German community in Ontario came from the United States. In the 1930's, John Frederick Doering and Eileen Elita Doering studied the folk beliefs and practices of Western Ontario, where the influence of Pennsylvania Dutch had intermarried with the English, Scottish and Irish strains of the early settlers.[2] The Doerings collected a number of provincialisms and unusual meanings: *halb leinich,* half linen cloth; *gowl,* a horse; *smear cheese,* cottage cheese; *shimmel,* a white horse; *lotwak,* apple butter;[3] *rutsa,* a young scamp; *beebee,* chick; *dummy,* an electric engine; *boomer,* a wildcat mine; *pulled,* sued; *mushle,* shuffle (cards); *mug-ups,* meals; *corduroy roads,* log rods; *shin-plaster,* a twenty-five cent bill in Canadian currency; *button-duck,* a female worker in a button factory; *paradise apple,* tomato; *kutsing,* belching; *brauch,* charming; *gush,* mouth; *kellar keel,*[4] fairly cool; *getackled,* attacked; *stand up,* get up in the morning; *buck,* mistake; *gool,* goal. The Doerings appear to have been somewhat misled in the course of their labours by certain terms like *corduroy roads* and *shin-plaster,* which are no more derived from Pennsylvania Dutch than from Bantu. One such word is *hydro,* a noun produced by shortening the adjective *hydro-electric.* When capitalized it refers to the Hydro Electric Power Commission, a public body responsible for developing and distributing electrical power in the province. In lower case, it is a standard Ontario term for electricity. As for *mug-up,* the *DA* dates it back to 1897 in the sense of "to eat heartily" and calls its origin unknown.[5] The *DC's* earliest citation is 1933.

Another important German community has long existed in western and central Saskatchewan, where a number of Germans and Russo-Germans settled just before and after the first world

---

[1] *Winter Studies and Summer Rambles in Canada,* cited in Craig, *Early Travellers,* p. 64.
[2] "Some Western Ontario Folk Beliefs and Practices," *Journal of American Folklore,* 1938, pp. 60–68.
[3] The Pennsylvania German is *lotwaerick.*
[4] This and a number of other examples are given in approximately phonetic spelling.
[5] The *DA's* earliest citation is from *Captains Courageous:* "No reg'lar meals fer no one then. 'Mug-up' when ye're hungry, an' sleep when ye can't keep awake."

war. Although all were literate and spoke and read only High German, the transition from German to English in the younger generation was rapid. Robert Somerville Graham found that "the German-speakers of Saskatchewan neither display a marked language loyalty nor regard their language as a symbol of survival and this more than counterbalances the favourable environment for linguistic survival. Thus we find a rather rapid progression from German, through bilingualism to English." [1] The European-born generation continues to use German as its usual language, but the second generation tends to assimilate as fast as possible.[2] Although traces of German pronunciation persist even among younger speakers, these are becoming more unusual. Some speakers do not clearly distinguish between *bull* and *pull*, *crate* and *grate*, *trunk* and *drunk;* and even younger speakers pronounce *village* and *very* with an initial *w* sound, or more often, with the sound of *f*. Most speakers were unable to distinguish between *raised* and *raced*, *rise* and *rice*. Graham found that no German loanwords persisted in the speech of the younger generation, although such expressions as "come right away quick" and "he is there already yet" were common. Conversely, the speech of native English speakers was not influenced by the speechways of the German community, although a few German expressions had some currency among English-speaking school children, among them *wie geht's, was ist los,* and *ich bin ausgespielt.*

VI The Chinook Jargon

The investigations of A. F. Chamberlain and others reveal how little was the effect of the Indian languages on North American English. Apart from place names, very few native words were carried over into the white man's tongue, and fewer still managed

---

[1] "The Transition from German to English in the German Settlements of Saskatchewan," *J.C.L.A.*, 1957, pp. 9–13.

[2] For an account of the easy assimilation of Germans in Canada, see Heinz Lehmann, *Zur Geschichte des Deutschtums in Kanada*, Vol. 1, Stuttgart, 1931, Vol. 2, Berlin, 1939.

to survive, often in mutilated form. Moreover, we have little knowledge of the opposite process, that is to say, the effect of English or French upon the Indian languages, although this seems to have been relatively slight, perhaps because of the rapid advance of the conquerors and the absence of prolonged intercourse with the native tribes.[1]

That the result might have been otherwise if the Indian and the white man had maintained more extensive social and economic relations is suggested by the Chinook Jargon, the only pidgin English ever to exist in North America.[2] The Jargon, a trade language composed chiefly of Indian, French, Spanish and English words, flourished throughout the nineteenth century from Oregon to Alaska. The Hon. H. L. Langevin reported in 1872 to Baron Lisgar, second Governor-General of the new Dominion, that "a knowledge of it is indispensable to all who trade with the Indians," and he appended a brief glossary of Chinook terms "as showing what transformations the Indian, English, and French languages have undergone on the Pacific coast in consequence of the relations of the whites with the Indians." [3] At that time, only a few months after British Columbia had entered Confederation and some years after the gold-fever was at its height, the population of that province comprised 8,576 whites, 462 Negroes, 1,548

[1] See Pascal Poirier, "Des vocables algonquins . . . qui sont entrés dans la langue," *Transactions of the Royal Society of Canada*, Ser. III, 1916, Vol. I, p. 339.

[2] A second native jargon, *Mobilian*, also known as the Chickasaw trade language, was spoken by the Indian tribes along the Gulf of Mexico and up both sides of the Mississippi River as far as the mouth of the Ohio. Mobilian was not a true pidgin English, being composed of Indian words only, chiefly Choctaw. No one ever thought of preserving any written record of Mobilian, and it became extinct about 1850: Edward Harper Thomas, "The Chinook Jargon," *American Speech*, 1927, pp. 377–384. Einar Haugen suggests that the broken English of the North American Indians might be considered a kind of pidgin: "Bilingualism in the Americas," *26 Proceedings of the American Dialect Society*, November, 1956, p. 36. The word *pidgin* itself is said to be a Cantonese corruption of "business," recalling that the expression originated in the South China trade ports. *Trade language* would be a close translation; the term *lingua franca* in addition to being more pretentious is not confined to jargon with an English content. To this class belong the *Petit Nègre* of French West Africa; *Créole* in Haiti, Martinique and Mauritius; the *Bêche-la-Mar* of Tahiti; *Tagalog* in the Philippines and the *Papiamento* of Curaçao.

[3] Report by the Hon. H. L. Langevin, C.B., Minister of Public Works, Ottawa, 1872. A "full vocabulary" of the Chinook Jargon appeared in the *San Francisco Bulletin* of June 4, 1857. It was reprinted in William Carew Hazlitt, *British Columbia and Vancouver Island*, London, 1858, pp. 241–243.

Chinese and an indeterminate number of Indians estimated at between 30,000 and 55,000 souls. From these many sources, including the numerous Indian tongues,[1] notably the language of the Chinook Indians of Oregon and, Mencken suggests, with contributions from the Russian,[2] there developed a trade language which Lewis and Clark found in widespread use when they reached the Pacific in 1804, and which was still understood within living memory in Oregon country.

The Chinook Jargon was a barbarous, debased speech, largely devoid of grammar, and shot through with marks of lexical miscegenation. Thus, in addition to several hundred words of the ancient language of the Chinooks, Chinese or at any rate the Chinese pronunciation of English phonemes found its echoes in *bloom*, broom, *cly*, cry, *dly*, dry, *glease*, grease, *lice*, rice, *lope*, rope, *lum*, rum and *to-mo-la*, tomorrow; French in *coo-lay*, to run, *co-sho*, pork, *co-sho glease*, lard, *la hash*, axe, *la ween*, oats, *le mah*, hand, *le mah-to*, hammer and *mah-sie*, thank you; English in *cole*, cold, *kaupy*, coffee, *peh-pah*, paper, *shem*, shame and *shut*, a shirt. In common with all languages, the Jargon relied upon onomatopoeia for many word formations: *hee-hee*, to laugh, *hoh-hoh*, to cough, *humm*, a bad odour, *ko-ko*, to knock, *kweh-kweh*, the mallard duck, *piu-piu*, to stink, *poh*, to blow out, *poo*, the sound of a gun and *toh*, spit. *Boston* signified an American, no doubt because of the prevalence of New England sailormen along the western shores, and *Boston illahie* (*illahie* = the ground, the earth), the United States. English was rendered as *King George*, and accordingly an Englishman became *King George man* (pronounced *kin-chotch-man*) and the English language *Kinchotch wawa*, although by the time of Langevin's report the last monarch of that name had been more than forty years in his grave. The French were known as *Passiooks*, and an Indian was a *Siwash*, from the French *sauvage*.

"The pronunciation of Chinook," says J. K. Gill in the introduction to his *Dictionary of the Chinook Jargon* (Portland, Ore., 1909) "can only be thoroughly learned by conversation with the

[1] Some of these were the languages of the Haida, Hygany, Massett, Skittgetts, Hanega and Cumshewas tribes and the Cheheelis, Nootka, Klikitat and Wasco Indians.

[2] *The American Language*, 1936, p. 150n.

Indians, whose deep gutturals and long-drawn vowels are beyond the power of our alphabet to represent. Most of their words are unaccented, the stress of voice falling upon the emphatic word of a sentence rather than upon particular syllables." [1]

Although the Chinook Jargon is said to have been spoken at one time by more than a hundred thousand persons in their everyday relations,[2] Douglas Leechman reported that by 1926 its use had greatly declined.[3] People versed in the Jargon were dying out, and as all Indian children were by then being taught English, many of them refused to speak the native language before strangers. The better part of its original vocabulary of more than five hundred words had fallen into disuse, and in the following year Edward Harper Thomas affirmed that "except for a few words and phrases [the Jargon] is now almost in the limbo of the lost." [4] According to Thomas, the Jargon was in extensive use down to about 1907, but by the 1920's it had sunk to low estate indeed, only a handful of words then remaining in use and those chiefly perpetuated by writers of popular Western stories.

---

[1] For a study of the phonetics of the Jargon, see Melville Jacobs, "Notes on the Structure of Chinook Jargon," *Language*, 1932, pp. 27–50. See also Douglas Leechman, "The Chinook Jargon," *American Speech*, 1926, pp. 531–534; E. H. Thomas, *Chinook: A History and Dictionary*, Portland, Ore., 1935; E. H. Thomas, "The Chinook Jargon," *American Speech*, 1927, pp. 377–384. A very full bibliography (37 titles) of writings on the Chinook Jargon may be found in A. G. Kennedy, *A Bibliography of Writings on the English Language (to 1922)*, Cambridge and New Haven, 1927, pp. 416 and following; also J. C. Pilling, *A Bibliography of the Chinookan Languages*, Washington, 1893, pp. 30–76.

[2] E. H. Thomas, "The Chinook Jargon," *American Speech*, 1927, pp. 377–384.

[3] "The Chinook Jargon," *American Speech*, 1926, pp. 531–534.

[4] Melville Jacobs based his "Notes on the Structure of Chinook Jargon," *Language*, 1932, pp. 27–50, on material collected in the course of field researches in 1930, at which time he noted that "the Jargon is being forgotten rapidly; a new *lingua franca*, English, is replacing it."

CHAPTER FIVE

PRONUNCIATION

Good English is plain, easy, and smooth in the mouth of an unaffected English Gentleman. A studied and factitious pronunciation, which requires perpetual attention and imposes perpetual constraint, is exceedingly disgusting. A small intermixture of provincial peculiarities may, perhaps, have an agreeable effect, as the notes of different birds concur in the harmony of the grove, and please more than if they were all exactly alike.

SAMUEL JOHNSON

PRONUNCIATION

1

MOST LAY DISCUSSIONS ABOUT THE PRONUNCIATION OF CANADIAN English resolve themselves into an argument about the respective vices and virtues of an English accent as opposed to an American accent, with something called a Canadian accent roughly in the middle—an ill-defined, pallid thing drifting helplessly about between the two, not knowing where to lay its head. The aimlessness of such contention results not only from a failure to define clearly what is being talked about, but also from an attempt to formulate value judgments about matters which are to a large degree social and emotive. It is further complicated by the fact that until recently there was almost no scientific investigation of spoken Canadian, so that even serious observers have had little more to go on than prejudice and the limited ambit of their own personal observation. Thanks in large measure to the work of the Canadian Linguistic Association in focussing attention upon how Canadian English is spoken, it is becoming possible to define at least the dominant tendencies of Canadian pronunciation in relation to the recognized standards of British and American English.

By convention among most experts, the standard of English speech is the language of the English upper classes. This is, according to Mario Pei, "the sublimated Londonese of the English aristocracy and upper bourgeoisie, a tongue fashioned out of a mixture of southern and east Midlands dialect, and refined by centuries of Court usage." [1] For many years, scholars have rated all other varieties of English well below this dialect, which has been given many names. Professor H. C. K. Wyld labelled it *Received Standard*, all else being, in his view, "the vulgar English of the Towns, and the English of the Villager who has abandoned his native Regional Dialect," to which he gave the name *Modified Standard*.[2] Dr. Daniel Jones called it *Standard Pronunciation*,[3] pointing out that it is "most usually heard in everyday speech in the families of southern English persons whose menfolk have been educated at the great public boarding-schools," [4] hence the common practice of referring to it as *Public School English*. Professor Wyld agrees that it owes its uniformity to "the custom of sending youths from certain social strata to the great public schools." [5] It is not, however, a class dialect only, in the view of Stuart Robertson, but "a form of speech that is limited geographically as well as socially, and limited geographically almost entirely to London and what are known as the 'Home Counties.' "[6] Professor Alan S. C. Ross of Birmingham University stirred up a small hornet's nest some years ago when he resorted to the single letter *U* to designate this upper-class usage, all else being non-U.[7] For convenience here, we shall call this dialect *Standard English*.

Despite its great repute among scholars, Standard English has provoked and been denounced by many eminent men of letters, among them George Bernard Shaw (an Irishman), Dr. J. Y. T. Greig (a Scotsman) and Robert Bridges (an Englishman, educated at Eton and Oxford). Dr. Greig, one of its sternest critics, complained, in *Breaking Priscian's Head*,[8] that it is "artificial, slovenly to a degree, absurdly difficult for foreigners to acquire, and except to ears debased by listening to it, unharmonious."

[1] *The Story of English*, Philadelphia, 1952, p. 154.
[2] *A History of Modern Colloquial English*, London, 1921.
[3] *The Pronunciation of English*, Cambridge, 1950.
[4] *English Pronouncing Dictionary*, 1924, p. vii.
[5] *A History of Modern Colloquial English*, p. 3.
[6] *The Development of Modern English*, New York, 1954, p. 402.
[7] "U and Non-U: An Essay in Sociological Linguistics," in *Noblesse Oblige*, London, 1956.
[8] London, 1929.

Standard English drove D. H. Lawrence almost to frenzy in "The Oxford Voice:" [1]

> When you hear it languishing
> and hooing and cooing and sidling through
> the front teeth,
> the oxford voice
> or worse still
> the would-be oxford voice
> you don't even laugh any more, you can't.

His feeling is shared, as we shall see, by a large number of Canadians.

No one dialect in the United States occupies the same position of prestige as Standard English. This has been ascribed to the absence of a "public school" system of education on this continent and the "vaguer social boundaries and the easier circulation between classes" which impeded the development of a class dialect of this kind.[2] Some observers would divide American speech into three parts: the English of New England, Southern English, and Western or General American. Of these the most important is General American which is spoken by perhaps two-thirds of the population of the United States residing in the Atlantic states (excluding New England and the South) and the Middle and Western states. General American, G. P. Krapp has pointed out, is the product of many influences, the most important being the mingling of Scots, Irish and both northern and southern English. The resultant speech is much closer to the speech of central and northern England than it is to that of southern England. This dialect, which is so prevalent throughout the entire continent that it might almost be called North American, has had an increasing influence upon the English spoken in every other country in the world. Something very close to it is used in Canada by a large proportion of the English-speaking population, in most places by a preponderance.

---

[1] In *Pansies*, 1929.

[2] Henry Alexander, *The Story of Our Language*, Toronto, 1940, pp. 174–175.

The differences between Standard English and General American are considerable, the principal phonetic distinctions being somewhat as follows:[1]

(1) The sound represented by *r* has been completely lost in Standard English in final position and before other consonants, as in *car, first* or *card*, with the result that words like *alms*, and *arms*, *father* and *farther* are identical in pronunciation. The only exception occurs when *r* is followed by a vowel sound in the same or following word. In General American *r* is sounded in all these positions, although many Eastern and Southern speakers prefer the English pronunciation.

(2) In Standard English, the so-called "broad *a*" prevails in *bath, laugh, grass*, and so on, whereas in General American the "short *a*" as in *cat* or *man* is more common, except in *father, psalm, alms* and sometimes *calm*. "Many educated speakers on this continent," say Larsen and Walker, "attempt a compromise between the two sounds."

(3) The two pronunciations differ in the sound of vowels followed by *r*. In Standard English, all long vowels are modified by the insertion of a vowel sound before the *r* somewhat like the vowel sound in *the*, particularly when the *r* is suppressed as in *fear*, but also when the *r* is sounded as in *fearing*. This vowel sound is never prominent before *r* in General American, except after long *i* and *ow*. American speakers usually give the vowel sound in *four* to the first syllable of words like *forest, foreign, forehead*, which Standard English pronounces with a shorter *o*. "There is also great uncertainty in America," say Larsen and Walker, "about the sound of the stressed vowels in words like *squirrel* and *stirrup*, *hurry* and *worry*. In Standard English, they are given the sound of short *i* and short *u* respectively. In General American, both are pronounced like the vowel sound in *the*."

(4) The tendency in England is to pronounce with long *i* such words as *direction, civilization* and *organization*, and also most

---

[1] The tabulation which follows is largely summarized from Henry Alexander, *The Story of Our Language*, Toronto, 1940, and Thorlief Larsen and Francis C. Walker, *Pronunciation: A Practical Guide to Spoken English in Canada and the United States*, Toronto, Oxford, 1930.

words which end in -*ile*, as *agile* and *docile*. In General American, the short *i* is almost universal in these positions.

(5) American English also tends to reduce the last syllable of words ending in -*ile*, such as *fertile*, to rhyme with "Myrtle." The ending -*ine* as in *genuine* is usually pronounced in Standard English to rhyme with "pin" and by some American speakers to rhyme with "pine."

(6) The vowel sound in *not*, *block*, *rod* is in Standard English close to the vowel sound in *nor;* in General American, it is usually shorter than the *a* in *father*.

(7) Speakers of Standard English are careful to sound a full *u*, or in effect to insert a *y-sound* before the sound of *u* following *d*, *n*, *t*, and sometimes *l*, as in *duke*, *duty*, *new*, *student*, *studio*, and following *s* or *z*, as in *assume*, *presume*. In American speech generally, not excepting that of New England, the *oo* sound is heard in all these words.

(8) One of the most striking differences between the two languages is the slurring of vowels in Standard English, where General American enunciates with "full" vowels. Thus a Standard English speaker somehow manages to reduce *extraordinary* to the two syllables "kstrordnri," while a General American speaker enunciates five syllables, and sometimes even six. This accounts for the criticism by Americans that an English speaker "swallows" his words, while American speech sounds monotonous to the cultured English ear. Other words of this class are *medicine*, pronounced "medsn" and *interesting*, pronounced "intrsting" by English speakers but carefully given their full complement of syllables by most Americans.

(9) Miscellaneous differences in vowel sounds exist. Thus the first syllables of words like *Berkeley*, *Berkshire*, *Derby* are pronounced *ar* in Standard English and *er* in General American. *Been* is pronounced by Standard English speakers as "bean," and by most American speakers as "bin." *Shone* is always pronounced to rhyme with "on" in England and usually with "known" in America. *Leisure* rhymes with *pleasure* in Standard English, but with *seizure* in General American. *Either* and *neither* are "eye-ther" and "nye-ther" in England, and "ee-ther" and "nee-ther" in America. *Patent* is usually "pay-tent" to an Englishman and "pat-ent"

E

to an American. *Tomato* is "to-mah-to" in Standard English, but almost always "tomayto" to a General American speaker. And *vase* usually rhymes with the first syllable of "Boswell" in England and sometimes with "case" in America.

(10) In Standard English, no distinction is made between initial *w* and *wh*. Such pairs as *which* and *witch*, *when* and *wen*, *whether* and *weather*, are pronounced alike. In General American, *wh* is usually more heavily aspirated than *w* at the beginning of a word.

(11) Minor variations in the consonants exist, as in *schedule* (Standard English "shed"—General American usually "sked"), *herbs* (Standard English sounds the *h*, while General American frequently suppresses it), *raspberry* (pronounced *z* in Standard English, sometimes *s* in General American), *lieutenant* (Standard English "left-," General American "loot-").

(12) The General American tendency is to place the accent on the first syllable in such nouns as *address*, *inquiry*, *magazine*, *recess*, *romance*, *spectator*, whereas Standard English usually accents the second or a later syllable.

It is clear that Canada does not possess anything like a standard pronunciation. The limited samplings which have been made reveal that considerable variation exists not merely from speaker to speaker, but often in the same speaker. This divided usage is probably typical of Canada as a whole; it is certainly general in Ontario, a province which some observers consider representative of English-speaking Canada. A survey conducted by Walter S. Avis revealed considerable diversity among Ontario speakers in their pronunciation of many everyday words,[1] which led him to conclude:

---

[1] W. S. Avis, "Speech Differences Along the Ontario-United States Border, III: Pronunciation," *J.C.L.A.*, 1956, pp. 41–59. Dr. Avis's investigation, which is the most ambitious field survey of Canadian usage yet published, also included "Vocabulary" (*J.C.L.A.*, October, 1954, pp. 13–18) and "Grammar and Syntax," (*J.C.L.A.*, March, 1955, pp. 14–19). The information came from two multiple-choice questionnaires circulated at Queen's University and Royal Military College, Kingston, Ontario, in 1949–1950 and 1954–1955. Within its self-imposed limits of educational level (senior matriculation standing or higher) and size of groups tested (from 102 to 159 informants), the survey produced much valuable information about Canadian usage, and was followed and largely confirmed by D. E. Hamilton, "Notes on Montreal English," *J.C.L.A.*, 1958, pp. 70–79, and H. B. Allen, "Canadian-American Speech Differences Along the Middle Border," *J.C.L.A.*, 1959, pp. 17–24.

Where clear-cut predominance is shown for any one pronunciation, the preferred form is apt to parallel British usage
when the word is literary and consequently of limited
currency in speech, and American usage when the word is in.
widespread general use. The implications seem to be that
British forms are apt to have greater currency at the top of
the social pyramid, American forms greater currency at the
popular level. But the most significant conclusion to be drawn
from this survey is that Ontario English (and surely Canadian
English generally) is neither American nor British, but a
complex different in many respects from both in vocabulary,
grammar and syntax, and pronunciation. The high degree
of diversity apparent in Ontario speech suggests that any
hopes of achieving a cut-and-dried speech standard are
forlorn.

It is not difficult to understand why Canadian pronunciation
should share many of the characteristics of both British English
and American. To begin with, there are very good historical
reasons for the similarities: English-speaking Canada was largely
colonized from Great Britain and the United States, and Canadian
pronunciation could be expected to show the influence of this
mixed parentage. There are also social and educational reasons,
although these are difficult to assess. Eric Partridge has recalled
that few educated and cultured persons went to North America,
South Africa, Australia and New Zealand until those countries
were fairly well established. Consequently, "there arose, quite
soon in every colony, a predominant pronunciation differing considerably from that of educated and cultured persons in England:
and in pronunciation must be included not only vowel-value and
accent, but stress and intonation and enunciation." [1] Despite the
intervening years, such differences have persisted. "Even among
the educated," Partridge adds, "especially the educated persons
of culture, pronunciation in the Dominions, as in the United
States, differs appreciably from that of the corresponding persons
in Britain. Moreover, the Dominions differ among themselves.
And the United States differs from all of them."

[1] *British and American English Since 1900,* London, 1951.

The influence of the Canadian school system in standardizing pronunciation remains to be investigated. Certainly very few Canadian school teachers are Standard English speakers, and no Canadian public school teaches either the broad *a*, or the suppressed *r* in terminal position and before consonants, which are two of the characteristic features of Standard English. Nevertheless, an official preference for Standard English persists, to the extent that this can be reproduced by Canadian speakers. It may be seen in the conscious choice by the Canadian Broadcasting Corporation of British rather than American pronunciation for words admitting of two variants, such as *schedule* which CBC announcers sedulously pronounce "shed-yule" in preference to the American "sked-yule," although the latter is still the dominant Ontario pronunciation. Only one-third of Ontarioans tested preferred "shed-yule" to "sked-yule," and many informants admitted to being fairly recent converts to the British form. "In this category, no doubt," says Avis, "is the CBC announcer who, in broadcasting the late news, spoke of a train wreck being the result of the engineer falling behind ["skedule"] and who five minutes later informed his hearers that the CBC broadcasting ["shedule"] was ended for the day." In Montreal, three out of four English speakers tested chose "sked-yule."

Opposed to this pro-British attitude, however, which is commonest among the upper classes, there has always been at the popular level a strongly Anglophobe sentiment which left its mark on Canadian speech. In Ontario, this goes back to the days of the Family Compact, when, as has been pointed out, because of their association with the old colonial regime Englishmen were suspect and their distinctive accent taboo.[1] To this day, the possessor of a marked English accent often finds himself *persona non grata*, even in the heartland of Ontario, and is not infrequently castigated in news items and letters to the editor.[2] In the result, authentic or even quasi-Standard English is usually heard only on the lips of transplanted Englishmen and some CBC people.

[1] Eric Partridge, *British and American English Since 1900*, London, 1951.
[2] See, for example, two articles by Brian Nicholson, "Pure B.B.C. Accent Is Handicap Here, English Girl Finds," Toronto *Telegram*, July 22, 1953, and "Why It Hurts— To Have an English Accent," July 23, 1953.

As a public body the Canadian Broadcasting Corporation comes in for a good deal of criticism, which does not deter it from hewing to its own standard of pronunciation. The professed aim of the CBC as set out in a pamphlet entitled *Handbook for Announcers* is wholly commendable: "In the pronunciation and accentuation of English words the policy of the CBC is to recognize any variants that are generally current among educated people. English speech uses are not rigid; they vary from place to place and from time to time, and it would be presumptuous for any one body to insist that the standards of any particular locality are correct and all others incorrect." [1] There follows a list of words and their recommended pronunciations which "is intended as a guide, and in no sense as the dictates of an infallible authority." When one comes to examine this list, however, it appears that the policy so fairly enunciated a moment earlier has been abandoned. When Standard English and General American usages differ, the CBC "recommended" pronunciation almost invariably follows Standard English, regardless of whether or not a majority of Canadians commonly use General American pronunciation for the same words.

The following examples are drawn from *Handbook for Announcers*, the second column showing the CBC "recommended" pronunciation, and the third column the commonly heard Canadian alternative, which is often also General American:

	Recommended Pronunciation	*Alternative Pronunciation*
abdomen	abdō'men	ab'domen
address	address', n. & v.	a'ddress, n.
ally	ally', n. & v.	a'lly, n.
appendicitis	-sightis	-seatis [2]
aristocrat	a'ristocrat	aris'tocrat
Asia	āsh-ă	āzh-ă
bouquet	boo-kay'	bō'kay
carburettor	-rĕttor	-ray-tor
decadent	dec'ădent	decā'dent [3]

[1] Revised edition, Toronto, 1946, p. 13.
[2] General American usage is almost always "appendi-sight-is."
[3] Usually "dec'adent" in the United States.

	Recommended Pronunciation	*Alternative Pronunciation*
deterrent	de-terr-ent as in "terrible"	de-turr-ent
diphtheria	diff-theria	dip-theria
diphthong	diff-thong	dip-thong[1]
dynasty	dĭn-	dyne-
economic	ēc-	ĕc-
envelope	en-	on-
evolution	ē-	ĕ-
finance	fĭnance′	fī′nance
frontier	frun′teer	fronteer′
incognito	incog′nito	incognee′to
inveigle	-vee-	-vay-
leisure	like "pleasure"	like "seizure"
often	off-n	oft-en
ordinarily	or′dinarily	ordinā′rily
plebiscite	plebi-sit	plebi-site
premature	prĕm-	preem-
program	-gram	-grum[2]
research	research′	rē′search
route	root	rowt
senile	sea-nile	sĕn-ile
simultaneous	sĭm-	sīm-
status	stay-tus	stătus
stratum	stray-tum	strătum[3]
suave	swāve	swahv
unprecedented	unpress-	unprees-
vacation	vuh-kay-shun	vay-kay-shun
valet	va′lett	va-lay′
version	-sh-	-zh-

Although reliable statistics on pronunciation are hard to come by, it is probable that more Canadians say "aris′tocrat," "āzha,"

---

[1] In the United States, "dip-theria" and "dip-thong" are uncultivated usage.
[2] "Pro-grum" is uncultivated American usage.
[3] Cultivated American usage is "stay-tus," "stray-tum," and "day-ta."

PRONUNCIATION 123

"carbu-raytor," "dip-theria," "onvelope," "fī′nance," "rē′ search," "stătus," "strătum" and "ver-zhion" than use the forms recommended by the CBC. Avis, who has taken one of the few Canadian samplings, reported that although a small but appreciable minority of Ontarioans tested said "prŏ-cess" rather than "prō-cess," more than half of them pronounced *genuine* to rhyme with "wine" rather than "win," and preferred American "prŏgress" (noun) to British "prōgress." With words of the class *Asia, version* and so on, Canadian usage almost always coincides with General American.

The CBC is said to be modifying much of its former inflexibility and admitting "any pronunciation common to Canadians providing it is recognized by a reputable dictionary." [1] But this aim is somewhat frustrated by the absence of any dictionary, whatever its repute, containing such representative Canadian pronunciations as "artic" for *arctic* and "vaze" for *vase*.[2] In practice, if not in theory, the CBC standard largely continues to be Standard English both for new words and old ones revived. Thus *missile*, which only a few years ago meant nothing more than a thrown or hurled object and was pronounced by every Canadian schoolchild to rhyme with "thistle," has now become an intercontinental engine of destruction and is carefully pronounced "miss-īle" by CBC announcers.

It is doubtful whether many of the Canadians who use the General American rather than the Standard English pronunciation of such words do so knowingly. Several factors may influence usage: one, the tendency which they share with most Americans to adopt a spelling pronunciation, resulting in such variants as "dyne-asty," "off-ten," "plebi-site," and *leisure* pronounced to rhyme with "seizure." There may also be a striving toward what is considered a more refined diction. Thus some speakers prefer "on-velope" to "en-velope" and "va-lay′" to "va′lett." One should also remember that many Canadians have no wish to

---

[1] "Canada Gets Own Dictionary," *Toronto Daily Star*, December 21, 1959.

[2] W. S. Avis in "Canadian English Merits a Dictionary," *Culture*, 1957, pp. 245–256, offers the following examples of words which educated Canadians pronounce in a way not usually recorded in any imported dictionary: *absolve, absurd, culinary, evil, finale, isthmus, jackal, longitude, machination, official, placate, plenary.*

sound like Americans and, indeed, if taxed with the offence would insist with some heat that they do not. When a particular pronunciation is clearly identifiable as American, the majority of Canadians tend to shun it without hesitation; if any public figure were to pronounce *khaki* as "kakkee," he would be laughed off the platform. The fact that a great many Canadians pronounce their words in the same way as General American speakers does not temper the disfavour with which American speech habits are treated. The late W. L. Mackenzie King, as authentic a Canadian as ever drew breath, habitually pronounced *news* as "nooze," and was sharply taken to task for this sin *post mortem*,[1] although fully one-third of those Ontarioans tested shared his guilt.

For other words, the CBC *Handbook* gives both a "recommended" and a "permissible" pronunciation, thus:

	Recommended	*Permissible*
adult	ad-ult′	ad′ult
again	agen	agane
artisan	artisan′	ar′tisan
carillon	karry-lon	ka-rill-yon
clerk	clark	clerk
combat	com′bat, v. & n.	combat′, v.
depot	dep′o	dee′po
docile	doe′sile	dŏ′sill
doctrinal	dok-trin-al	dok-try′nal
fertile	fer-tyle	fer-till
gala	gayla	gah-la
iodine	iodeen	iodyne
pariah	par′ïa	par-eye′ah
patent	pay-	pat-
patriot	pat-	pay-
precedence	pre-see′dence	press′edence
princess	prin-cess′	prin′cess
tomato	tomahto	tomayto

This list clearly illustrates the divided nature of Canadian usage, although many Canadian speakers might be inclined

---

[1] G. H. M., "Copycat Canadians," *Toronto Daily Star*, March 18, 1957.

to reverse the order of "recommended" and "permissible."
Some of the CBC "recommended" pronunciations are simply
never used by Canadians, for example, "clark" and "pay-tent"
while "tomahto" is not a majority pronunciation. On the other
hand, CBC standards are not always as unbending as they seem.
Although holding firmly against such pronunciations as *detergent*
accented on the first syllable, and *mattress* and *inventory* accented
on the second, the CBC sometimes permits speakers the liberty
of *often* pronounced either "off'n" or "off-ten," and *schedule*
as either "shedule" or "skedule," notwithstanding its official
preference for the former. It has even gone so far on occasion as to
approve of "crick" for *creek* and "grainary" for *granary*, although
neither pronunciation is authorized by the *SOED*.[1]

The pro-British bias of much of Canadian education, however,
backed by the resolute stand of the CBC is still no match for the
geographical proximity of the United States, the effect of which is
felt everywhere across the land. The cultural and linguistic
penetration of Canada by the United States is today almost
complete, and the fact that the speech of these two countries is
still distinguishable can chiefly be ascribed to the natural conservatism of languages generally, reinforced by Canada's own
conservatism as a nation, which has made its citizens highly
resistant to linguistic change. Canadian speech is constantly
being Americanized, although we have as yet no accurate notion
of the extent and speed of this process. Some idea of what is
happening may be gathered from a study conducted about 1955
by M. H. Scargill, then of the University of Alberta.[2] This investigation of six hundred Canadians born and educated in Alberta,
having the same age and educational level ("up to and a little
beyond the last grade of high school"), revealed that almost two-
thirds of the informants had a predominantly American pronunciation, only one-half of one per cent had a pronunciation
which was predominantly British, and the remaining one-third
had what Scargill calls a "free pronunciation"—one using both

[1] "C.B.C. Uses Two Dictionaries, Can't Go Wrong, Critics Told," *Toronto Daily Star*, January 13, 1949.
[2] "Canadian English and Canadian Culture in Alberta," *J.C.L.A.*, 1955, pp. 26–29.

E*

British and American pronunciations freely, with neither predominant.

Scargill found that in general the influence of American pronunciation declined with the distance from the American border.
Thus the towns of Cardston and Raymond which lie close to the
international boundary showed more than 84 per cent American
predominance, although the southwestern part of the province
which includes Lethbridge had an American predominance of
only 75 per cent. At Calgary, which is farther north, the index was
48 per cent, and in the Peace River area only a little more than
39 per cent of informants had a predominantly American pronunciation.[1] In general, Scargill perceived in the pronunciation of
cultured native Albertans "a definite trend towards American
predominance" which seems likely to continue, while those with a
"free" pronunciation will diminish as time goes on.

The phonology of Canadian English still awaits extensive
scientific investigation. One study, conducted by R. J. Gregg
of the University of British Columbia, although of considerable
value is limited by the size of the group tested.[2] Gregg found
evidence, particularly among younger speakers, of the development of a distinct regional standard pronunciation which in his
view was probably applicable to most of English-speaking Canada.
One prominent feature was the lack of any consistent differentia-
tion between the "long" vowels in *seal, aunt, taught, fool* and the
"short" vowels in *sill, ant, tot, full.* In Standard English, these two
sets of vowel sounds differ in both quality and quantity; they
comprise one of the most distinctive features of southern English
speech. In Canadian English as in General American, Gregg points
out, "there is no constant relationship between quality and
duration in vowels with relatively strong stress, the traditionally
short vowels being frequently lengthened especially in association

[1] The results of Scargill's sampling are not so regular as these examples might
imply. Thus Red Deer, which is more than 200 miles north of the international
boundary, showed exactly 50 per cent American predominance, while Calgary which
is halfway between Red Deer and the American border showed a coefficient of 48
per cent. On the other hand, at Edmonton in the north west, American predominance
was 53.6 per cent. The size of the community may be of some significance.

[2] "Notes on the Pronunciation of Canadian English as Spoken in Vancouver,"
J.C.L.A., 1957, pp. 20–26.

with a change of pitch, for example the falling or rising pitch at
the end of an utterance." Thus the short vowels in *is, Sam, cot, pull*
will not be distinguished in length from the vowels in *ease, psalm,
caught, pool*,[1] and the lengthening of the short vowel sound may
produce such homophones as *cot* and *caught*, or *sod* and *sawed*.
In lengthening the short vowels, there is also a tendency to insert
what is called "a centring diphthong," to produce an effect not
unlike a second syllable. Gregg notes that this transformation of
the short vowel by centring diphthongs, as well as the tendency
to abandon the traditional distinction between long and short
vowels, may also be observed among younger speakers in southern
England.[2]

In general, Vancouver speech and, by extension, a good part
of the speech of English Canada, tends at times to correspond
with Standard English and at times with General American,
although there is no apparent pattern. In matters of disputed
pronunciation, Canadian usage sometimes follows the English
standard, so that a Canadian *lieutenant* is always and only a
"leftenant" (with the stress on the second syllable) and never a
"lootenant." On the other hand, a majority of Canadians un-
questioningly say "haf past" instead of "hahf pahst." And yet
there are times when Canadians eschew both the English and
American pronunciations of a word and devise one of their own.
One of the terms frequently commented upon is *khaki*, pronounced
something like "kahkee" or "kawkee" in England and "kakkee"
in the United States.[3] The only permissible Canadian pronunciation, although it lacks the sanction of either Webster or Oxford,
is "karkee."[4] Typically Canadian is the tendency toward "voiced"
rather than "unvoiced" consonants, which results in such pronunciations as "lug-zhury" and "signifigant," and confounds

[1] It should be noted that the quality of the vowels in *is* and *ease*, and the other pairs
of words quoted, still remains different. As Gregg points out, length is non-phonemic
in General American in contrast to Standard English.
[2] Daniel Jones, *The Phoneme, Its Nature and Use*, Cambridge, England, 1950, p. 169.
[3] See editorial, "Say It in Canadian," *Toronto Daily Star*, February 9, 1957. The
term comes from the Urdu *khaki* = dusty.
[4] See W. S. Avis, "Speech Differences Along the Ontario-United States Border,
III: Pronunciation," *J.C.L.A.*, 1956, p. 44.

pedal and *petal*, *feudal* and *futile*, and turns *pretty little* into "priddy liddle."

Notwithstanding a leaning toward some British speech forms, Canadian English exhibits frequent inconsistencies. Thus a clear majority of Ontario speakers pronounced *suggest* as "suh-djest," following British usage, rather than the American "sug-djest." On the other hand, *figure* was given the American pronunciation "figyer" by 68 per cent over the British "figger," a clear indication, says Avis, "that the prestige of British usage is fighting a losing battle, probably because connotations of slovenliness have become associated with the British form." Yet this view should be accepted with some caution, for the metaphor of a losing battle is more than a little reminiscent of Mencken's theory, discussed earlier, that American English drove the original British English out of Canada. There is, of course, no evidence that "figger" was first in the field. Avis is correct in recalling that school teachers have long inveighed against "figger" as being slovenly, while trying to instil the American pronunciations "fig-yer" and even "fig-yure." The pattern is complicated, however, by the fact that some speakers try to distinguish between two common uses of *figure*. One who would never speak of a lady's "figger" may not hesitate to say "I can't figger it out."

Even when words have no marked social connotations, Canadian usage is often divided, a classic example being *either* and *neither*. There is a curious theory, almost certainly without foundation, that the older pronunciations "eye-ther" and "nye-ther" were introduced into England by the early Georges, who, being Hanoverians, spoke English with a German accent.[1] In any event, the accepted pronunciation in England is now "eye-ther" and "nye-ther" and, although not more correct, has almost wholly displaced "ee-ther" and "nee-ther" in educated speech.[2] The American pronunciation, however, is firmly and resolutely "ee-ther" and "nee-ther," although just after the first world world war G. P. Krapp remarked that "eye-ther" and "nye-ther"

---

[1] The point has been discussed at length by Dr. Louise Pound in "On the Pronunciation of 'Either' and 'Neither,' " *American Speech*, 1932, pp. 371–376.

[2] H. W. Fowler, *A Dictionary of Modern English Usage*, ed. Sir Ernest Gowers, Oxford, 1965, p. 147.

existed in the United States "often as a consciously refined pronunciation," [1] and this still seems to be so. In Ontario, among the
group of speakers tested, almost two-thirds preferred the American
pronunciation to the British. There is sometimes a combination,
not discussed by Avis, in which usage is divided as between *either*
and *neither*, the same speaker pronouncing one "eye-ther" and the
other "nee-ther" or vice versa. In the case of *leisure*, however, the
British pronunciation rhyming with *pleasure* is clearly preferred
by some 60 per cent of Ontario speakers over the American pronunciation rhyming with "seizure."

Sometimes the preference of Canadian speakers for an American
pronunciation is almost complete. Thus less than one per cent of
Avis's informants used the British pronunciation of *greasy* which
rhymes with "easy," the use of the unvoiced *s* sound in this word
being almost unanimous in Canada. As for *garage*, the predominant
Canadian and General American pronunciation slurs the first
syllable, puts the accent on the second, and rhymes the word with
"mirage," or less commonly with "lodge." There is also a possibly
distinctive pronunciation often heard in Canada, although never
in the United States, rhyming with "badge." Canadians seem to
favour the pronunciation "kwest-" for the first syllable of questionnaire rather than the English "kest-." In the case of *privacy*,
we pronounce the first syllable to rhyme with *alive* rather than
give, and we pronounce *says* to rhyme with *fez* as do Americans,
and not with something approximating *plays*, which is a British
English variant. In common with American speakers, we omit the
l sound in *solder*, although it is pronounced in British English.
Finally, in the large class of words ending in *-ary* and *-ory*, as
dictionary, *necessary*, *obligatory*, *ordinary*, *reformatory* and *secretary*,
most Canadian speakers follow the North American custom of
enunciating each syllable distinctly and placing a secondary stress
on the penultimate syllable. This stands in marked contrast to the
British practice of slurring all but the stressed vowels in words of
this class.

How, then, may the pronunciation of Canadian English be
characterized? It is certainly closer to General American than

---

[1] *The Pronunciation of Standard English in America*, New York, 1919, p. 164.

to Professor Wyld's Received Standard, although it has much in common with both dialects. Wyld would probably have included it under the heading "Modified Standard," as being one of "a large number of Social or Class Dialects, sprung from what is now Received Standard, and variously *modified* through the influence of regional speech on the one hand, or, on the other, by tendencies which have arisen within certain social groups." Eric Partridge, perhaps the leading exegete of the Wyld school, finds no Received Standard pronunciation in Canada "except among Public School men and women resident there." He concludes, a little sadly, that Canadians may be said to speak Modified Standard, upon which he hopes "the clarity and subtlety of the best Standard English will always exercise a beneficent influence." [1]

The hope is perhaps vain. In discussing standards of English, it is, of course, difficult not to find some inherent superiority in the form of English which one happens to speak, or which one would like the rest of the world to believe one speaks naturally. H. C. Wyld stoutly took the position that Standard English is better than all comers,[2] and English Received pronunciation is preferred to General American by most English and some Canadian commentators. Thorleif Larsen and Francis C. Walker held that it is more beautiful, more resonant in tone and richer in effect, hence its adoption "as the speech of the stage both in America and England."[3] With something like the attitude of Calvinists towards salvation they do not "advise any one who has not already acquired the speech characteristics of English Received pronunciation in a natural way to attempt to acquire them artificially." Then, relenting slightly, they urge upon their readers a more general use of the *ah* sound in *path, grass, pass* and similar words. This generally is the view expounded in Palmer, Martin and Blandford's *Dictionary of English Pronunciation with American Variants*.[4] Yet many and equally well-qualified authorities firmly reject any question of values. As Henry Alexander remarks of

---

[1] *Usage and Abusage*, 5th ed., London, 1957, p. 315.
[2] *The Best English*, Society for Pure English, Tract No. 39.
[3] *Pronunciation: A Practical Guide to Spoken English in Canada and the United States*, Oxford, 1930, p. 14.
[4] Cambridge, 1926.

Standard English, "it is simply one dialect of English, which, it must be admitted, carries with it a certain amount of social prestige. On the other hand, many speakers who do not possess this dialect have risen to the highest offices of state and church. No true Scotsman would admit that his Scottish dialect was inferior to Standard English." [1]

2

One of the greatest points of difference between speakers of Standard English and Canadian English is the way in which they pronounce the vowel sound in such words as *half, ask, clasp, past, grass* and *path*.

In refined southern English speech, this sound takes the form of the so-called "broad *a*" which the refined Englishman pronounces much like the *a* in *father*. In Canadian speech, as in General American, the so-called "flat *a*" or "short *a*" as in *that* or *man* is sounded by a majority of speakers in all these words.

Oddly enough, the "broad *a*," despite its great prestige, turns out to be a comparatively modern habit, the "flat *a*" along with the strongly rounded *r* having been characteristic of southern English speech until late in the eighteenth century. The "broad *a*" became fashionable in polite London discourse about 1780, and has since constituted for many persons the *cachet* of cultured English speech. The "flat *a*" is almost universally used by Ontarioans and, it would seem, Canadians in general, in such words as *class, dance, bath* and the rest. The close approximation to American usage here has been remarked for many years. "This similarity," writes Avis, "along with the presence of a similar /r/ phoneme contributes much of the 'American' colouring attributed to Canadian English by Britishers. In words of this class, and there are quite a number of them ... the so-called 'broad *a*' is relatively rare, although it does occur occasionally ... usually in the speech of

[1] *The Story of Our Language*, Toronto, 1940.

those who consciously adopt British usage because of its prestige value in certain circles." If this is so in Ontario, which, along with British Columbia, is the most English of the provinces, it would not be surprising to find the same pattern repeated throughout Canada.

More than 90 per cent of the Ontario speakers tested pronounced *class, dance, bath* and *laugh* with "flat *a.*" In the case of certain other words, however, the incidence of the "broad *a*" varies. Thus while *aunt* was pronounced with "broad *a*" by less than 10 per cent of the informants, *drama* was so pronounced by twice as many, and *rather* by a socially impressive 33 per cent. In such words as *calm* and *palm*, the "flat *a*" occurs, frequently among uneducated speakers in Canada as in the United States, but Avis points out that in this context the "broad *a*" is "the more acceptable vowel socially, just as it is in both Britain and America." Only 4 per cent of the Ontario speakers tested pronounced *calm* and *palm* with "flat *a*" although there can be little doubt that a less restricted sampling—all the informants were of senior matriculation standard or higher—would have revealed a higher percentage of "flat *a*" speakers for this class of words.

Montreal usage shares the North American preference for flat *a* in words of this class. D. E. Hamilton found that the number of his informants who claimed to use broad *a* exceeded 10 per cent for only four words: *aunt, calm, drama* and *rather*, the same words and substantially the same percentage that were reported from southern Ontario, except for *calm*, which 15 per cent of Montrealers would pronounce "kam," as opposed to only 4 per cent of Ontarioans.[1] Despite the presence of many transplanted Standard English speakers in British Columbia, a group of Vancouver students ranging in age from sixteen to twenty-two followed substantially the same speech pattern as did the Ontarioans.[2]

Canadian usage is much divided over the pronunciation of *vase.* In descending order of popularity, half of the Ontario speakers tested offered a pronunciation rhyming with "maze," one-third would rhyme it with "Oz," the Standard English version, and

[1] "Notes on Montreal English," *J.C.L.A.*, 1958, pp. 70–79.
[2] R. J. Gregg, "Notes on the Pronunciation of Canadian English as Spoken in Vancouver," *J.C.L.A.*, 1957, pp. 20–26.

most of the remainder rhymed it with "face," the common American pronunciation, while less than two per cent preferred a pronunciation rhyming with "has." The British form, as Avis points out, "undoubtedly enjoys prestige in some Canadian and American circles, a situation recognized by the informant who claimed to use ["vaze"] for the garden variety and ["vaws"] for the Ming variety." Among Montreal speakers, the dominant version is that which rhymes with "Oz," thus offering one of the few reported instances where Montreal speakers favour the Standard English form over the American. The other Montreal pronunciations of *vase* in descending order of frequency are those rhyming with "maze," "has," and "face."[1] Along the "middle border" from Fort William to Saskatchewan, a very limited sampling indicates a preference for the "Oz" pronunciation, although this is considered to be affected by many speakers who prefer the form rhyming with "maze." [2]

The pronunciation of the sound designated by *e* in most positions is similar in England and America, but there are a few exceptions. The English prefer a long *e* in *evolution* and *epoch*, where most General American speakers would use a short *e*. Canadian usage is divided, but a clear majority agree with General American pronunciation, preferring the *e* of "stem" in *evolution* and *epoch*, and the long *e* of "see" in *ego* and *egotism*, two words which Standard English speakers pronounce with short *e*. Many educated Canadian speakers pronounce the first syllable of *senile* to rhyme with "then," although no leading British or American dictionary sanctions anything but the pronunciation rhyming with "sea."

Another word which apparently has a distinctive sound in Canada is *zebra*, pronounced by more than half the Ontario informants with the short *e* of "bet" instead of the long *e* of "beat," the latter pronunciation prevailing in both Britain and the United States. Canadian usage contrasts sharply with American in the case of *been*, which most Ontarioans rhyme with "bean" and General American speakers with "bin;" and *again*, which most Canadians

[1] D. E. Hamilton, "Notes on Montreal English," *J.C.L.A.*, 1958, pp. 70–79.
[2] Harold B. Allen, "Canadian-American Speech Differences Along the Middle Border," *J.C.L.A.*, 1959, pp. 17–24.

rhyme with "main" instead of the dominant American version with the vowel sound of "men." There is also a tendency in Vancouver to import the short *e* sound into words like *Barry* and *parry*, making them homophones of *berry* and *Perry*. The speakers who do this may also treat *Harry* and *marry* as homophones of *hairy* and *Mary*.[1] The dominant Canadian preference is for the long *e* sound in *creek* and *sleek*, which many Americans pronounce as "crick" and "slick."

The division of Canadian usage between British and American is well illustrated by the class of words ending in *-ile*, as *docile, fertile, futile, projectile, senile, virile*. British usage prefers the long *i* of "while" in the last syllable of all these words, where General American sometimes uses the short *i* of "will," an unstressed vowel sound corresponding roughly to the second syllable of "sofa," or almost completely suppresses the vowel to rhyme with "w'll." In all words of this class except *fertile*, Ontario usage prefers the long *i*, but not unanimously, and considerable variation exists from speaker to speaker. On the other hand, a majority of Ontario speakers used the American pronunciation of *fertile* rhyming with "myrtle." A similar pattern of divided usage appeared in Montreal, but with British usage predominant in all words of this class. Only in the case of *futile* and *fertile* was usage fairly evenly divided. One word that does not conform to this class is *profile*, the common British and American pronunciation of which is "pro-file," although "pro-feel" also has wide acceptance in England. Not one Ontario or Montreal speaker tested offered "pro-feel," although two Ontarioans professed to use "pro-fill," a secondary English pronunciation.

Usage is also divided in the group of words ending in *-ine*, the sample words being *bovine, quinine* and *sanguine*. The usual British and American pronunciation of *bovine* is with long *i*, rhyming with "vine," and this is the pronunciation favoured in both Ontario and Montreal, although one-third of those tested professed to rhyme the word with "fin," an American variant. *Sanguine* is usually pronounced with short *i* in England and

---

[1] R. J. Gregg, "Notes on the Pronunciation of Canadian English as Spoken in Vancouver," *J.C.L.A.*, 1957, pp. 20–26.

America, and a majority of Canadian speakers follow suit, although about one speaker out of four in Ontario and Montreal preferred the ending in long *i*. The pronunciation of *quinine* is the least stable of any of the words in this group, the following variants in descending order of popularity being current in Ontario: "quĭ-nīne," "quĭ-neen," the preferred British form, and "quī-nīne," the American form.

An interesting sidelight on usage is provided by the prefixes *anti-*, *multi-* and *semi-*, the second syllables of which in both Ontario and England are usually pronounced to rhyme with "see." This is also the common American pronunciation, but a variant rhyming with "sigh" is sometimes heard just south of the international border. The difference is so striking, says Avis, that Canadian teen-agers refer to their American neighbours as *semis*, rhyming with "size."

Phonologists draw a fine distinction between the English and American pronunciations of the vowel sound in such words as *block* or *pot*. Larsen and Walker describe the English version as "a lightly rounded vowel, not usually found in General American speech, though it is close to the short form of the American *aw* heard in the opening syllables of *authentic* and *autocracy*," whereas the American pronunciation is "the shortened *ah*-sound usually heard in *what*, *not*, as pronounced in General American speech."[1] Mencken has called attention to a third variant, in American English, a downright *aw* sound, so that, for example, *God* may be variously pronounced *God* (rhyming with "nod"), *Gahd* or *Gawd*.[2] "The first of the three, I believe," he goes on, "is commonly regarded as the most formal, and I have often noticed that a speaker who says *Gawd* in his ordinary discourse will switch to *God* (or maybe *Gahd*) when he wants to show reverence." Such subtleties are largely lost on the average Canadian who pronounces all these words with a short *o* sound somewhere between the limits of Standard English and General American. Most

[1] *Pronunciation, a Practical Guide to Spoken English in Canada and the United States*, Toronto, Oxford, 1930.
[2] *The American Language*, New York, 1936, p. 343.

Canadians make no distinction between the vowel sounds of *cot* and *caught*, and *collar* and *caller*.

Where there is a clear choice between long and short *o*, that is, between the *o* in "roll" and the *o* in "lot," Canadian speakers tend to follow British usage rather than American. Thus the nouns *process* and *progress* are pronounced with long *o* by a majority of Ontarioans, although about one-third of those tested preferred the short *o* in *progress*. Despite this, the Canadian versions of *process* and *progress* sound very different from their equivalents in Standard English, because a Canadian pronounces long *o* in the same way as a General American speaker, that is, as a full sound spoken through rounded lips. A Standard English speaker, on the other hand, gives the vowel quite a different value: it is more nasal and diphthongized with the lips drawn back and slightly pursed rather than rounded to produce a somewhat thinner and flatter sound.

Most Canadian speakers have no hesitation in following British rather than American usage in the class of words ending in "-ough" or "-ought." Thus *drought* is almost universally pronounced to rhyme with "out" in Ontario, this being the form common to both Standard English and General American, less than one per cent of speakers rhyming the word with "mouth," a form widely used by uneducated speakers in the United States and there frequently spelled *drouth*. Ontario speakers also followed British usage in pronouncing *slough* to rhyme with "brow," although almost one-quarter of them pronounced it "sloo" in the General American fashion, which is also the pronunciation current in the Prairie Provinces, where the word is in common use to describe "any fairly large body of residual water." The pronunciation of *slough*, which is only a literary word east of the Great Lakes, is one of the ways to distinguish between a westerner and a person from central or eastern Canada.

Canadian speakers do not consistently choose between the Standard English pronunciation of *u* in certain words, sometimes called the "bugle *u*," and the "American" or "Websterian *u*": that is to say between the pronunciations "dyuke," "styudent" and "Tyuesday" on the one hand, as opposed to "dook," "stoodent" and "Toosday" on the other. British usage requires a "*y*" sound before the *u* in all words of this class. In the United States, particularly in the northern speech area adjacent to Canada, the usual pronunciation of *u* in such words is "oo": thus "noo," "nood," "enthoosiasm," "stoopid," "soot" and "dooty" are all good American. As Mencken notes, "*nyew, nyude, enthyusiasm, styupid* and *syuit* would seem affectations in most parts of the United States. The schoolmarm still battles valiantly for *dyuty*, but in vain." [1]

In Canada, usage is very much divided and unsettled. Yet there is little doubt but that the British practice enjoys prestige, the diphthong being widely used by educated speakers, at least after /t/, /d/, and /n/; but after /s/ and /l/, as in *suit, lute, superstitious, absolute*, the British diphthong is unusual. Thus the sampling of educated Ontario speakers revealed that the English or "bugle *u*" was preferred in *news, Tuesday, dew, duke* and *tune* by well over half of those tested. At that point, the line can be drawn, however, and in the case of *due*, the next word in the series, slightly more than half of those tested professed to say "doo," the same preference being shown in the case of *student*. It is interesting to note that a greater percentage of speakers pronounced *lute* and *suit* as "loot" and "soot" than pronounced *news* and *Tuesday* as "nyews" and "Tyuesday."

Only a few speakers were consistent in their pronunciation of *u*, however, which suggests that many of them had adopted the British or prestige pronunciation without extending it uniformly throughout the whole series of words. For example, some informants while saying "nyews" and "Tyuesday" also said "stoodent" and "toon," and many distinguished between *dew* and *due* by pronouncing the former "dyew" and the latter "doo," although the two words are homophones in Received Standard English.

So far as Ontario is concerned, the "dook," "toon," "noos" pattern seems to occur in inverse ratio to the cultural level of the speaker. It is, of course, true that, Mencken notwithstanding, the "dyuke," "tyune," "nyews" pattern also exists in the United States as a recognized social variant. The difference is that in the

[1] *The American Language*, New York, 1936, p. 345.

United States "both pronunciations are recognized as standard speech acceptable at all levels of society," whereas in Canada social pressure is noticeably in favour of the British *u*, and pronunciations such as "dook" and "noos" are considered inelegant by many people—"including, it seems, those who furnish dictionaries for use in Ontario schools." [1] Indeed, the snob appeal of the "bugle *u*" is such that some Ontario speakers would import it into words where it never belonged; thus for *moon*, *noon* and *too*, one may sometimes encounter the pronunciations "myoon," "nyoon" and "tyoo," although fortunately such extremes are rare.

Montreal usage appears to follow that of Ontario in preferring the "bugle *u*" for most words, although many Montrealers choose the pronunciations "soot" and "stoodent," but usage is very divided, even in the speech of individual informants. [2] Among the younger generation in Vancouver, the tendency is to follow the American pattern. [3] In some areas, among them the "middle border" between Fort William and Saskatchewan, the initial "tyoo" sound of *Tuesday* and *tube* may be assimilated to "choo," producing the variants "choosday" and "choob," which are also to be heard in the United States as a minority pronunciation. [4]

3

In common with English and American speakers, Canadians do not sound the *h* in *heir*, *honest*, *honour* or *hour*, but thereafter their pattern of *h*-aspiration is very inconsistent. Thus in Canada, *herb* is "hurb" as it is in England, and not "urb" as in America, and the first syllable of *humour* is "hew" and not "you," the latter a secondary American and British pronunciation. On the other

[1] W. S. Avis, "Speech Differences along the Ontario-United States Border: Pronunciation," *J.C.L.A.*, 1956, p. 49.

[2] D. H. Hamilton, "Notes on Montreal English," *J.C.L.A.*, 1958, pp. 70–79.

[3] R. J. Gregg, "Notes on the Pronunciation of Canadian English as Spoken in Vancouver," *J.C.L.A.*, 1957, pp. 20–26.

[4] Harold B. Allen, "Canadian-American Speech Differences Along the Middle Border," *J.C.L.A.*, 1959, pp. 17–24.

hand, we drop the *h* in *honorarium*, although it is still retained in England. In *hostel* and *hospital*, Canadians usually sound the *h* clearly, although it is pronounced lightly or not at all by Standard English speakers. CBC announcers when they are on their best behaviour say *an historical*, which is good English usage, but some of them spoil the effect by aspirating the *h* at the same time; many Canadians stick resolutely to *a historical*.[1]

The same tendency shows itself in the presence of an aspiration preceding the *w* in such words as *whales, whether* and *whine*. In Standard English the *h* sound is suppressed, so that such pairs as *when* and *wen, whether* and *weather, while* and *wile* are homophones. In the northern United States, the aspiration is usually although not always sounded to distinguish one member of the pair from the other, and this practice appears to be followed in Canada. When Ontario speakers were confronted with the following pairs: *which* and *witch, whether* and *weather, where* and *wear, whales* and *Wales, white* and *wight, whine* and *wine*, a majority distinguished all or some of the pairs, although about one-third of the informants claimed to make no distinction at all. Elsewhere, however, any uncertainty seems to have resolved itself in favour of suppressing the *h* sound, and in Vancouver and the Prairie Provinces there is little attempt to distinguish between the members of such pairs.

One of the most distinctive features of southern British English, after the "broad *a*," is the "suppressed *r*." Starting as early as the fifteenth century and confirmed in the eighteenth largely by the authority of Samuel Johnson, who called *r* "the rough, snarling letter," the practice arose in southern England of universally omitting to sound the *r* before consonants and at the end of words unless the following word began with a vowel.[2] Standard English retains *r*, according to H. C. Wyld, "initially and when preceded by another consonant, before vowels," as in *rag* and *great*, "in the middle of words between vowels," as in *erect* and *heretic*, and "at the end of words when the next word begins with a vowel, and there is no pause in the sentence between the words," as in *over all*

[1] See Raven I. McDavid, Jr., "*H* before Semi-Vowels in the United States," *Language*, 1952, pp. 41–62.
[2] H. C. Wyld, *A History of Modern Colloquial English*, London, 1921, p. 298.

and *for ever*, although according to Wyld the rule is not often observed in the last position. The confusing result of all this is to turn into homophones such pairs as *ah–are*, *alms–arms*, *lorn–lawn*, *paw–pore*, *sauce–source*, *stalk–stork*, *taught–tort*.[1]

As opposed to this *r*-less dialect, Canadian English like General American sounds the *r* in all positions. Indeed, some Canadian speakers go out of their way to give fullest value to this consonant. George E. Buckley of the University of Western Ontario once observed: "Our great Canadian *r* makes its little roar heard throughout our conversation. It even erases syllables. Thus *horrible* becomes 'horrble' and *recreation* 'recration.' "[2] Is this resounding *r* an American import? There seems little evidence either way. It is true that Henry James, not an unbiased observer, upon returning to the United States from abroad described the widespread use of *r* by his countrymen as "a morose grinding of the back teeth;"[3] but in fact fully a third of Americans do not pronounce the letter distinctly or at all, notably in and around Boston and throughout the South.[4] It may be that the well-sounded Canadian *r*, which appears to be as prevalent in British Columbia as it is in Ontario, is in part a legacy from the ubiquitous Scottish immigrants of the last century.

When British and American usage differs in the pronunciation of *s* and *sh* sounds, Canadian speakers as a rule prefer the cisatlantic version. Thus *issue* and *tissue* are usually "ish-oo" and "tish-oo" as in the United States, and not "iss-you" and "tiss-you," which are fairly common English variants. The second *s* of *sensual* is pronounced like the *sh* of "shop," or sometimes like the *s* in "pleasure," but never like the *s* of "sea," which is the version preferred by the *SOED*. A *geyser* is usually a "gī-zer" in Canada and the United States, and either a "gī-zer" or a "gē-zer" in England; and we pronounce the second half of *impresario* as "-sär-io" not "-zär-io." Occasionally, we follow British usage in preferring "glā-sïal" to the American "glā-shǎl," although we decline both "glă-sïer" (Br.) and "glā-sher" (Am.) in favour of

[1] Robert Bridges, *On English Homophones*, Oxford, 1919.
[2] Toronto *Globe and Mail*, April 18, 1952.
[3] *A Question of Our Speech*, Boston, 1905, p. 29.
[4] John S. Kenyon, "Some Notes on American R," *American Speech*, 1926, p. 333.

"glā-sĭer." Of late, CBC announcers have taken to pronouncing *racial* as "rāce-ĭ-ăl," rather than "ray-shăl," heretofore the dominant Canadian version.

One of the most interesting and distinctive aspects of North American speech is the tendency to give to the sound /t/ when it occurs between two vowels a pronunciation approximating "d." This phenomenon has yet to be fully investigated; many people still consider it nothing more than slovenliness in speech, although it may represent an important linguistic change in North American English. "Since this process is far from being complete," Avis writes, "and since it affects a very wide range of words indeed, there is a great deal of diversity from speaker to speaker and from word to word. The situation, moreover, is made more complex by the currency of several consonants intermediate between fortis, voiceless /t/ and lenis, voiced /d/." [1] The Ontario survey exposed the informants to a series of paired words: *bitter-bidder, bleating-bleeding, kittie-kiddy, latter-ladder, Ottawa-oddawa.* Almost half the persons who took the test admitted pronouncing at least some of the pairs alike, and the practice may be even more widespread than this sampling would indicate. The reluctance of some informants to confess that they were guilty of this speech habit arose from its connotations of social inferiority, the practice being considered "bad form." Thus some Ontario speakers vigorously denied pronouncing *demonstrated* as "demonstraded" and *Ottawa* as "oddawa," although in fact they often used such pronunciations.

The tendency is by no means recent. The word *potatoes* has been commonly pronounced "podaydoes" in and around Ottawa for many years, and the Chateau Laurier was always "The Shadow." A similar phenomenon has been observed in Vancouver speech, where the pairs *hit it* and *hid it*, and *matter* and *madder* are pronounced the same. Indeed, the habit is so widespread as to influence the spelling of many words of this class. Thus Vancouver children sometimes misspell *patio* as "padio," and *teeter-totter* as "teeder-todder," reflecting the prevailing pronunciation of these words. [2]

[1] "Speech Differences Along the Ontario-United States Border: Pronunciation," *J.C.L.A.*, 1956, pp. 41–59.
[2] R. J. Gregg, "Notes on the Pronunciation of Canadian English as Spoken in Vancouver," *J.C.L.A.*, 1957, pp. 20–26.

A similar process occurs when the consonant cluster *nt* occurs between a pair of vowels or their equivalent, and is modified to *nd*, as when *twenty* becomes "twendy." In Vancouver and elsewhere, the process has been carried a step further by the elimination of the *d* sound, so that one may now hear something like "senner" for *centre*, "innerview" for *interview*, "plenny" for *plenty*, "twenny" for *twenty* and "winner" for *winter*. Contrariwise, the sound of *t* is sometimes inserted where none grew before, so that words like *also*, *sense* and *Wilson*, may be pronounced "altso," "sents" and "wiltson." One of the best-known examples of the suppressed *t* may be found in the popular pronunciation of the name *Toronto*. Most Americans and other outsiders give the word three clearly enunciated syllables. Canadian pronunciation on the other hand runs a wide gamut, starting close to the American version, although with a lighter stress on the middle syllable, and a progressive weakening of the first syllable to produce such variants as "Tronto" and "Tronno," often with some modification of the vowel sounds to "Trŏnna," "Trahna" and "Trănnah." The pronunciation of *Saskatchewan* provides a less well-known shibboleth, most non-Canadians preferring four distinct syllables, the first two equally stressed and pronounced with the *a* of "hat." Canadians, on the other hand, tend to slur the first syllable and accent the second to produce something like "suss-katchewan," or the vowel sound may be almost entirely suppressed to "ss-skatchewan."

CHAPTER SIX

SPELLING AND SYNTAX

As felicitous an instance of futile classicism as can well be found is the conventional spelling of the English language. English orthography satisfies all the requirements of the canons of reputability under the law of conspicuous waste. It is archaic, cumbrous and ineffective; its acquisition consumes much time and effort; failure to acquire it is easy of detection.

THORSTEIN VEBLEN

SPELLING AND SYNTAX

I Spelling

FEW LINGUISTIC CONVENTIONS HAVE BEEN MORE BLINDLY FOLLOWED in our day than the so-called rules of English orthography, and fewer still have evoked as much controversy. It is hardly surprising that this should be so, for some of them are little more than an invitation to disagreement. "The real difficulty about our spelling," writes G. H. Vallins, "is its inconsistency. There are no reliable rules, and even the guiding principles—of which there are more than we imagine—are apt sometimes to fail and mislead both ear and eye." [1] At the same time, the modern attitude toward spelling is only a trifle this side of veneration since, as Professor Vallins adds, "the ability to spell according to the conventionally fixed pattern has been looked on as the outward sign of a literate man."

Prior to the seventeenth century, men spelled much as they chose, and it was not until the spread of printed books that printers and publishers began to impose a standard system of orthography. Modern spelling as we know it is primarily the legacy of two great men: Samuel Johnson (1709–1784) and Noah Webster (1758–1843). The enormous authority of Johnson's *Dictionary* fixed English spelling in substantially the form which it still has; it was he who ordained the *-our* ending for words of the *labour* and *honour* class, and most of the other conventions which

---

[1] *Spelling*, London, 1954, p. 17.

145

he advocated have withstood the test of time. Webster's influence
on American spelling was no less important through his spelling
book, one of his important contributions being the deletion of *u*
from the *-our* ending.

The differences between English and American spelling have
been given undue importance, particularly by some Englishmen
who, John W. Clarke points out, regard American spelling variants
as not merely ugly but also crude, ill-bred and bumptious.[1]
Strangely enough, few Americans are aroused to the same extent
by British spelling, perhaps because it is older and has the weight
of much authority behind it, but in any case they cling stubbornly
to their own brand of orthography. The standard American view,
as expressed by Mencken, is that American spelling is quite
simply better than English spelling and will prevail.

The most distinctive characteristic of modern American spelling
is a simplification of certain English spelling practices. This most
commonly takes the form of eliminating one or more letters, either
in the middle of a word (British, *aluminium, carburettor, flunkey,
chilli;* American, *aluminum, carburetor, flunky, chili*), or at the end
(British, *axe, annexe, furore, gelatine;* American, *ax, annex, furor,
gelatin*). The best-known example of this process is the reduction
of *-our* to *-or* in all polysyllables except *saviour*, which, especially
when capitalized, is usually so spelled in America.[2] Thus English
ardour, behaviour, clamour, favour, neighbour are always and only
ardor, behavior, clamor, favor, neighbor in America.

Although Englishmen profess to turn from this practice with
horror, they forget that the same development has been taking
place in England since Johnson's day when even *authour, horrour*
and *terrour* were so spelled, to the point where, as H. W. Fowler
has remarked, British words ending in *-our* are much fewer in
proportion to words ending in *-or* than one would have supposed.
Moreover, adds Fowler, "there seems to be no discoverable line
between the two sets so based on principle as to serve any useful
purpose."[3] Thus an Englishman writes *ardour* but *pallor; favour*

[1] G. H. Vallins, *Spelling*, pp. 174–175.
[2] H. W. Fowler, *A Dictionary of Modern English Usage*, 2nd ed., Oxford, 1965, p. 428.
[3] *Glamour*, being of Scottish derivation, is usually so written in the United States.

but *horror; odour* but *tremor.* And from *humour* comes *humorous*, from *vapour, vaporous* and from *vigour, vigorous* and *invigorate.* G. H. Vallins points out that although in 1926 Fowler had said dogmatically "*humorous* but *humourist*," the *u* has since fallen by the wayside and the *COD* gives *humorist* only, although the *u* is still preserved in *humourless.*[1]

Another American development was the virtual elimination of many doubled consonants, the commonest example being -*ll*- and -*pp*-, as in American, *paneled, graveled, jewelry, parceling* (British, *panelled, gravelled, jewellery, parcelling*); American, *kidnaped, worshiped* (British, *kidnapped, worshipped*). Despite Webster's pruning, however, many inconsistencies remain: thus Americans sometimes double a consonant that is single in British English, as *distill, fulfill, instill, installment* (British, *distil, fulfil, instil, instalment*). As offensive to most Englishmen as -*or* instead of -*our* is the American preference for -*er* in the place of -*re*, which requires *caliber, fiber, luster* and *saber* (British, *calibre, fibre, lustre, sabre*); also the dropping of *ae* and *oe* in favour of *e*, which reduces the British *foetid, haemoglobin, mediaeval, manoeuvre* to the simpler *fetid, hemoglobin, medieval, maneuver.*

Strangely enough, not all American spellings are shorter, as witness the English *cantaloup, forbears, pedlar, racoon, stymy*, which Americans spell *cantaloupe, forebears, peddler, raccoon, stymie.*[2] The remaining differences relate chiefly to the choice of alternate letters, as in American *defense, offense, pretense* versus British *defence, offence, pretence*, and the British preference for *em-* and *en-* instead of the American *im-* and *in-*, and -*ise* for -*ize*, although -*ize* is fast becoming the dominant British form. There are also a few miscellaneous differences, such as the English *cheque* (Am. *check*), *gaol* (*jail*), *closure* (*cloture*), *grey* (*gray*), *kerb* (*curb*), *mollusc* (*mollusk*), *pyjamas* (*pajamas*), *plough* (*plow*), *toffee* (*taffy*).

G. P. Krapp wrote:

When one begins to examine the details of British spelling

---

[1] *Spelling*, London, 1954. The second edition of Fowler revised by Sir Ernest Gowers (1965) accedes to *humorist* but requires *humourless* and *humoursome.*

[2] These and earlier spelling comparisons are taken from Margaret Nicholson, *A Dictionary of American-English Usage, Based on Fowler's Modern English Usage*, Oxford, 1957.

it soon becomes apparent that it is a wise and rare Britisher
who knows what British spelling is. . . . In the style book of
the Oxford Press . . . we learn that *advertise* and *affranchise*
must be spelled with *s* not *z*, but *anglicized*, *appetize*, and
many others, must be spelled with *z*, while *apprise* 'to
inform' must have *s*, and *apprize* 'to value,' must have *z*.
Only one whose business it is to remember technical details
would think of burdening his mind with minutiae of this
sort, and certainly when the Britisher's heart glows with
pride and patriotism as he rises to the defense or defence of
the beloved institution of British spelling, it cannot be with
such matters that his mind is filled. It is filled merely with
those half dozen words like *honour*, *centre*, *defence*, *waggon*,
traveller, which indeed serve sufficiently as rocks on which to
found his faith.[1]

Torn between British and American example, Canadian
spelling does not follow a consistent pattern. On what one may
call the "official" level, British spelling is mandatory in Canada.
Mencken has recalled that as long ago as 1890 an Order-in-
Council required government officials to indite their correspondence in British spelling, and this patriotic stand was duly endorsed
in 1931 by the combined weight of the Royal Society of Canada,
the Canadian Geographical Society and the Canadian Historical
Association.[2] It was also so ordained, at least for *-our* words, in
the bible of officialdom, *Preparation of Copy for the Printer*, issued
by the then King's Printer at Ottawa, although that work made
a number of concessions to current inconsistencies: thus the American *aluminum* will do for commercial writing, but the English
aluminium is required for scientific prose. American usage is also
to be followed in *cipher*, *dryly*, *jail*, *net*, *program* and *wagon* instead of
the English *cypher*, *drily*, *gaol*, *nett*, *programme* and *waggon*.[3] Even

---

[1] *The English Language in America*, Vol. 2, pp. 349–350.

[2] H. L. Mencken, *The American Language*, p. 396, citing an article in the Baltimore
Evening Sun of August 5, 1931, "Canada Won't Even Import American Spelling."

[3] Many of these "British" spellings seem to be passing out of current use in England,
or are confined to commercialese. Thus Fowler, *Modern English Usage*, prefers *cipher*,
jail, *net*, *program*. According to the *OED*, *program* was the regular spelling in England
until the nineteenth century; hence, no doubt its inveterate use in Canada and the
United States.

alright, that bugbear of Fowler and others, is given the stamp of approval. Apart from minor deviations, however, it is still true to say that "the British standard is the declared official standard of the Dominion Government and is used in all government correspondence and printing. This statement with few and minor deviations applies to practically all provincial governments." [1]

Generally speaking, a concerted attempt is made to hold the British spelling line in Canadian schools, and this has been so for a hundred years and more.[2] The devotion of early schoolmasters to this cause was sometimes accompanied by a marked anti-American bias. Thus *The Canadian Spelling Book Intended as an Introduction to the English Language*, which was published at Toronto about 1840 and by 1856 had reached a printing figure of 130,000, followed British spelling throughout. In the preface, its author, Alexander Davidson, boasting a residence of nearly twenty years in Canada, deplored the large number of American schoolbooks to be found here. "While spelling books from England are to *us* necessarily defective," he wrote, "not being suited to our scenery and other localities, those of a foreign origin are liable to more serious objections." This attitude was followed by succeeding generations, and to this day it is almost impossible for many persons who have been educated in Canada to bring themselves to write *labor* and *center* rather than *labour* and *centre*. It can be truly said that "the British standard is taught to practically every Canadian school-child and used throughout school life. It is the standard of the great majority of Canadian universities and colleges." [3]

Despite this careful indoctrination, however, even before the young Canadian leaves school he is assailed on every side by American spelling. This comes not only from the flood of American newspapers and periodicals which inundates the entire

[1] Kennedy Crone, *British Spelling of English as the Canadian National Standard*, Montreal, N.D. (*c*. 1931).

[2] Mencken, *The American Language*, 1936, p. 396, was in error when he stated that American spelling "is also taught in most of the [Canadian] public schools."

[3] Kennedy Crone, *British Spelling of English as the Canadian National Standard*. A typical early school text was *The English Spelling Book, Accompanied by a Progressive Series of Easy and Familiar Lessons; Intended as an Introduction to the Reading and Spelling of the English Language*, by William Mavor, LL.D., published at Kingston, Upper Canada, in 1831, "from the 328th London edition."

F

country but from the domestic press as well, which is thoroughly Americanized in its spelling habits. About 1931, Kennedy Crone, then managing editor of the *Canadian Geographical Journal*, published a brief plea for a return to British spelling, making the point that not only was there no national standard of spelling in Canada but that we were further from having a national standard than any other English-speaking community in the world.[1] Crone found that Canadian orthography was of two kinds, one of which he named "British spelling" and the other "Americanized spelling." He rejected the contention that "the incomplete fusing of American forms into Canadian spelling of English has brought about a Canadian standard, neither British nor American, borrowing from both, and distinctly Canadian," and found no evidence whatever "that this fusing has any consistency or was well on the way to becoming the national habit."

Substantially the same conclusion can be reached today. British and American forms, sometimes for the same words, co-exist and contend with each other, and we are no nearer the consistency of a national standard than we were two generations ago. As Crone rightly pointed out, "the greatest single source of usage of these American forms in Canada is the Canadian press. An overwhelming majority of Canadian newspapers and magazines use them, more or less completely and in all sorts of combinations with British forms." Yet, he concluded, we are a long way from having a press standard, apart from words ending in -*or*. "Many periodicals are laws unto themselves, and there are even instances when differing standards of spelling are applied to the different pages of a periodical."

As evidence of the steady encroachment of American spelling, Crone compiled a table of "American forms incorporated into Canadian spelling of English." But he made clear that his list did not imply general acceptance of an American standard, since many American spellings, for example, *maneuver* and *kidnaped*, are almost never used in Canada, being proscribed along with such examples of "simplified spelling" as *thru* and *discust*. Crone's division of Canadian spelling into British and Americanized is

[1] *British Spelling of English as the Canadian National Standard*, Montreal, N.D.

equally applicable today and appears to follow no rational pattern. Thus Canadians prefer American *airplane, baritone, connection, font, gasoline* to British *aeroplane, barytone, connexion, fount, gasolene;* at the same time, Canadians use British *cauldron, cheque, furore,* rather than American *caldron, check, furor.*[1] They prefer American *jail, jimmy, jujitsu,* to British *gaol, jemmy, jujutsu,* while insisting upon British *glycerine, mollusc, syrup, toffee,* instead of American *glycerin, mollusk, sirup, taffy.*

If there is a reason why these things should be so, no one has yet suggested it. The preference for *-our* instead of *-or* in words of the *clamour, colour, favour, honour* class is almost universal, apart from the newspapers, as is *-au-* instead of *-a-* in such words as *caulk,* and *-ou-* instead of *-o-* in *moult, mould, smoulder.* Canadians prefer *-re* to *-er* in *fibre, lustre, sombre, theatre,* as well as the superfluous *-e* in *axe,* all of them preferences for British rather than American forms. On the other hand, some British forms have no currency whatever in Canada, among them the *-xion* ending in words of the class *connexion, inflexion,* which Canadian and American spellers always write as *connection* and *inflection.*

Unlike the United States where such things are endemic, Canada has offered scant aid and comfort to the cause of simplified spelling. One early voice in the wilderness was that of *The Fonetic Herald,* a periodical "devoted tu Orthoepi and Orthografi," which first saw the light of day at Port Hope, Ontario, in January, 1885. "Its chief object," announced the prospectus, "wil be tu elucidate and exemplify the *simplicity* and *practicability* of amending English orthografy on a fonetic basis. It shal not be the organ ov any party, sect or society; nor advocate any particular alfabet or other views, but wil treat the whole subject az one ov linguistic science, and therefore tu be approacht in the spirit ov general science, always unbigoted and cosmopolitan. Orthoepy, a sister subject ov orthografy, shal receiv a larj shar ov attention, az wil also, in les degree, etymology." *The Fonetic Herald,* which began rather inauspiciously by printing "The Last Roz ov Sumer" ("left bluming alon"), later moved to Toronto and managed to brave

[1] These and the following spellings are taken from Margaret Nicholson, *A Dictionary of American-English Usage,* Oxford, 1957.

the boreal blasts for some four years and forty-five issues before expiring in May, 1889, since which time spelling reform has made little stir in Canada. Even such mildly reformed expressions as *nite, thru, foto, sox, burlesk* and the like which have become part of American journalese—although lacking any academic imprimatur —are never used in Canada, not even on the sporting page. Our spelling resists reformation and remains as it was in the beginning, unsimplified.

In September, 1960, the Canadian Conference on Education commissioned a report "on the present state of the movement to reform the spelling of English." [1] The resultant monograph presented a balanced study of the case for and against spelling reform. In keeping with the avowed intention of the committee which prepared it to maintain a neutral attitude, the report carefully listed ten arguments in favour of spelling reform (including "reduction of delinquency and crime") and eleven against (including "public apathy and prejudice"). One of the major objects of the report was "to attract as much attention as possible to the subject." It is perhaps too early to say whether the report will bear fruit, although the general lack of interest in spelling reform which prevails throughout Canada does not bode well for the future.

II Morphology and Syntax

That Canadians and their American neighbours across the line speak substantially the same variety of North American English has been borne out by inquiries into grammar and syntax along the border.[2] Syntactical and grammatical usages are not easy to determine by means of a questionnaire, and the problem is

---

[1] *Some Arguments for and against Reforming English Spelling. A Report Prepared for the Canadian Conference on Education by a Committee Representing the Canadian Linguistic Association and the Association of Canadian University Teachers of English.* Kingston, Ontario, 1962.

[2] See, *e.g.*, Walter S. Avis, "Speech Differences Along the Ontario-United States Border: II, Grammar and Syntax," *J.C.L.A.*, March, 1955, pp. 14–19; Donald E. Hamilton, "Notes on Montreal English," *J.C.L.A.*, 1958, pp. 70–79.

obscured by the fact that differences are often social rather than regional; nevertheless, a marked preference existed in Ontario and Montreal for American idiom at all levels. Thus the American contraction *I won't* was overwhelmingly offered in Ontario by four-fifths of speakers tested in preference to the British *I shan't*. When a number of variants were in current use, it was often the American idiom which prevailed, a good example being the phrase *sick to the stomach*, preferred by more than half of Ontario and more than three-quarters of Montreal speakers. The standard English form *sick at the stomach* fared badly in Southern Ontario (about two-fifths) and worse in Montreal (less than two per cent), the remaining speakers offering either *sick in the stomach* or, infrequently, *sick of the stomach*.

Sick at the stomach with its prepositional variants *to*, *in* and *of* provide an interesting example of linguistic geography. The usual expression in the Northern speech area of the United States is *sick to the stomach*. *At* is the common preposition in the Midland and Southern areas, although *in* and *on* occur in Pennsylvania Dutch country. In Ontario, usage divides sharply between *sick at the stomach* west of Toronto and *sick to the stomach* from Toronto eastward, reflecting the difference in settlement history between Eastern and Western Ontario. In addition, *sick in the stomach*, one of the Pennsylvania Dutch forms, may be heard in the German areas of Western Ontario. *Sick to the stomach* is preferred by more than three-quarters of Montreal informants, thus confirming the eastward trend. In the French form, *mal à l'estomac*, the preposition *à* may be translated into English as *in*, *to* or *at*, so that it is difficult to say which one a French Canadian would prefer when speaking English, although the investigator's personal feeling was that it would be *at* or *in*, neither of them, as it happens, the prevailing Montreal form.

The same tendency to follow American usage appears in the use of preterites, notably *dove*, a classical and much-maligned Americanism which is still clearly preferred even at the college level by Ontarioans over the British *dived*, a few speakers using either without preference. *Drank* as the past participle of *drink* is the usual form in the Northern American speech area, as opposed to the Standard English *drunk*, even in New England, "the very citadel of prestige speech." [1] In Ontario, the participial form *drank* occurred even among educated speakers. Given the form "he has (*drank* or *drunk*) five glasses of beer already," more than a third of Ontario informants chose *drank*, while a few speakers used either *drank* or *drunk* indiscriminately. In Montreal, the number of speakers who offered the form *has drunk* fell to less than one-fifth, although the general conclusion was that Montreal English more closely resembled the northern variety of American English than did the speech reported from Southern Ontario. To bear this out, the form *has gotten*, a tried and true Americanism that has been the butt of British ridicule for a century and more, was offered by almost two-thirds of Montreal informants, as compared to much less than one-half in Ontario.

The verb *loan*, another Americanism for which the Standard English is *lend*, was used by less than one-third of Ontarioans, and this included a few who offered either form. Another expression where usage was divided is *bath* as in the sentence "I am going to *bath* (or *bathe*) the baby." More than a third of Ontario informants offered the American alternative *bathe*. Moreover, *bath* was preferred by older and *bathe* by younger informants, suggesting that the older British term is being supplanted by the American. In fourteen out of twenty-three grammatical and syntactical items, however, Montrealers preferred the American alternatives, and in five out of six expressions where a comparison with Ontario usage was possible, a larger number of Montreal speakers chose the American form.

Even an informal examination of Canadian English will bear out these findings. A Canadian lives *on* Blank Street like an American, and not *in* it as would an Englishman; he says *due to* instead of *owing to* and assures his listeners that there is *nothing to it* (Br. *nothing in it*). He often looks forward like an American to

---

[1] W. S. Avis, "Speech Differences Along the Ontario-United States Border: Grammar and Syntax," *J.C.L.A.*, March, 1955, p. 15. An earlier study by Avis, "The Past Participle 'Drank' in Standard American Usage," *American Speech*, 1953, pp. 106–111, drawing on *Linguistic Atlas* data for Ontario, indicated that four out of five cultured informants used *drunk* and one used either, but the later and more extended study "indicates that *drank* as participle is commonplace as a vulgate verb form in Ontario."

taking his first *vacation in* two years (Br. first *holiday for* two years).
He prefers such Americanisms as *all of the people* for *all the people;*
and like an American he *works nights*—an expression unknown in
England. One may also note *I want off*, which is common to many
parts of Canada and the Midland area of the United States.

On the other hand, some American locutions have almost no
currency in central Canada. The border has proved impervious
to such common Americanisms as the time designation *a quarter
of* (five); only a negligible number of Ontario and Montreal
speakers admitted to its use, the overwhelming preponderance
preferring *a quarter to*, or, occasionally, *a quarter till* (near Windsor)
and *a quarter before*. *A quarter of* is occasionally heard in New
Brunswick and Nova Scotia and *a quarter till* has some currency
among older speakers in Cape Breton Island. Similarly, the use
of *to* in the sentence "He lives *over to* the Browns," although
reported as being usual in the Northern United States,[1] was
offered by only 2 per cent of Ontario informants, the overwhelming
majority of speakers preferring *over at*.

An interesting division of usage was shown in the use of *(in) back
of* to signify *behind*, as in "the truck is *in back of* (or *back of*) the
barn." Only 13 per cent of Ontario speakers used the prevalent
American form *(in) back of*, although 29 per cent of Montrealers
used *in back of* and 9 per cent *at the back of*. The relative frequency of
in back of in the Montreal area may be due to the fact that it is a
literal translation of the French *en arrière de*, which English-
speaking Montrealers may unconsciously borrow from French
speakers who use English as a second language. On the prairies,
the expression *usen't to* is found "as acceptable standard colloquial,"
where Americans in adjacent border areas typically say *didn't use
to*.[2]

The shibboleth of Canadian syntax is unquestionably the *have
you* or *have you got* construction as a way of asking for things:
have you the time? or *have you got any matches?* which is as general in
Canada as the *do you have* idiom in the United States: *do you have*

---

[1] R. I. McDavid, Jr., "Midland and Canadian Words in Upstate New York,"
American Speech, 1951, pp. 248–256. Cultivated American speakers would say *over at*.
[2] Harold B. Allen, "Canadian-American Speech Differences Along the Middle
Border," *J.C.L.A.*, 1959, pp. 17–24.

the time? do you have any matches? The *do you have* construction enjoyed almost no currency in Ontario, only 10 per cent of the limited number of persons tested using the American form, while 3 per cent used both forms interchangeably. Significantly enough, several *do you have* users had lived in the United States, and Canadians living south of the border quickly fall into the *do you have* idiom without being aware of it, even though they might be impervious to Americanisms in general, so is the pervasive influence. The adopted form apparently persists when Canadians return home, although the *have you* (got) construction usually manages to re-establish itself in time as the only form enjoying general usage in Ontario. In Montreal, on the other hand, *do you have* was offered by 35 per cent of informants, the remaining speakers dividing their allegiance between *have you* (30 per cent), and *have you got* (35 per cent), although the latter is frowned upon by English teachers because of the redundant "got."

CHAPTER SEVEN

ITS NAMES

If some countries have too much history, we have too much geography.

W. L. MACKENZIE KING

F*

ITS NAMES

I Place Names

IN THE YEAR 1883, ONE E. A. FREEMAN, RECALLING HIS TRAVELS through North America, gave Canada a back-handed accolade:

> The truth is, that the great land of the United States has
> not yet got a name, a real local name, like England or
> France, or even like Canada or Mexico . . . . The want of a
> real name for the land, and the awkwardness to which one is
> driven for lack of it, struck me at every turn in my American
> travels. The thought even sometimes occurred, What if the
> name of New England, a name surely to be cherished on
> every ground, had spread over the whole Union? It would
> have been better than nothing; but a real geographical
> name would be better still.[1]

The name *Canada*, inevitable and pre-eminently suitable as it now seems, was the subject of considerable debate at and prior to the time of Confederation. Among many alternative names suggested for the new country were *Tupona* or *Tuponia*, drawn from the initial letters of The United Provinces of North America and, on the same principle, *Efisga*, an acrostic of England, France, Ireland, Scotland, Germany and Aborigines. Other scarcely less likely suggestions included *Transatlantia*, *Transylvania*, *Canadensia*, *Vesperia*, *Mesopelagia* and *Aquilonia*. Loyalty to the Queen

---

[1] *Some Impressions of the United States*, New York, 1883, pp. 31–32, quoted in Joseph Jones, "Hail, Fredonia!" *American Speech*, 1934, p. 12.

and her late consort inspired the portmanteau word *Albertoria*
and such neologisms as *Victoralia, Alexandrina, Victorialand* and
Albertsland. Of equally patriotic inspiration were *British North
America, Western Britannia, Britannia West, Britannica, Albona,
Albionora* and *New Albion*. Names evoking Canadian history were
also somewhat favoured, among them *Cabotia, Acadia, Hochelaga,
Laurentia* and *Niagarentia;* but there were few supporters for *Colonia*
to indicate a union of colonies, or such names of more abstract
conception as *Ursulia, Borealia, Superior* and *Norland*.[1]

There was probably never any real danger that such confec-
tions would be taken seriously, for the name *Canada* had a prior
claim of very long standing.[2] "It first appears in the narratives of
Jacques Cartier in 1534," says the *Encyclopedia Canadiana*, "when
it seems to have reference to the Indian community of Stadacona."[3]
According to Robert's map of 1638, it was applied to the St.
Lawrence River, and later became the popular name for the
colony of New France as distinct from *Acadie* or *Acadia*, which
comprised what are now the Maritime Provinces and parts of
Quebec and Maine. The name *Acadie* itself which became current
after 1604 was almost certainly a misreading of the earlier designation *Larcadie* appearing on Gestaldi's map of 1584.

After the cession of Quebec to England, its official name was
"The Province of Quebec" but, such is the persistence of old
geographical names, the name *Canada* continued in popular use.
When by the Constitutional Act of 1791 the old Province of
Quebec was separated at the Ottawa River, the two new provinces were called *Upper Canada*, now Ontario, and *Lower Canada*,
now Quebec, collectively often referred to as *The Canadas*. The
Act of Union of 1840 joined them again as the Province of Canada,
composed of *Canada East* and *Canada West*, although according to

[1] These are garnered from Isabel Skelton, "The Name 'Canada,'" *The Canadian
Magazine of Politics, Art and Literature*, 1921, pp. 312–314. See also Ivan Velyhors'kyj,
The Term and Name 'Canada,' Winnipeg, 1955.

[2] As Thomas D'Arcy McGee remarked: "One individual chooses Tuponia and
another Hochelaga, as a suitable name for the new nationality. Now I would ask any
member of this House how he would feel if he woke up some fine morning and found
himself, instead of a Canadian, a Tuponian or a Hochelagander:" *Confederation
Debates*, February 9, 1865.

[3] Vol. 2, p. 182.

contemporary accounts these names never caught on. Samuel
Phillips Day in *English America: or Pictures of Canadian Places and
People* noted that as late as 1864 the new designations were
scrupulously avoided both in legal documents and by the public
at large in favour of the older names. Any question of nomenclature was permanently settled by the British North America Act
of 1867, which decreed: "It shall be lawful for the Queen, by and
with the advice of Her Majesty's Most Honourable Privy Council, to
declare by Proclamation that, on and after a Day therein appointed, not being more than Six Months after the passing of this
Act, the Provinces of Canada, Nova Scotia and New Brunswick
shall form and be One Dominion under the name of Canada;
and on and after that Day those Three Provinces shall form and be
One Dominion under that Name accordingly."

It was fitting that the Province of Canada in passing out of
existence should confer its name on the new Dominion, being
not merely the name of the largest and most populous of the
provinces entering Confederation but also that by which the
central territory had been known long before the fall of Quebec.
For many years after Confederation, the official designation was
The Dominion of Canada although that phrase nowhere appears
in the British North America Act.[1] At the time of the second world
war, there was some agitation for the suppression of the word
Dominion on the theory that it had a servient connotation, and the
then Government quietly dropped it, to the periodically recurring
displeasure of some native Anglophiles who draw what comfort
they can from the fact that Sir John A. Macdonald wanted to call
the new nation "The Kingdom of Canada."[2]

The origin of the name *Canada* which long perplexed historians

[1] Sir Leonard Tilley is usually credited with having derived *dominion* from Psalms,
72, 8: "He shall have dominion also from sea to sea. . . ." Whence also the legend
on the Canadian Coat of Arms: *A mari usque ad mare.* However, the phrase "His
Majesty's Dominion in British North America" was used as early as 1858 by Sir
Edmund Head: Robert M. Hamilton, *Canadian Quotations and Phrases,* Toronto, 1952, p.63.
[2] The term *Kingdom of Canada* was originally used in 1822 by Sir John Beverley
Robinson, Chief Justice of Upper Canada, and one of the pillars of the Family
Compact. It was adopted by Sir John A. Macdonald in a handwritten draft of the
B.N.A. Act, 1867, but was dropped, according to Macdonald, "at the instance of Lord
Derby, then [1867] foreign minister, who feared [that the] name would wound the
sensibilities of the Yankees:" Robert M. Hamilton, *Canadian Quotations and Phrases,* p.23.

and philologists has given birth to a number of intriguing theories. Of these, the most fanciful relates that the early Spanish explorers, finding only ice and snow instead of the fabled wealth of the Indies, exclaimed in disgust *"Aca nada!"*—"Here nothing!" This expression was supposedly treasured by the Indians and repeated to later French voyageurs who concluded that it was the name of the country. The view of a majority of commentators, however, has long been that the name derives from the Indian word *kanata* meaning a village or collection of huts, the theory being that as Jacques Cartier's fleet of two small ships ascended the St. Lawrence the Indians pointed to their settlements saying *"kanata,"* which from its repetition the French took to be the name of the entire country.

A. Marshall Elliott set out long ago to demolish this theory on philological grounds, pointing out that Cartier had appended a list of Indian words to the narrative of his discoveries in which he correctly set down the meaning of *kanata* as village, with no suggestion that from this word had come the name of "la terre et province de Canada." [1] From this and a considerable weight of philological evidence, Elliott concluded that Cartier found the name *Canada* already in existence when he arrived at Stadacona in 1535. In Elliott's view, *Canada* is a Spanish or Portuguese adjective used as a noun, comparable to *Florida* (*terra florida*) and *Barbada* (*ihla barbada*). The Spanish word *cañada*, Elliott further noted, is the term for a glade, and is in wide use in Argentina to signify the fertile reed-grown banks of a river. Its earliest application to Canada was not in reference to the country as a a whole but only to a single province lying along the banks of the St. Lawrence. The Spanish origin of the word was further suggested by the existence, according to Elliott, of some fifty places in Spain bearing "this characteristically generic designation" as well as seven places on the map of France with the same name, notably an elevated promontory above Fécamp (Seine-Inférieure), which has borne this name "de temps immémorial."

[1] The various and conflicting theories are dealt with by this early student of Canadian linguistics in "Origin of the Name 'Canada,'" *Modern Language Notes*, 1888, pp. 327–345. See also J. G. Bourinot, "Canadian Historic Names," *Canadian Monthly*, 1875, pp. 289–300.

This theory of an Iberian origin for the name *Canada* is not without some precedent. When the French first arrived on the eastern coast of America, they found a great many places bearing Spanish or Portuguese names, since they had been anticipated in their travels by explorers from both these countries. Thus *New-foundland* was first known as *Terra Nova do Bacalhao* from the codfish which abounded in its waters, and *Labrador*, originally *Terra Cortereales*, a name given to that coast by Cortereal, was later called *Terra de Labrador* or *Laborador*, a name of obscure origin.[1]

Elliott's theory has been called in question largely because it failed to show how a Spanish word came to be in common use among a tribe of savages who had seen practically nothing of Spaniards.[2] Given the difficulty of rooting out an old geographical name among Indian tribes little accustomed to change, it seems improbable that a few visits by Spanish navigators, even if they had penetrated so far up the St. Lawrence, would be sufficient to revolutionize the native name of a district; nor does the name *Canada* appear on any early Spanish maps of the area. Ivan Velyhors'kyj, one of a group of Ukrainian students of onomastics dwelling in western Canada, lists three theories about the origin of the name *Canada*: first, that it is of local, probably Iroquois, origin and was applied, it would appear indiscriminately, to the country east of Lake Ontario, the St. Lawrence River, the Montreal district, a settlement, and so on; secondly, that it is of

[1] Formerly the name *Labrador* was thought to derive from "the adaptability of the natives for labour:" J. G. Bourinot, "Canadian Historical Names," *Canadian Monthly*, 1875, pp. 289–300, who added: "Labrador—Laboratoris Terra—is undoubtedly so called from the fact that Cortereal stole from the country some fifty-seven natives, whom he described in a letter to the Venetian Ambassador at Lisbon, as well-fitted for slaves: 'They are extremely fitted to endure labour and will probably turn out the best slaves which have been discovered up to this time.' " This theory, although repeated by Eloise Lambert and Mario Pei in *The Book of Place Names*, New York, 1959, p. 83, is no longer given credence by serious students of toponymy. M. A. Buchanan, "Notes on Portuguese Place Names in North-Eastern America," in *Estudios Hispanicos Homenaje a Archer M. Huntingdon*, Wellesley, Mass., pp. 99–104, suggests that the name recalls Joao Fernandes, an Azorean landowner or *laborador* in the service of Bristol. This view is consonant with an inscription on the Wolfenbuttel map of 1534: see *Encyclopedia Canadiana*, vol. 6, p. 32.

[2] Walter Bell Scaife, *America's Geographical History, 1492–1892*, Baltimore, 1892, pp. 83–88.

European, probably Spanish or Portuguese origin—or possibly French; thirdly, that it is of Oriental origin, being either imported from the East Indies or selected to honour the Hindu philosopher Kanada.[1] There seems to be no evidence to support the last of these, and most commentators are divided between the first two with the weight of opinion on the whole favouring the former.

Canadian in the sense of one of the aboriginal inhabitants of Canada is traced by the *DC* to 1664, as a native of French Canada to 1746 and as a native of Upper or Lower Canada to 1792. The word *Canadian*, as Lighthall long ago pointed out, is taken in its present form from the French.[2] "In a translation of Lahontan's *Travels* dated 1763 the English form used is 'Canadans.' Lahontan again, following others, applies 'Canadiens' like 'Canadois' in the Jesuit *Rélations* only to Indians of the country; thence it became the designation of all the French natives of this continent, including those of Louisiana; and now the native British residents enthusiastically accept the name." Lighthall also noted the dual pronunciation, "one 'Canadians;' the other less musical but older— 'Canajans.' " A traveller in 1840 observed that the name of the country was then pronounced "Kaugh-na-daugh."[3]

There have been few nicknames for Canadians, among them *Canuck* and its variants *Jack* or *Johnny Canuck*. The term *Canuck* has had a long history, although it is little used in Canada today except as a burned-out cliché by sports writers.[4] Historically, the word boasts many different variants: *Canuck, Canack* and *Cunnuck*, listed by Sylva Clapin in *A Dictionary of Americanisms; Kanuck, Kanuk* and *K'nucks*, cited in the *DAE* (along with *Canuck*), not to mention *Cannacker*, traced by the *DAE* to 1846; and *Conuck* in the *Boston Transcript* of February 7, 1840. The earliest use of *Kanuck* is given as 1835, when it apparently meant "a Dutch or French

[1] *The Term and Name "Canada,"* Winnipeg, 1955. A concise review of some of the theories may be found in *A Dictionary of Canadianisms on Historical Principles*, Toronto, 1967.
[2] "Canadian English," *The Week* (Toronto), August 16, 1889, pp. 581–583; and see H. L. Mencken, "Names for Americans," *American Speech*, 1947, p. 248.
[3] [Henry Cook Todd] *Notes upon Canada and the United States from 1832 to 1840*, Toronto, 1840, p. 160.
[4] Wilson MacDonald drew on the term for his satirical "Song of a Bloody Canuck" (1931).

Canadian," and of *Canuck* as 1855. The earliest citation in the *DC* is 1849. Walt Whitman wrote in "Song of Myself":

> Growing among black folks as among white,
> Kanuck, Tuckahoe, Congressmen, Cuff, I give
> them all the same.[1]

Although the word is used today, where at all, as a sobriquet for a Canadian, its meaning was not always so clear. The *SOED* says *Canuck* is of American origin, but defines it rather ambiguously as "a (French) Canadian." The *DAE*, citing Norton, *Political Americanisms* (1890), calls *Canuck*, also *Canack* and *K'nucks*, "in Canada the nickname for all Canadians." Clapin, a somewhat less reliable witness, defines *Canuck*, also *Canack* and *Cunnuck*, as "familiar and colloquial slang appellations for a native of Canada, although, within the Canadian border, a *Canuck*, is almost solely understood to be a French-Canadian." According to W. D. Lighthall, writing in 1889, French Canadians were called *Johnny Baptiste* in Ontario and *Canuck* in the English-speaking parts of Quebec.

The origin of *Canuck*, as the *DC* notes, is unclear. Clapin reported that it is "said to be derived from Connaught, which was a name given by the French Canadians to the Irish," but he gives no clue as to its subsequent divagations. This theory is repeated in the *Encyclopedia Canadiana*, which adds the suggestion that the word may be derived from the first syllable of *Canada* joined to the Algonquin noun ending -*uc*. *Canuck* in the sense of a Canadian horse is traced by the *DAE* to 1888 and in attributive use to 1862. In the sense of "the language of the Canucks," the *DA* traces it to 1904, and also turns up *Canuckia* (1889) as a jocular term for Canada, marked "rare."

Mencken divided American place names into eight general classes: "(a) those embodying personal names, chiefly the surnames of pioneers or of national heroes; (b) those transferred from other and older places, either in the Eastern States or in Europe; (c) Indian names; (d) Dutch, Spanish, French, German and

---

[1] Whitman's orthography is as usual idiosyncratic. In "Song of Myself," 16, he claims to be "At Home on Kanadian Snowshoes." In the lines quoted, a *Tuckahoe* is a Virginian and a *Cuff* (from the Gold Coast term *kofi*, a boy's name) is a Negro.

Scandinavian names; (e) Biblical and mythological names; (f) names descriptive of localities; (g) names suggested by local flora, fauna or geology; (h) purely fanciful names." [1] A similar division is applicable to Canada, although our somewhat different ethnic composition would require the substitution of Slavic for Dutch.

In the first class, our national onomastic hero is unquestionably Guy Carleton, Baron Dorchester, whose career as soldier and administrator in Canada extended from 1759 to 1796. [2] Every possible aspect of Carleton has been memorialized: his Christian name in Montreal's *Guy Street*, and *Guy Ward* in Saint John, New Brunswick; his family name in *Carleton Street* or *Carleton Avenue*, sometimes spelled *Carlton*, in Fredericton, Halifax, Quebec City, Montreal, Ottawa, Toronto and London, to name but a few, not to mention *Carleton Cape* in Nova Scotia, *Carleton County*, *Carleton Island* and *Carleton Place* in Ontario, *Carleton Parish* in Quebec, *Carleton Siding* in Prince Edward Island, *Carleton Township* in Manitoba and *Carleton Village* in both Quebec and Nova Scotia.

His title, Lord Dorchester, has conferred a *Dorchester Street* on Charlottetown, Saint John, Quebec, Montreal and London, as well as *Dorchester Port, Town* and *Crossing* in New Brunswick, *Dorchester County* in Quebec, and *Dorchester Township* and *Station* in Ontario. His wife's Christian name was Maria, perpetuated in *Maria Parish* and *Village* and *Maria Cape* in the Province of Quebec. Carleton's father-in-law was the Earl of Effingham, whence the village of *Effingham* in Ontario. His father resided in an Irish village named Newry at the time of his death, thereby giving to Ontario *Newry Station* in Perth County. He himself was born in Strathbane, County Down, and Ontario has a *Strathbane* post office in Wentworth County. Carleton was appointed governor of Claremont in Ireland, a name which has been reproduced in the County of Bothwell. His first military post was with the Earl of Rothes' regiment, and the name duly appeared in *Rothes' Settlement* in Ontario County. At the end of his career, Carleton retired

---

[1] *The American Language*, New York, 1936, p. 529.
[2] George Johnson, "Place Names of Canada: The Carletons," *The Canadian Magazine*, 1898, pp. 287–295.

to Basingstoke, England, and this name was duly used for a post office in Grimsby Township.

Few historical figures can compete with Carleton for sheer variety, although Queen Victoria is a strong contender, having contributed some forty Victorias, alone and in combination, to the roster of Canadian place names. One runner-up might be the Earl of Selkirk, who in 1811 received a grant from the Hudson's Bay Company of some 116,000 square miles in the Red River Valley, which he christened *Ossinaboia*. His activities as immigration agent peopled Canada with Scottish settlers and place names, sprinkling the map with his name from *Port Selkirk* in Prince Edward Island to *Cape Selkirk* overlooking the Arctic Ocean.[1]

The map of Canada provides a catalogue of once-famous men: Frenchmen in *Roberval* (the first Governor of Canada), *Montcalm*, *Vaudreuil*, *Iberville*, *Joliette*, *Charlevoix*, *Frontenac*, *Gatineau*, *Cartier*, *Marquette;* Englishmen and a few Englishwomen, in *Simcoe*, *Wellington*, *Eldon*, *Monck*, *Dufferin*, *Dalhousie*, *Bathurst*, *Cavendish*, *Edith Cavell*, *Haig*, *Keppel*, *Lansdowne*, *Nightingale*. Some place names have more than a touch of caprice about them, as *Belleville*, "named after Bell, the familiar name of Governor Gore's Lady." [2]

The strongly British leanings of Ontario from earliest days appear in its choice of place names. A reading of Herbert F. Gardiner's inquiry of some seventy years ago into the origin of the county and township names of Ontario reveals that 38 of 48 counties and 354 of some 550 townships derive their names from English persons and places.[3] The abundant offspring of George III alone supplied well over a dozen: all six of his daughters found their echo in the names of Ontario townships—*Matilda*, *Augusta*, *Elizabethtown*, *Marysburg*, *Sophiasburg* and *Ameliasburg*—and most of his nine sons both directly and through the names of their dukedoms: *Williamsburg*, *Clarence*, *Edwardsburg*, *Alfred*, *Ernestown*, *Cumberland*, *Fredericksburg*, *Adolphustown*, *Cambridge* and *York*. Some twenty-three Ontario Townships boast royal names, only one,

[1] George Johnson, "Place Names of Canada: Selkirk," *The Canadian Magazine*, 1899, pp. 395–406.
[2] J. G. Bourinot, "Canadian Historic Names," *Canadian Monthly*, 1875, pp. 289–300.
[3] *Nothing But Names*, Toronto, 1899. The lady's given name was Arabella.

Alice (the daughter of Queen Victoria) more recent than William IV.

By contrast, Canadian notables fare less well in Ontario: only three counties and districts and 129 townships bear what might be called Canadian names. Strangely enough, few Ontario county and township names are of Indian origin—only 32 out of some 600 place names of this class. This is not to be explained by any general shortage of native names in Ontario, for according to one estimate there are more than a thousand Indian place names in the province,[1] but rather because the naming of most counties and townships took place at the time of the settlement of Upper Canada by the United Empire Loyalists, who asserted their devotion to England by the generous use of British place and personal names to identify the new political divisions. It may be noted in passing that although the place naming was predominantly British, the township form of government and much of its terminology was borrowed from New England.

The same choice of names had, of course, occurred in the American colonies a hundred and more years earlier when the first settlers in many cases ignored long-established Indian place names in favour of an English nomenclature. Their ambition was not to make themselves over in the image of the Indian but rather to transfer to their new homes something of the feeling and atmosphere of the Old World. In Upper Canada, a comparable ambition was doubtless present, although the choice of English place names had also strong political overtones. It was at the same time a repudiation of the Loyalists' late connection with the rebellious colonies and an assertion of their solidarity with the mother country, an attitude thus described by Dr. William Canniff in *The Settlement of Upper Canada* (1869): "The practice of naming places, rivers, etc. after Royal personages and those occupying prominent places in the public service, naturally arose from the intense loyalty which reigned in the bosoms of all who had forsaken their old homes to settle under the flag in the wilderness."

[1] Louis Blake Duff, *The Romance of Our Place Names*, Fort Erie, N.D. (1934).

In Mencken's second class, borrowings from the place names of Great Britain predominate. The choice of such names was dictated by memories of the old country in the hearts of recent arrivals, or the desire to indicate a fellow-feeling with the motherland, and perhaps even by the ease with which such names fell from the lips, for the place names of old countries such as England have been worn smooth by centuries of friction, with all hard or awkward sounds eliminated. Thus we find in Canada many an English name that has existed almost from time immemorial: *Ashby, Bath, Brighton, Cheltenham, Don, Essex, Flamborough, Grimsby, Guildford, Harwich, Humber, Kent, Lancaster, Newcastle, Norwich, Oxford, Plympton, Ryde, Saltfleet, Stratford, Tottenham, Uxbridge, Warwick, Yarmouth, York.* From Scotland were borrowed *Athol, Ayr, Banff, Dumfries, Glamorgan, Glengarry, Greenock, Iona, Kincardine, Lanark, Paisley, Perth, Renfrew, Seaforth, Tavistock;* and from Ireland *Belfast, Cavan, Coleraine, Enniskillen, Erin, Galway, Innisfil, Killarney, Limerick, Malahide, Mayo.*

There are far fewer borrowings from other countries. From France, we have taken *Arras, Beauce, Cambrai, Chateauguay, Douai, Paris, Seine, Soulanges;* from the United States, *Alton, Delaware, Elmira, Orono;* and from the continent of Europe, a small but mixed bag: *Athens, Bergen, Copenhagen, Dresden, Espanola* (= *Hispaniola*), *Hooge, Lunenburg* (= *Lüneberg*), *Minden, Osnabruck, Palermo, Stockholm, Toledo.* This comparative lack of non-British place names stands in marked contrast to the American penchant for such classical borrowings as *Utica, Rome, Syracuse, Troy, Memphis* and the like. Those foreign place names which do occur in Canada have usually been chosen because of their intimate association with famous English personages or events. Thus Continental European wars of the nineteenth century in which Englishmen took part are well-represented in Ontario: the Peninsular Wars by *Moore, Corunna, Douro, Vittoria, Sorauren, Roncesvalles;* and so with their protagonists, Nelson by *Trafalgar, Nelson, Palermo, Bronte, Burnhamthorpe,* and the Duke of Wellington by *Arthur, Wellesley, Wellington, Mornington, Apsley, Walmer.*[1]

[1] See William Alexander McFall, M.D., *Relation of Wars of Europe to the Place Names of Ontario*, Toronto, N.D. (1945?), from which these names are culled.

The Crimean War was a prolific source of Canadian place names, being commemorated in *Sebastopol, Raglan, Caradoc, Alma, Inkerman, Balaclava* and *Odessa*, not to mention *Bruat, Brudenell, Cathcart, Griffith, Kars, Kertch, Lucan, Malakoff, Nolan, Redan, Sviaborg* (a port on the Gulf of Finland, Canadianized as *Sweaburg* in Oxford County) *Varna* and *Welsford*.[1] By way of anticlimax, the most noteworthy linguistic achievement of the first world war was to change the name of *Berlin*, Ontario, to *Kitchener*, a metamorphosis which corresponded with the change of *Berlin* in Michigan to *Marne*.

In the third class, one of the most fertile sources of our place names has been the languages of the Indian nations, to which we probably owe the name *Canada* itself, the names of four of the ten provinces, four of the five Great Lakes, four capital cities including the national capital, many lakes and rivers and thousands of city, town and local names. Some of our most melodious names are of Indian origin, describing a geographical feature or commemorating a notable event.[2] To this class belong *Abitibi* (halfway water); *Bobcaygeon* (rocky portal); *Chinguacousy* (where young pines grow); *Esquimalt* (a place gradually shoaling); *Gananoque* (rocks rising out of the water); *Illecillewaet* (swift water); *Kakabeka* (high fall);[3] *Lillooet* (wild onion); *Manitoba* (the strait of the manito or spirit, or perhaps, more prosaically, the water or lake of the prairie); *Niagara* (thunderer of waters, resounding with a great noise); *Ontario* (sparkling water); *Passamaquoddy* (a great water for pollock); *Quebec* (where the river narrows); *Rimouski* (the home or retreat of dogs); *Shubenacadie* (where nuts grow in abundance); *Wetaskiwin* (hills of peace); and *Yukon* (the river). The majority of these names furnish a convincing refutation of the view reported by G. P. Krapp that Indian place names are rarely poetic when one discovers their true etymology.

There is a close connection between the good relations of

---

[1] W. J. Wintemberg, "The Crimean War and Some Place Names of Canada," *Royal Society of Canada, Proceedings and Transactions*, 3rd ser. XXI, 1927, pp. 71–79.

[2] G. H. Armstrong, *The Origin and Meaning of Place Names in Canada*, Toronto, 1930, with a short bibliography down to 1928.

[3] The "high fall" may appropriately be found on the *Kaministikwia* (river with short bends and many islands).

Indians and white men and the survival of Indian place names. As W. F. Ganong pointed out many years ago: "If there is friendly intercourse with the natives many of the names are adopted, but if there is enmity from the start, few of these can be learned. New Brunswick and Nova Scotia where French and Indians long were friends are rich in native names, while New-foundland has hardly one." [1] In Newfoundland, "the brutal efficiency of the early settlers erased the persons of the original Beothic population, and with them disappeared the native place names;" as a result the only surviving native place name is apparently the *Shannoc River*.[2]

Indian place names afford some of the shortest examples of Canadian toponymy—*Oka* (the doré, a fish commonly called *John Dory*, from the French *jaune dorée* meaning "yellow gill"), *Erie* (cat), *Gaspé* (the end or extremity), *Naas* (satisfier of the stomach) —and also some of the longest, such as *Kennebecasis* (pronounced Ken-ne-bec-ay-shus and of uncertain meaning), *Memphremagog* (great extent of water), *Ashuapinuchuan* (where we watch for the deer), *Penetanguishene* (place of white falling sands),[3] and two names that bid fair to rival the famous Welsh railway station: *Kakekekwabi* and *Kapikikikakik*.[4]

The sounds of Indian names are always intriguing and often possessed of much beauty, as *Pugwash* (a bank of sand), *Shickshock* (rocky mountain), *Coboconk* (high fall), *Temiskaming* (from *timi*, "deep," and *skami*, "a great extension of water where the current in the river is slow"); *Athabaska* (where there are reeds), *Kapus-kasing* (branch river), and *Nipigon* (lake that you cannot see the end of). W. F. Ganong remarked that the Indian place names of New Brunswick were "melodious, dignified and unique;" [5] they

[1] "A Monograph of the Place Nomenclature of the Province of New Brunswick," *Royal Society of Canada, Proceedings and Transactions*, 1896, 2nd Ser. Vol. II, pp. 125–289 at p. 183.

[2] G. M. Story, "Research in the Language and Place Names of Newfoundland," *J.C.L.A.*, 1957, pp. 47–55.

[3] These names and their meanings are found in G. H. Armstrong, *The Origin and Meaning of Place Names in Canada*, 1930.

[4] H. L. Mencken, *The American Language*, 1936, p. 533n.

[5] "A Monograph of the Place Nomenclature of the Province of New Brunswick," *Royal Society of Canada, Proceedings and Transactions*, 1896, 2nd Ser. Vol. II, pp. 125–289.

include *Restigouche, Aroostook, Oromocto, Matapedia, Cleuristic*. Long ago, the rhythms of these Indian river names were hymned by James De Mille:

> Sweet maiden of Passamaquoddy,
> Shall we seek for communion of souls
> Where the deep Mississippi meanders,
> Or the distant Saskatchewan rolls?
> Ah, no! In New Brunswick we'll find it,
> A sweetly sequestered nook,
> Where the smooth gliding Skoo-da-wab-skook-sis
> Unites with the Skoo-da-wab-skook.[1]

Some Canadian place names have gone through a confusing series of changes under the impact of successive and at times coeval cultures. Thus *Lake Simcoe* in Central Ontario was so named by Lieutenant-Governor Simcoe in memory of his father Captain John Simcoe, R.N., who died in the expedition of 1759 against Quebec. Formerly, however, the lake had been known at various times as *Sheniong, Ouentironk, Toronto* and *Lac aux Claies* (Hurdle Lake).[2] Creuxius calls Lake Simcoe *Lacus Ouentaronius* or *Ouentarontus*.[3] Toronto was, of course, formerly called *York*, a name which still attaches to its home county. The word *Toronto*, originally, it is said, *Deondo*,[4] "is an Indian term referring to a place of meeting, and was originally applied to the peninsula between Nottawasaga Bay, Sturgeon Bay, the River Severn, Lake Couchiching and Lake Simcoe—a locality much frequented by the native tribes, especially by the Wyandots or Hurons."[5]

The island of *Anticosti*, about which little seems known to the world, was first discovered by Jacques Cartier on Ascension Day

---

[1] Quoted in Bruce Hutchinson, *The Unknown Country*, New York, 1942, who added a few more New Brunswick river names for good measure: *Miramichi, Tobique, Upsalquitch* and *Nipisigint*. The original poem appeared in *New Dominion and True Humorist*, Saint John, April 16, 1870, p. 171.

[2] J. G. Bourinot, "Canadian Historic Names," *Canadian Monthly*, 1875, pp. 289–300.

[3] John Langton, "On the Early Discoveries of the French in North America," *Canadian Journal* (N.S.), 1857, pp. 393–406. Langton was a Vice-Chancellor of the University of Toronto.

[4] W. F. Moore, *Indian Place Names in the Province of Ontario*, Toronto, 1930, p. 45. He favours the meaning "trees growing out of the water."

[5] J. G. Bourinot, "Canadian Historic Names," quoting Dr. Scadding, "that indefatigable local historian."

in 1534 and accordingly called by him *L'Ile de l'Ascension*, later
named by Thevet *L'Ile de l'Assomption*. The Indian name, according
to the latter, was *Naticousti*, which the French changed to *Anticosti*.
It may be derived from *Natiscotec*, meaning "where bears are
hunted." [1] *Annapolis* was formerly *Port Royal*, and the *Bay of Fundy*
was originally *La Baie Française*, the lower part according to one
theory having been called *Fond de la baie*, which eventually became
corrupted into *Fundy*.[2] An equally persuasive theory, however, relates the name to *Rio Fondo* = deep river, that is, extending far
into the land, a term which is said to appear on Portuguese maps
of the sixteenth century. *Prince Edward Island* was called by
Champlain *L'Ile de Saint Jean*, and the Anglicized form *St. John*
was retained after possession passed to the British. In 1798 by an
Act of the provincial legislature, this was changed to the present
name of the province, honouring the future father of Queen
Victoria. The Micmac name of the Island is *Epagwit* or *Abegweit*
(at rest on the water).[3]

The names by which the Ottawa River has been known over
more than three hundred years are many, among them the
earliest, *Algomequi*, mentioned in the Jesuit *Rélations* of 1612–1614,
La Rivière des Algommequins, *La Rivière des Algonquins*, *La Rivière des
Prairies*, *La Rivière du Tessouac* or *Tessouat* after an Algonquin chief,
La Grande Rivière or *Great River*, *La Rivière Creuse* or *Deep River*, and
Ottawa, or *La Rivière des Ouatouais*, the last from the Indian tribe
dwelling along its banks, whose name probably came from *adawe*,
"to buy and sell," its men being noted as intertribal traders and
barterers.[4] "The ghosts of the old chiefs must surely chuckle,"
wrote Rupert Brooke, "when they note that the name by which
Canada has called her capital and the centre of her political life,
Ottawa, is an Indian name which signifies 'buying and selling.'

---

[1] G. H. Armstrong, *The Origin and Meaning of Place Names in Canada*, Toronto, 1930.

[2] W. F. Ganong, "A Monograph of the Place Nomenclature of the Province of
New Brunswick," cited above.

[3] Benjamin Bremner, *Tales of Abegweit*, Charlottetown, 1936. This work contains
an appendix of Island place names with their origins and meanings.

[4] W. J. Wintemberg, "Early Names of the Ottawa River," *Transactions of the Royal
Society of Canada*, 1938, Vol. 32, Ser. 3, Sect. 2, pp. 97–105. This includes a bibliography.
For an earlier account, see J. G. Bourinot, "The Ottawa Valley: Its History and
Resources," *The Canadian Monthly*, 1875, pp. 41–55.

And the wanderer in this land will always be remarking an un-
explained fragrance about the place names, as from some flower
which has withered, and which he does not know." [1]

The spellings of *Algonquin* are many and varied. Samuel de
Champlain called the natives *les Algoumequins* (1603), a form which
successive generations rendered *Algonquins* (1667), *Algonkins* (1770),
and *Algonquians* (1907). [2] The commonest usages today appear to
be *Algonquin* and *Algonkin*, with some effort to fasten on *Algonkin*
as the official term, the spelling preferred by the *Encyclopedia
Canadiana* (1957). The language of these tribes was first called
Algonkine (1705) in Virginia, and later *Algonquin* by Francis
Parkman (1869). Current usage is divided between *Algonquian*
and *Algonkian*, both pronounced "-kian," the last mentioned being
adopted by the *Encyclopedia Canadiana*. [3] As a geological term for
pre-Cambrian rocks, *Algonkian* has pre-empted the field since 1897.
For the forms *Algonquin* or *Algonkin*, the pronunciation "-kin" is
the only one given by the *DA*, but in Canada "kwin" is used for
the name of the tribes, as well as such place names as *Algonquin
Park* in northern Ontario.

In many places, the white man substituted his own often unimaginative place names for the older Indian names which were
soon forgotten. Sometimes the new name was simply a translation
of the old, as in the case of the *Oldman River* in British Columbia,
named by the Indians "Old Man's Playing Ground." Another
example from Alberta is the *Pipestone River*, the original Cree name
signifying "blue pipe-stone river," from the presence of a blue
clay used by the Indian tribes for the manufacture of pipes. [4]
Another translation is *Chaudière* from *Asticon*, a cauldron.

Many Indian place names have come down to us unchanged
except for their spelling, as *Winnipeg, Manitoba, Saskatchewan;*
others have been perpetuated in English translations, as *Medicine
Hat* (from the Blackfoot *saamis*, "hat of the medicine man"), or

[1] *The Prose of Rupert Brooke*, ed. Christopher Hassall, London, 1956, p. 53.

[2] These and subsequent citations are taken from the *DA*.

[3] Both are given, without indication of preference, in Margaret Nicholson, *A
Dictionary of American-English Usage*, Oxford, 1957.

[4] James White, "Place Names in the Rocky Mountains Between the 49th Parallel
and the Athabaska River," *Proceedings and Transactions of the Royal Society of Canada*,
1916, Ser. III, Vol. 10, pp. 501–535.

Swift Current (a literal translation of the Cree *kisiskatchewan*, whence
also the name of the province); a few are French translations of
Indian originals, as the *Qu'Appelle River* (from *katepwe*, "who calls").
Some names which have an authentic Indian ring turn out to be
purely synthetic, as *Usona*, a single acrostic of "United States of
North America," *Irricana*, a contraction of "irrigation canal," and
one of the most euphonious of all Canadian place names, *Kenora*,
fashioned unromantically enough from the first two letters of three
adjoining communities, *Keewatin*, *Norman* and *Rat Portage*, whose
amalgamation formed the town.[1] The difficulties of transliteration from Indian to English and the faulty ear of some observers
have conspired to produce many variants. Thus the name *Ottawa*
is said to have thirty-two different spellings,[2] the poet Thomas
Moore favouring *Utawa* with the accent on the second syllable:

> Utawa's tide! this trembling moon
> Shall see us float o'er thy surges soon.[3]

The Canadian record was claimed for *Niagara*, which may be
spelled in forty different ways including *Onguiaatira* and its contraction *Ongiara*, *Nicariagas*, *Niagari* and *Ohnyakara*, not to mention
Oneangarall. More recently, however, this has been bettered by
Gananoque, which lays claim to no fewer than fifty-seven varieties,
among them such tongue-twisters as *Gaunuhnauqueeng* and *Guan-
isgnouga*.[4] Still other Indian place names have been shortened out
of all recognition to their present forms: thus *Kashe Lake* in
Ontario was formerly *Kosheshebogamog* (lake of many channels)

[1] C. Meredith Jones, "Indian and Pseudo-Indian Place Names in the Canadian
West," Winnipeg, 1955 (*Onomastica*, No. 12). Another such name is *Flin Flon*, Manitoba,
which is said to have been called after Professor Josiah Flintabbatey Flonatin, the
hero of a novel, *The Sunless City*, by J. E. Preston-Muddock which was alleged to have
been found on a portage near the present town in 1915. The story is considered to be
of doubtful authenticity.

[2] Capt. W. F. Moore, *Indian Place Names in Ontario*, Toronto, 1930, p. 13. James
White in a monograph *Place Names in Quebec* published in the Ninth Report of the
Geographical Board of Canada, 1910, Pt. 11, cites no less than thirty different
spellings for the name *Ottawa*, including the Canadian French *Ouatouais*, and then
suspends his enumeration and our credulity by adding "and some hundred and
fifty others."

[3] Thomas Moore visited Canada in 1804, his *Epistles, Odes and Other Poems* containing
the "Canadian Boat Song" appearing in 1806.

[4] Frank Eames, *Gananoque: The Name and Its Origin*, Aouan Island, 1942.

and *Mackinac*, pronounced "mackinaw," is the abbreviated form of *Michilimackinac*. Sometimes the original name and the shortened form are both in current use, as *Penetanguishene* and *Penetang*.

In the fourth class, no province is richer in foreign place names than British Columbia, where at least six languages colour the pages of the official Gazetteer—Mongolian, Russian, Indian, Spanish, French and English.[1] Some Mongolian names survive unchanged, as *Tsacha*, *Tchai-kazan*, *Uhal-gak*, while the Oriental derivation of others gives evidence of early Mongol settlement. Russian names are few, in testimony of the short-lived Russian occupation, but the many Spanish place names recall the discovery of the coast by Perez in 1774, although most of them proved too unwieldy to survive in a terse age. Thus *El Gran Canal de Nuestra Senora del Rosario la Marinera* became the *Strait of Georgia;* but other names still survive to lend an exotic flavour to the coastal areas, among them *Alberni*, *Port Angeles*, *Bonilla*, *Camanoa*, *Espinosa*, *Galiano*, *Hernando*, *Juan de Fuca*, *Lopez*, *Rada de Solano*, *San Jacinto*, *Sonora*.

British Columbia also has a fine taste for unusual names: thus *Kicking Horse Pass*, celebrating the spot where an early traveller and his steed had a difference of opinion; *Katz*, "where a cat on one of the early steamboats stopped to give birth to kittens;" and *Piebiter Creek* near Lillooet, named after a famous pie-eating miner. The Gold Rush days left a pungent heritage along the Fraser River whence F. H. Goodchild has collected such names of creeks as *Crazy*, *Damfino*, *Deadeye*, *Hoodoo*, *Hunger*, *Hell*, *Jack of Clubs*, *Joker*, *Lockup*, *Misery*, *Poison*, *Suicide* and *Whisky*. Old days in the Canadian North-West provided an impressive roster of trading posts, among them *Whoop-Up*, *Stand-Off*, *Slide-Out* and *Robbers' Roost*.[2]

French place names have contributed generously to the map of North America, mostly in the Province of Quebec, although a goodly number exist elsewhere, often Anglicized beyond recognition. At its height in the seventeenth and eighteenth centuries, the

[1] Fred H. Goodchild, *British Columbia, Its History, People and Industry*, London, 1951. For a lighter introduction to British Columbian place names, see Harrison Brown, *Admirals, Adventurers and Able Seamen*, Vancouver, 1956.

[2] John McLean, *The Indians, Their Manners and Customs*, Toronto, 1889, pp. 197–201.

influence of France stretched from Cape Breton to Louisiana, and to this day one can follow the route of the French missionaries and voyageurs by the names they left behind them, as witness *Detroit, Coeur d'Alene, Des Moines, Dubuque*. Often the only clue may be found in the American pronunciation of Indian names, many of which first entered English through French: such pronunciations as *Iroquois, Illinois, Arkansas* and *Sioux* could only have established themselves on the basis of French pronunciation.

The manhandling of French names occurred in many unlikely places and at a very early date. Thus the British member of a Boundary Commission in 1839 remarked that the name of an island in Lake Michigan had been corrupted from *Bois Brulé* to *Bob Ruly's Woods*.[1] A similar conversion is *Bob-lo Park* on an island in the Detroit River, derived from *Bois Blanc*. Other changes were *Tarblue*, a stream in Missouri, from *Terrebleu*, and *Swashing Creek* from *St. Joachim;* while the *Embarras*, a stream in Indiana, so called because of an obstruction in its bed, became the more poetic *Ambrosia*. In similar vein, the *Rio Purgatoire* along the Santa Fe trail became transmogrified into *Picket-wire River*, the French pronunciation of *-oire* clearly showing through, and *Chemin Couvert* became first *Smack Cover* and finally *Smackover*.[2]

Canadian place nomenclature has tended to be pedestrian, with infrequent excursions into the rare and remote. One small but permanently exotic note was struck by Sir Peregrine Maitland, an early Governor of Upper Canada, who, fresh from Waterloo and Wellington's Peninsular campaigns, scattered Spanish names like foreign coins across the young province: *Orillia, Rama, Oro, Mono, Zorro, Lobo, Oso* and *Sombra*. Lady Maitland, not to be outdone by her husband's fantasy, conferred upon three Ontario townships the names of her poodle dogs: *Tiny, Floss* and *Tay*. We can also boast of a few Latin names, *Marmora, Ops* and *Vespra*, a few Greek ones, *Alpha, Delta, Proton*, and at least one Hebrew, *Thorah*.

[1] *Excursion Through the Slave States, 1844*, reported in Mamie Meredith, "Language Mixture in American Place-Names," *American Speech*, 1930, pp. 224–227.
[2] Helen Blish in *American Speech*, 1930, p. 78.

Unlike the United States, Canada has drawn few place names from her Dutch or Scandinavian settlers, their place being taken by names from middle and eastern Europe. The "block settlement" of immigrants from central and eastern Europe in the Prairie Provinces resulted, according to Watson Kirkconnell, in the creation of "facsimiles of the European communities that they left behind," many of which still bear decidedly Slavic names.[1] Thus there are scores of communities throughout the West such as *Antonivka, Babyna, Chortitz, Dobrovodu, Franko, Gorlitz, Hryhoriv, Ivasyuky, Khutir, Lanivci, Makovsk, Novyj, Oleskiw, Peshkiv, Rak, Slawa, Tere-bovla, Ukraina, Vostok, Yarmolynci* and *Zbaraz.*

These block settlements—which embrace not only the Ukrainian communities in Manitoba and Alberta, but also Mennonites and Hutterites in the same provinces, and Doukhobors in Saskatchewan and British Columbia—have stubbornly resisted assimilation although, with the spread of education and the impact of the second world war, young people have begun to drift away from the attitudes of their parents. Kirkconnell feels that "the European-Canadian culture groups as such will probably have been completely digested in another century."[2] But the Ukrainian place names persist. According to J. B. Rudnyckyj, there is one such name in British Columbia (*Poletica*), two in Quebec (*Sheptetski* and *Ukraina Camp*), three in Ontario (*Busko's Corner, Odessa* and *Poltava*), sixty-two in Saskatchewan, sixty-four in Alberta and sixty-five in Manitoba.[3]

In Mencken's seventh class of names, the flora and fauna of Canada, both real and imaginary, are well-represented: *Amaranth, Asphodel, Euphrasia, Oaklands, Rice Lake, Porcupine, Birtle* (formerly *Bird Tail*) and *Osprey.* The mineral wealth of the land is suggested by *Cobalt, Copper Cliff, Coppermine, Diamond* and *Petrolia.*

Some of the most fanciful and striking place names are to be found in the Maritime Provinces. Surely nowhere else in Canada

[1] *Canadian Toponymy and the Cultural Stratification of Canada*, Winnipeg, 1954.
[2] The same, p. 12.
[3] *Canadian Place Names of Ukrainian Origin*, Winnipeg, 1957. Dr. Rudnyckyj has investigated Canadian onomastics generally in *Classification of Canadian Place Names*, Winnipeg, 1958, pp. 7–11.

and perhaps in the world are names to equal those of New Brunswick: *Bumfrau* (said to be a corruption of the Acadian *bois franc*, hardwood), *Chockpish* (now called *Ste. Anne*), *Cocagne*, *Manawaganish* (contracted by folk etymology to *Mahogany*), *Paticake Brook* and *Yoho*.[1] Even these, however, pale beside the luxuriant growth to be found in Newfoundland, whose long history as a fishing station has attracted names from half the maritime nations of Europe. As G. M. Story remarks, "French and English predominate; but mixed with them are Gaelic, Scandinavian, Spanish, Portuguese, Basque and Channel Islands names, ample evidence of the varied sea-faring peoples who have frequented our shores."[2] Certainly many of them supply a freshness and humour sadly lacking in more recently settled regions.

To one observer, Newfoundland place names were full of surprise and enjoyment, with none of the slavish repetition of British or French names found elsewhere, and a refreshing absence of such cliché communities as Centerville, Smithtown or Fairview.[3] The hard, dangerous life of the island was reflected in such names as *Bad Bay*, *Gripe Point*, *Famish Cove* and *Empty Basket*, not to mention *Bleak Island*, *Misery Point*, *Wild Bight*, *Slave Harbour* and *Breakheart Point*. Yet other names are not without charm: *Winterland*, *Blue Pinion*, *Maiden Arm*, *Little Heartease* and *Honey Pot Harbour*. Pungent place names abound on this rugged island: *Damnable Bay*, changed through clerical intervention to *St. Chad's; God Almighty Cove; Hell's Mouth; Cuckold Cove;* two islets in the Strait of Belle Isle (locally called *The Straits*) known as *Our Lady's Bubbies;* names like *Ha Ha*, *Blow-me-Down* and *Stepaside;* and such determined puns as *Snake's Bight*, *Scilly Cove*, *Bumble Bee Bight*, *Lushes Bight* and the *Annieopsquotch Mountains*.[4] Alas, here too the

---

[1] W. F. Ganong, "A Monograph of the Place Nomenclature of the Province of New Brunswick," *Royal Society of Canada, Proceedings and Transactions*, 1896, 2nd Ser. Vol. II, pp. 125–289.

[2] "Research in the Language and Place Names of Newfoundland," *J.C.L.A.*, 1957, pp. 47–55.

[3] H. L. Keenleyside, "Place Names of Newfoundland," *Canadian Geographical Journal*, 1944, pp. 255–263.

[4] Pronounced "an-ni-op-skwotch," according to "A Guide to the Pronunciation of Canadian Place Names," *C.B.C.*, Toronto, 1959.

strong arm of convention wielded by the Nomenclature Board has changed *Broom's Bottom* to *York Harbour*, *Mother Hicks* to *Regina* and *Maggoty Cove* to *Hoylestown*. No locality in Newfoundland is too small to merit a name; even fishing berths are commemorated by some signal happening. In this vein, G. M. Story records *The Gulch Where the Vessel Was Lost*, *Stem and Stern*, *No Man's Land*, *Roof of the House*, *Hanging Cliff* and *Where the Man Fell Over*.

The continual mispronunciation of French place names in Newfoundland resulting in actual changes in spelling—*Lawn* from *L'Aune*, and *Lords* from *Lourdes*—came, it is said, from the longstanding rivalry and enmity between Frenchmen and Newfoundlanders and the consequent lack of fraternization between them.[1] Following a concerted attempt by France to conquer Newfoundland in the sixteenth and seventeenth centuries, French fishermen were by treaty given the right of seasonal occupation on the Newfoundland coast, which they enjoyed until 1904 when France withdrew completely, leaving behind the name *French Shore* to the west coast of the island.[2] A modest legacy of French place names, often somewhat corrupted, is about all that remains of the *présence française*.

In this connection, it is interesting to observe how geographical names, particularly along the coast, have been affected by successive Spanish, Portuguese, French and English influences. Often the early French names have become all but unrecognizable: thus *Cap de Bonne Viste* and *Saincte Katherine*, two names given by Cartier during his expedition of 1534, have filtered down through Spanish or Portuguese and emerged as *Bonavista* and *Catalina*. Many Breton names have been completely Englished as *Twillingate* (originally *Toulinquet*).[3]

To consider the mutation of French vocables alone would be a lengthy study: thus *Tasse à l'arpent* became *Tostlejohn*; *Beau Bois*

---

[1] R. J. Miffin, "Some French Place Names of Newfoundland," *American Speech*, 1956, pp. 79–80.

[2] Also called *French Coast* and *Treaty Shore*: C. J. Lovell, "A Sampling of Materials for a Dictionary of Canadian English on Historical Principles," *J.C.L.A.*, 1958, p. 22.

[3] For an extended study, see E. R. Seary, "*The French Element in Newfoundland Place Names*," *J.C.L.A.*, 1958, pp. 63-69.

became *Boby; Baie de Vieux* was Anglicized to *Bay-the-View* and
Lance au Diable to *Nancy Jobble; Baie du Diable*, however, became
Jabbouls. Often the metamorphosis produced a place name of quite
different meaning, as when *Baie du Livre* was turned into *Bay
Deliver*, or *Baie des Boules* into *Bay of Bulls*, while sometimes the new
name had exactly the opposite meaning; thus *Baie d'Espoir* became
Bay Despair.[1] This process is not, of course, confined to Newfound-
land. Elsewhere, *Mill Rush* on the St. Lawrence was once *Mille
Roches;* in Cape Breton, *Big Lorran* was *Grande Lorraine* and the
River Margarie was originally the *Marguerite*. In time, *Chateauguay*
became *Shattagee*.[2]

Many Canadian cities have achieved, or had thrust upon them,
what G. P. Krapp once called "poetic and oratorical second
designations." Such appellations are often unflattering, in spite
of which they acquire acceptance and may even be worn with a
certain civic pride. Thus Toronto has for a long time been widely
known by some as *Toronto the Good*, and by others as *Hogtown*, the
latter name indicating not a meat-packing industry—as Cincinnati
was once called *Porkopolis*—but an alleged greed for influence and
material wealth.[3] In the same way, Ottawa is sometimes referred
to as *Bytown* to imply not merely a link with the past, recalling
the original name of that city and its founder, Colonel By, but
also a certain small-town, nay, parochial outlook—qualities by
no means confined to capital cities. Ottawa may be called the
Capital, but not the *Capitol*. On the other hand, *Calgary* is referred
to as *the Oil Capitol* (or *Capital*) *of Canada*. Fact may follow fiction,
as when Orillia is sometimes designated *Mariposa*, the name used
by Stephen Leacock in *Sunshine Sketches of a Little Town*. Other
names seem obscurely pejorative—as when Rudyard Kipling once

---

[1] These are garnered from A. Marshall Elliott, "Origin of the Name 'Canada,' "
Modern Language Notes, 1888, pp. 327–348.

[2] W. D. Lighthall, "Canadian English," *The Week* (Toronto) Aug. 16, 1889, pp.
581–583. For some account of the reverse process, that is, the Gallicization of English
names, see Adjutor Rivard, *Etudes sur les parlers de France au Canada*, Quebec, 1914,
p. 214.

[3] Bruce Hutchinson in *The Unknown Country*, New York, 1942, says that the name
was conferred on Toronto "because it fattened on the rest of the surrounding country
through a protective tariff."

G

referred to Medicine Hat as *the City with all Hell for a Basement*.[1]

The whole field of civic nicknames still awaits exploration, although the major classifications may be described somewhat as as follows:

(1) Names derived from a geographical location, as Yarmouth, called *the Gateway to Nova Scotia;* North Bay, *the Gateway City* or *the Gateway of the North;* Halifax, *the Old Port City;* Portage la Prairie, *the Plains City;* Swift Current, *the Frontier City;* Brockville, *the City of the Thousand Islands;* Calgary, *the Sunshine City of the Foothills*, or sometimes *the Foothills City;* and the many "Hub" cities, including Nanaimo, *the Hub City of Vancouver Island;* Saskatoon, *the Hub City* or *the Hub of the Hard Wheat Belt;* and Moncton, *the Hub of the Maritimes*.

(2) Names indicative or reminiscent of some botanical or horticultural attribute, as when Fredericton is designated *the City of Stately Elms;* Chatham, *the Maple City;* London, *the Forest City;* Victoria, *the Garden City;* Blenheim, Ontario, *the Heart of the Golden Acres*.

(3) Names derived from a mineral or cognate product associated with the city, as Kingston, *the Limestone City;* Sudbury, *the Nickel City;* Trail, *the Silver City;* Medicine Hat, *the Gas City;* Sarnia, *Chemical Valley;*[2] or from an agricultural product as Kelowna, *the Apple Capital of Canada*, or *the Orchard City;* Armstrong, *the Celery City;* Brandon, *the Wheat City of the West*, and Leamington, *the Tomato Capital of Canada*.

(4) Names recalling some man-made object, as Brantford, *the Telephone City;* Peterborough, *the Lift Lock City;* Welland, *Canal*

---

[1] The Canadian record for municipal sobriquets is shared by Vancouver and Toronto. At various stages in her corporate career, Vancouver has been called *Canada's Golden Gate* (1912), *From Stumps to Skyscrapers* (1936), *Gas Town* (after one, John "Gassy Jack" Deighton, builder of a hotel on Burrard Inlet in 1867), *The Gateway to the Orient* (1906), *The Lion-Guarded City* (1925), *Queen of the Coast*, *The Sunset City* and *The Terminal City*. Not to be outdone, Toronto has laid claim to being *The Athens of the Dominion*, *The Belfast of America*, *The Choral Capital of North America*, *The City of Churches* (1890), *Hog Town*, *The Green City*, *Toronto the Good* (1890) and *Tory Toronto*. See Robert M. Hamilton, *Canadian Quotations and Phrases*, Toronto, 1952, p. 37. In the same vein, Galt has been called *The Manchester of Canada;* Hamilton, *The Birmingham of Canada;* Medicine Hat, *The Chicago of Western Canada;* Sydney, *The Pittsburg of Canada;* and Waterloo, *The Hartford of Canada*.

[2] Sarnia was formerly called *The Imperial City* named for the Imperial Oil Company according to B. A. M. Thomas, City Clerk.

Town; Cornwall, *the Seaway City;* Saskatoon, *the City of Bridges;* or a particular industry, as when Moose Jaw is referred to as *the Mill City* because of the presence of a large flour-mill. Peterborough was for many years also known as *the Electric City* because it was the first town in Ontario to have its streets illuminated at night.[1]

(5) Names claiming association with a member of the animal kingdom, sometimes extinct, as in the case of Drumheller, Alberta, *the Home of the Dinosaurs*, or apocryphal, as Kelowna, British Columbia, *the Home of Ogopogo.*

(6) Names formed by abbreviating the formal name of the city or town. When the name consists of two or more words, one word is often used, usually preceded by the definite article. This practice is particularly evident in Ontario where Arnprior is familiarly known as *The Prior*, North Bay as *The Bay*, Port Credit as *The Port* or *The Credit*, and Sault Ste. Marie as *The Soo*. Similarly Portage la Prairie is abbreviated to *Portage* and Medicine Hat to *The Hat*. Prince Albert, Saskatchewan, however, is known as *P.A.* When the city name consists of only one word, the first syllable may be chosen for the colloquial designation; thus Gananoque has become *Gan*, and Kapuskasing is known locally as *Kap.*

(7) Names largely panegyrical, as when Kelowna styles itself *the City of Champions*, Fredericton, *the Celestial City*, and Halifax, *the Warden of the Honour of the North.*[2] In the same self-laudatory vein are Cornwall and Belleville, both claiming to be *the Friendly City;* Lethbridge, *the City of Opportunity;*[3] Woodstock, *the City Beautiful;* Regina, *the Queen of the Plains*, and Weyburn, Saskatchewan, which holds itself out as *the City with a Future.*

(8) Names descriptive of the history or founding of the city. Thus Saint John styles itself *the Loyalist City* and Galt, *the Scotch Town*, recalling that the former was first settled by United Empire Loyalists and the latter by Scotsmen, while Charlottetown likes to be remembered as *the Cradle of Confederation* because the conference of Maritime delegates held there in 1864 led eventually

---

[1] I am indebted for the last reference to E. A. Outram, City Clerk.

[2] Kipling so styled it in "The Song of the Cities—Halifax" (1896).

[3] T. L. Ferguson, the City Clerk, informs me that the Chamber of Commerce refers to Lethbridge more prosaically as *the Irrigation Capital of Canada.*

to the union of 1867. In the same vein, Quebec city is known as *the Ancient Capital*, a mistranslation of *L'ancienne capitale*.

Many Canadian cities and towns have never achieved familiar designations, sometimes for good and apparent reason. Thus the City Clerk of Antigonish, Nova Scotia, in response to an inquiry wrote: "The place has no nickname, perhaps the real name is sufficient." The same view was taken by the Town Clerk of Chilliwack, British Columbia, who advised that "there doesn't seem to be a nickname for either the municipality or its residents. Our official name seems to be distinctive enough in itself."

The designations which are applied to residents of various cities and towns have also been little studied. Although there seem to be few hard-and-fast rules governing the formation of such words, they fall generally into the following categories:

(1) If the name ends in *-a*, the name of an inhabitant is formed by adding *-n;* thus, *Ottawan.*

(2) If the name ends in *-ia*, add *-n;* thus, *Orillian, Sarnian, Victorian.*

(3) If the name ends in *-y*, change the *y* to *i*, add *-an* and shift the stress; thus, *Sudburian, Calgarian.*

(4) If the name ends in *-on*, usually add *-ian;* thus, *Edmontonian, Saskatoonian, Hamiltonian, Kingstonian, Frederictonian, Monctonian.*

(5) If the name ends in *-outh*, add *-ian;* thus, *Yarmouthian, Dartmouthian.*

(6) If the name ends with a vowel other than *-a*, add *-ite*, sometimes with a hyphen and sometimes without: thus, *Barrie-ite, Fernie-ite, Nanaimoite*, and *Sooite* for a resident of Sault Ste. Marie.

(7) If the name ends with a consonant, in some cases add *-er;* thus, *Antigonisher, Medicine Hatter*, or just plain *Hatter, Montrealer, Saint Johner, Wellander, Winnipeger;*[1] in other cases add *-ite*, sometimes with but more often without a hyphen; thus, *Arnpriorite, Atikokanite, Banffite, Bayite* for a resident of North Bay, *Chathamite, Cornwallite, Drumhellerite, Guelphite, Kapuskasingite, Moosominite, Port Coquitlam-ite, Renfrewite, Trailite, Weyburnite, Windsorite.*

These rules are no sooner suggested, however, than exceptions

[1] I owe this spelling to the courtesy of G. W. Gardner, City Clerk. Mencken, *The American Language*, New York, 1936, p. 549, gives *Winnipegger.*

clamour for recognition. A resident of Kenora is not, as one would expect, a *Kenoran* but a *Kenoraite*. Although a burgess of *Moncton* is called a *Monctonian*, if he moves to Brandon he becomes in due course a *Brandonite*, while in Flin Flon he is a *Flin Floner* and in London a *Londoner*. A resident of Portage la Prairie is a *Portager*, but one from Lethbridge is a *Lethbridgeite*. A man from Brockville is a *Brockvillian*, but one from nearby Belleville is a *Bellevonian*. Again, while an inhabitant of Saint John, New Brunswick, calls himself a *Saint Johner*, one from Saint John's, Newfoundland, is known as a *Saint John's man*.

There is also a group of designations which bend to no apparent rule, having in common only the suffix -*onian*. Thus a resident of Charlottetown is a *Charlottetonian*, of Galt a *Galtonian*, of Halifax a *Haligonian*, of Woodstock a *Woodstonian*, and of Pictou a *Pictonian*. To add to the confusion, an inhabitant of Picton, Ontario, is also a *Pictonian*.[1] In the case of some cities, there are conflicting names for residents. Thus Major J. S. Matthews, the City Archivist of Vancouver, writes out of the experience of more than sixty years' residence there: "Sometimes we are called 'Vancouverians,' and sometimes 'Vancouverites;' my preference is for 'ians,' a name applied to the people of Vancouver Island a hundred years ago, forty or fifty years before the City of Vancouver existed; that is, they were 'Vancouverians,' the people of Vancouver's Island." C. J. Lovell confirms that *Vancouverian* was an early designation for an inhabitant of Vancouver Island, but adds that "modern usage for a citizen of the British Columbia city is *Vancouverite*." [2]

The names of many provinces have been manhandled in popular speech. Thus Newfoundland is often called *Newfie*, as is a Newfoundlander, although upon that island's becoming the tenth province the rest of the country was solemnly requested to shun the name as being calculated to offend. At the same time, we were told that the pronunciation accented on the penultimate syllable which had been taught in Canadian schools a generation

---

[1] I am indebted for this and most of the foregoing city and town names to the clerks of the respective municipalities.

[2] "Whys and Hows of Collecting for the Dictionary of Canadian English," *J.C.L.A.,* October, 1955, p. 7.

earlier was now incorrect, the island province being called by its inhabitants "New-fn-land," the stress falling on the final syllable.[1]

Other provinces have also their second names. Thus Nova Scotia is *The Mayflower Province*,[2] and New Brunswick *The Loyalist Province*. Together with Prince Edward Island, they are collectively known as the *Maritime Provinces* or, more familiarly, the *Maritimes* or the *East Coast*. When Newfoundland is included, the designation becomes the *Atlantic Provinces*. Prince Edward Island is affectionately referred to by natives as *Spud Island*, also *The Garden of the Gulf* and *The Million Acre Farm*. Manitoba, Saskatchewan and Alberta are usually designated as the *Prairie Provinces*[3] or, colloquially, *The West*, while British Columbia is called, without much originality, the *West Coast*. Ontario, called *The Banner Province*, and Quebec are still occasionally referred to by their pre-Confederation names of *Upper Canada* and *Lower Canada*, but the terms have had no real currency for many years, and are chiefly resorted to by journalists in search of variety.

Those provinces with double or triple names find them commonly reduced to initial letters for postal and similar purposes: *B.C.*, *N.B.*, *N.S.* and *P.E.I.* are usually so written when addressing a letter, although infrequently in formal prose. They have, however, some currency in such forms as *B.C. fir* or *P.E.I. potatoes*. New Brunswick and Nova Scotia are never, and Prince Edward Island only rarely, abbreviated to their initial letters in the spoken language, but British Columbia is quite commonly called *B.C.* In the same way, that portion of Canada lying north of the western provinces and known as the *Northwest Territories* is digested to *N.W.T.* as a postal address, but rarely otherwise. The names of the remaining provinces are abbreviated for postal and

[1] Mario Pei, in *The Story of English*, Philadelphia, 1952, p. 130, suggests that *Newland* has some currency, at least in headlines. A popular name is *The Ancient Colony*. Newfoundlanders sometimes refer to the rest of Canada as *Up Along*. The matter is dealt with in some detail in William Kirwin, "Labrador, St. John's and Newfoundland: Some Pronunciations," *J.C.L.A.*, 1960, pp. 115–116.

[2] The reference is to the provincial floral emblem. The province was called *Nova Scarcity* about 1783 by disgruntled Loyalists.

[3] Manitoba was called *The Postage Stamp Province* after 1870 because of its original shape and size. It was later known as *The Prairie Province* from the title of a book by J. C. Hamilton (1876). After 1905, the term was pluralized to include Saskatchewan and Alberta.

general commercial purposes by chopping off their tails: thus Saskatchewan is trimmed to *Sask.*, Manitoba to *Man.*, Ontario to *Ont.*, Quebec to *Que.* or *P.Q.*, and the Yukon to *Yuk.* or *Y.T.*, although Alberta without any apparent logic is disembowelled to produce *Alta.* None of these abbreviations is commonly used in formal prose or the spoken language.

A good deal of research has been done into the origin of Canadian street names. Those of Saint John[1] have been classified thus according to their sources:

Prominent local citizens	30
Local objects and features	29
Imperial statesmen	19
Royalty	17
Civic officials	8
Governors and administrators	7
Saints	6
Military and naval	6
Old Country names	5
Trees	5
Battles	4
Seasons	4

This classification, although not necessarily in the order given, is probably applicable to many Canadian street names, the better part of which betrays a sad lack of colour and originality. In many instances, earlier essays at a more picturesque nomenclature were ruthlessly stamped out by civic leaders of a later day. Thus Toronto during the 1860's saw the disappearance of such lusty street names as *Grog Lane*, *Whisky Alley*, *Fish Lane*, *Pig Street* and *Deadbeat Lane*, and their replacement by the more pedestrian successors which we know today.[2] In Toronto as elsewhere, a few leading families sprinkled their given names and surnames and the names of their English estates over the young city; in this way, the Denisons spawned *Bellevue*, *Borden*, *Lippincott*, *Denison*, *Dovercourt*, *Ossington*, *Fenning* and *Rolyot*, while the equally prolific

[1] John Willet, "Epitomized History of St. John, N.B." in *New Brunswick Historical Society, Collections*, 1927, Vol. 4, No. 11, pp. 143–205.

[2] T. A. Reed, "The Historic Value of Street Names," in *Ontario Historical Society, Papers and Records*, 1929, Vol. 25, pp. 385–387.

Macaulays produced *James*, *Elizabeth*, *Hayter*, *Alice*, *Edward*, *Louisa*, *Hagerman* and *Buchanan*.

The founding fathers of Barrie, Ontario, on the other hand, showed an unusual affinity for British naval officers who served in Canadian waters during and after the War of 1812, no fewer than 35 of its street names being derived from their surnames.[1] Winnipeg inclines toward historical personages, many of them not intimately connected with Canada, as *Disraeli* and *Gladstone*, while Halifax, in addition to the usual bag of members of the royal family and early British statesmen, has retained a number of street names recalling the early German settlers of the mid-eighteenth century.[2] The newer generation of street names in outer suburbia has been researched barely at all, but these seem to differ from their urban predecessors chiefly in being more pretentious. In place of the older *street* and *avenue*, we find a proliferation of *circle*, *crescent*, *garden*, *drive* and the like, the pomposity of the names increasing with the drabness of the subdivision, and often graced by no more poetic inspiration than the name of the builder who has tried to assert his title to immortality by erecting half a hundred ranch bungalows.

Local usage often permits some leeway in the pronunciation of place names. Thus, *Apohaqui*, New Brunswick, may be said either "ăp-o-hawk′kwi" or "ăp′o-hawk;" *Baleine*, Nova Scotia, is either "bă′lēn" or bă-lăn′," the former being the more common local version. *Capreol* may be "kāp′re-ŏl" or "kăp′re-ŏl" in descending order of popularity; *Craigellachie*, British Columbia, prefers the Scots

[1] Lt. Col. D. H. MacLaren, "British Naval Officers of a Century Ago; Barrie and Its Streets, A History of Their Names," *Ontario Historical Society, Papers and Records*, 1919, Vol. 17, pp. 106–112.

[2] The following are a number of monographs on Canadian street names: Mary J. L. Black, "Fort William Streets," in *Thunder Bay Historical Society, Annual Report*, 1924–1926, pp. 22–25; John N. Mackendrick, "Local History in the Street Names of Galt," in *Waterloo Historical Society, Annual Report*, 1919, pp. 67–72; George H. Smith, "The Street Names of Port Colborne," in *Welland County Historical Society, Papers and Records*, 1938, Vol. 5, pp. 192–198; George Tait, "Street and Place Names and Early Reminiscences of Bridgeburg," in *Welland County Historical Society Publications*, 1927, Vol. 3, pp. 104–113; Mrs. E. J. Canfield, *Street Names of Woodstock*, Woodstock, 1932; Mary Hislop, *The Streets of Winnipeg*, Winnipeg, 1912; George Wm. Hill, "Nomenclature of the Streets of Halifax," *Nova Scotia Historical Society Collections*, 1911, Vol. 15, p. 3.

"ch" as in *loch*, and, according to the speaker's choice, may be "kră-ge-lăk′ï" or "kră-gĕl′a-kï;" similarly one can pronounce *Gaspereau*, Nova Scotia, as "găs′pe-rō" or "gas-pe-rō′," and *Iberville*, Quebec, as either "ï′ber-vïl" or "ē′ber-vïl." [1] French names suffer much at our hands, the first casualty being stress. This results from the action of what H. W. Fowler called a recessive accent, that is, the drift of accent or stress towards the beginning of a word. Thus such French place names as *Beausejour* in Manitoba, New Brunswick and Ontario; *Brosseau*, Alberta; *Caraquet*, New Brunswick; *Chapleau*, *Crapaud*, Prince Edward Island; and *Lardeau*, British Columbia, which should proudly wear their accent on the last syllable are instead reduced to "bō′ze-zhoor," "broo′sō," "kă′ra-kĕt," "shăp′lō," "krăp′ō," and "lar′dō" respectively. French pronunciation suffers a similar affront as *Bienfait*, Saskatchewan, becomes "bēn′fāte;" *Boissevain*, Manitoba, is Englished to "boiz′ e-vāne;" *Desaulniers*, Ontario, is "dĕz-ō′nï-ă;" *Framboise*, Nova Scotia, becomes "frăm′boiz;" *Mainadieu*, Nova Scotia, is pronounced "măn-a-doo′;" *Paincourt*, Ontario, is "păn′kor;" and *Port Mouton* in Nova Scotia becomes "port ma-toon′."

Sometimes the original pronunciation is partly retained in one locality and lost in another: thus *Fauquier*, Ontario, is still "fō′ke-ā," although *Fauquier*, British Columbia, has become "fo-kēr′" to rhyme with "deer." Sometimes the two pronunciations coexist, as when *Chauvin*, Alberta, is not only "shō′vin" but also "shaw′vin," and *Brule* is "broo′lā" in Cape Breton and New Brunswick but "brool" in Nova Scotia and Newfoundland. *Dalhousie* in New Brunswick is called "dăl-how′zi," as is Dalhousie University, although *Port Dalhousie*, Ontario, is "dăl-hoo′zi."

The pronounciation of Indian place names usually follows their spelling, although the stress occasionally falls in unexpected places. To this class belong *Chiputneticook*, New Brunswick, (ship-oot-nĕt′ i-cook); *Illecillewaet*, British Columbia, (ïl-ï-sïl′ï-wït); *Kikkertaksoak*, Quebec, (kïk-er-tăk′sō-ăk); *Malagawatch*, Nova Scotia, (mal′a-gah-wotsh); *Manawagonish*, New Brunswick, (man-a-waw′gon-ish); *Miminigash*, Prince Edward Island, (mïm′ïn-ĕ-gash); and

---

[1] All these are drawn from "Handbook for Announcers," Toronto, 1946, pp. 30–43, and "A Guide to the Pronunciation of Canadian Place Names," Toronto, 1959, both published by The Canadian Broadcasting Corporation.

Opinipiwan, Manitoba, (ō-pin'i-pi-won). Other native names are
less predictable, among them a strange collection beginning with
the letter *k*: *Kawawong*, Ontario, (kăg'a-wong); *Kedjimkujik*, Nova
Scotia, (kēj-e-ma-koo'je); *Kitwanga*, British Columbia, (kit-wun-
gah') and *Kouchibougwack*, New Brunswick, (koosh'i-be-kwăk).

The drastic abridgement of many names recalls not a little the
"Cholmondeley-Chumley" pattern. Thus *Clayoquot* in British
Columbia becomes "klăk'wŭt;" in New Brunswick, *Magaquadavic*
is shortened to "măg-ă-dā'vik," and the final *k* sound is often
omitted locally; while *Pokesudie* and *Youghall* are reduced to
"pŭk'shoo" and "yawl" respectively. The small tribe of place
names with the termination *-ish* usually bears the accent on the
last syllable in Nova Scotia, as *Antigonish'*, *Igonish'*, *Merigomish'*, or
in Prince Edward Island, as *Tignish'*; but *Manawa'gonish* in New
Brunswick carries its stress on the antepenult. Our relatively
small stock of foreign place names provides a few distinctive pronunciations: *Agincourt* in Ontario is "ā'jin-cort;" *Calais*, New
Brunswick, is pronounced "kăl'as;" and Delhi, Ontario, is
"dĕl'hī"—not, like the Indian capital, "delly." [1]

II Personal Names

As in the case of many other branches of Canadian linguistics,
the study of personal names still remains largely unexplored. One
student of birth announcements published in the Toronto *Globe
and Mail* during 1959 attempted certain conclusions which may
well be applicable to other Canadian cities.[2] He discerned a
return to older more traditional names for children, and a corresponding decline in the custom of naming offspring after movie
and television stars. But the effect was one of pallid conformity,
and a far cry from some exotic Newfoundland names collected by
Grace Tomkinson in 1940, which included surnames such as *Cake*,

[1] C.B.C. "Handbook for Announcers," Toronto, 1946.
[2] Eric Dowd, "What's In a Name?" *Globe and Mail*, January 22, 1960.

Courage, Coveyduck, Dearlove, Pretty, Rabbits and *Sweetapple*, and among Christian names *Virtue* and *Pearl Button*.[1] One may also recall that back in the 1880's personal names meant something in the Canadian West and a Methodist missionary of the time reported the following: *Gum-Shoe Jack, Tangle-Foot Ben, Rutabaga Bill* and *Waggon-Box Julia*.[2]

Elsewhere we have considered the mutation of French Canadian surnames under the stress of social and economic circumstances.[3] The same process was reported by M. B. Emeneau from Lunenburg, Nova Scotia, where a small pocket of German soldiers who settled there after the American Revolution maintained their identity for more than 150 years, although little today attests to their memory except a small residue of Germanisms.[4] In time, surnames went the way of the rest of their language; thus *Spannagel* became *Sponagle*, *Schweinheimer* is written *Swinnimer*, *Maurer* is now *Myra*, and *Jung*, *Koch* and *Schmidt* are pronounced and spelled *Young*, *Cook* and *Smith*. Only *Knickle* and *Knock* have retained their original pronunciation with sounded *k*, although once the owners remove themselves from Lunenburg their names quickly become *Nichol(s)* and *Knox*.

Later colonists elsewhere lost their distinctive patronymics even more quickly. Thus Robert Somerville Graham has traced the Anglicization of German family names in Saskatchewan, where over a period of fifty years the German speech of the original settlers has been all but lost, particularly in the case of children born since 1920.[5] It is noteworthy that few families legally changed their names; in the community of 350 under examination there were only two: *Volk* and *Butwilofsky*, which became *Follick* and *Budd*. For the rest, the German spelling was retained in all cases although the pronunciation had become completely Anglicized by way of concession to the rest of the community. As a result, English speakers often wrote the names according to the spoken

---

[1] "Shakespeare in Newfoundland," *Dalhousie Review*, 1940, pp. 58–70.
[2] John McLean, *The Indians: Their Manners and Customs*, Toronto, 1889, pp. 197–201.
[3] See *Speaking Canadian French*, Toronto, 1967, pp. 87–90.
[4] "The Dialect of Lunenburg, Nova Scotia," *Language*, 1935, pp. 140–147.
[5] "The Anglicization of German Family Names in Western Canada," *American Speech*, 1955, pp. 260–264.

version. Thus *Euric* became *Yurick*, *Gruen* became *Green*, *Hauk* became *Hook*, and *Heidt* became *Hyde*. In the same way *Heuermann* was reduced to *Herman*, *Kuechel* to *Keekel*, *Laure* to *Lowrie* and *Rietsche* to *Ritchie*. *Rohnke* was rendered as *Ronkey*, *Sauer* as *Sowers* and *Schneidt* as *Shyde*. Frequently the change was slight as when *Schlichtman* became *Slickman*, *Schmale* became *Smalley*, or when *Uebel* was changed to *Youbel*, *Werner* to *Warner* and *Wierhacke* to *Wierhockey*.

Turning from surnames to the names of ethnic or regional groups, we find that Canadian English boasts far fewer native terms of opprobrium than the United States which has a large stock, as Mencken pointed out, chiefly directed at aliens.[1] Indeed the Canadian vocabulary is singularly poor in this respect, those few terms which are in general use being imported from the United States along with most of our street and gutter language. Our largest group of non-English speakers is, of course, French Canadian and here the pickings are very lean. Mencken observed that *frog*, used generally in England and America to designate a Frenchman, presumably because of his custom of eating frogs' legs, is not applied in Canada to a French Canadian. "The common name for him is *Joe*," he added, "but it is not used often." While this may once have been so, the expression *Joe* is now completely out of fashion, and has not been replaced with any commonly accepted designation, although the *DC* can muster a few citations for *pea-soup* and *pea-souper*. The only generic term with any currency, unimaginative though it is, seems to be *the French*, counterbalanced on the part of French Canada by *les anglais*. The fightingest expressions in this vein are echoes of each other: *les maudits anglais* on the one hand, and on the other *the goddam French*. The term *Jean Baptiste* is occasionally met with, in reference to the patron saint of Quebec, but the expression is uncommon in English-speaking Canada. The *DC* traces it back to 1818, but can give only one citation since 1878.

[1] *The American Language, Supplement 1*, 1945, p. 595. Mencken rescued from the limbo of learned periodical literature the term *acthronyms* to describe "derisive names for various peoples."

For their part, the early French Canadians were much less temperate. In 1864, Samuel Phillips Day reported:

The settlers from Great Britain and Ireland were not favourably received by the *habitans*. They were called by the offensive but ingenious appellation of *Bas de Soie*, owing to their not wearing any stockings .... The French Canadians, in order to distinguish between the Scotch and English settlers, used to designate them by a term more graphic than elegant, '*Les Ecossais Sauvages.*' Nor were the Americans regarded much more favourably; for Jean Baptiste used generally to speak of them with *mauvaise plaisanterie* as '*Sacré Yankee Crapo,*' or '*D – – d Yankee toads.*' [1]

For some reason, only partly apparent at this distance, nineteenth-century Canadians reserved the better part of their spleen for Scotsmen and Americans. Thus John Howison, one of the early travellers, wrote in 1821: "It is a remarkable circumstance, that, in Upper Canada, the *ne plus ultra* of vanity, impudence and rascality, is thought to be comprised under the epithet *Scotch Yankey.*" [2] It may be noted in passing that *sauvage* is the common expression in Canadian French for an Indian, although not for an Eskimo. It often has a pejorative connotation, as in "mentir comme un sauvage," also "boire comme un sauvage" where Standard French would say "boire comme un polonais." French Canadians say "partir en sauvage" where a Frenchman would say "filer à l'anglais," and an Englishman "take French leave." To these may be added, by way of supreme insult to a fellow white man, *sauvage!* and *maudit sauvage!*[3]

As in the United States, such expressions as *wop, dago, mick,* and the like are heard across the land, but less frequently than they used to be. One term which still has some vogue is *hunkie* (or *hunky* or *hunkey*) a derivative of *Bohunk*, itself a portmanteau word formed from the first syllables of Bohemian and Hungarian, and

[1] *English America: or, Pictures of Canadian Places and People*, London, Vol. 2, pp. 222–223.
[2] *Sketches of Upper Canada, Domestic, Local and Characteristic*, Edinburgh, 1821, quoted in Craig, *Early Travellers in the Canadas, 1789–1867*, Toronto, 1955, p. 62.
[3] Gaston Dulong, "Le Mot *Sauvage* en Franco-Canadien," *J.C.L.A.*, 1961, pp. 161–163.

sometimes abbreviated to *Hunk* or *Honk*. The word is used in
Canada, according to Mencken, "to designate Poles, Ukrainians
and miscellaneous Slavs, maybe because actual Hungarians are
scarce." [1] It also extends to Macedonians, although not to Greeks.
The expression *hunkey-wedding* has some currency, at least in
Ontario, to describe the marriage celebrations of eastern Europeans in general and Slavs in particular.[2] As is the case with
many acthronyms, members of the group referred to may apply
the term to themselves in conversation within the group, often in
a friendly or semi-humorous manner, but its use by an outsider
constitutes a deadly insult. One interesting term reported by an
observer about the turn of the century was *hickories*, applied to
Pennsylvania Germans who had settled in Ontario many years
earlier, but it was even then passing out of use. It is said to have
been first applied to them in Pennsylvania, perhaps in reference
to the fact that they voted for Andrew Jackson, styled "Old
Hickory," for President.[3]

New Englanders over the years have devised a number of unflattering designations for their Maritime neighbours in Canada:
thus *herring-choker* for a Newfoundlander or Nova Scotian, *newfy*
or *cod-hauler* for a Newfoundlander and *novy* for a Nova Scotian
were reported long ago by Mencken.[4] Maritimers generally were
called *Herring-backs* about 1875.[5] Perhaps the best-known of such
terms is *bluenose* defined by the *DAE* as "a native of Nova Scotia

---

[1] *Supplement 1*, pp. 601–602.

[2] Professor A. R. M. Lower recalls in *Canadians in the Making*, Toronto, 1958,
p. 372, that the term *New Canadian* came into existence early in the present century,
"perhaps because it was not so insulting as 'bohunk' or 'dago.'" He appends the
following catechism on *bohunk* from a northern bush camp:

> "Is a French-Canadian a *bohunk?*"
> "Certainly not."
> "Is a Swede a *bohunk?*"
> "No."
> "How about Germans?"
> "No, about the same as Swedes."
> "Are Finns *bohunks?*"
> "Well, they might be."
> "Are Galicians [later Ukrainians]?"
> "Oh, yes, of course they are—Poles, too."

[3] W. J. Wintemberg, *Journal of American Folklore*, 1903, p. 128.

[4] *The American Language, Supplement I*, p. 611.

[5] Robert M. Hamilton, *Canadian Quotations and Phrases*, Toronto, 1952, p. 133.

or New Brunswick." [1] Apparently it was originally applied to a New Englander, but from the last century on the word has been used only in reference to Canadian Maritimers. The usual modern sense, according to the *DC*, is a Nova Scotian. There is some dispute about the origin of the term, and no really satisfactory explanation has yet been advanced. Thomas Chandler Haliburton in *Sam Slick* says that it "is the name of a potato which [the Nova Scotians] produce in great perfection, and boast to be the best in the world. The Americans have, in consequence, given them the nickname of *blue-noses*." The earliest use of *bluenose* is given by the *OED* as 1837 and by the *DA* as 1830, but the *DC* has traced the word back to 1785 when it was applied to the original inhabitants of Nova Scotia in contrast to the Loyalists.[2]

Canadians have also invented a few disparaging or humorous names for particular groups. Thus the inhabitants of Peterborough, Ontario, have been called *Peterboors* by those who accuse them of being "indifferent to arts, letters, and the finer graces of society." Residents of Moose Jaw, recalling the Indian name of their town, are said to enjoy referring to themselves as *Moosichapiskanisippians*, and those of New Westminster were at one time ingloriously called *Salmon-bellies*.[3] In the same category is *Spud Islander*, for an inhabitant of Prince Edward Island, recalling the potatoes which are produced in such superb quality and abundance by the island province.

Canadian railway nicknames display a strong vein of irony, often reflecting either the discomfort of passengers or the dissatisfaction of employees. Tardiness and unreliability, whether real or fancied, have been two of the commonest sources of inspiration. Thus the Canadian National Railways, popularly referred to as the *C.N.R.*, has been dubbed *Certainly No Rush*. Other past and present railway acrostics include, for the Cumberland Railway and Coal Company, *Can't Run and Can't Crawl;* Grand

---

[1] The *SOED* confines the word to Nova Scotians.

[2] See also C. J. Lovell, "A Sampling of Materials for a Dictionary of Canadian English Based on Historical Principles," *J.C.L.A.*, Spring, 1958, p. 12.

[3] H. L. Mencken, "Some Opprobrious Nicknames," *American Speech*, 1949, pp. 25–30. Pre-Confederation British Columbians used to call the Canadians *North American Chinamen* "because of their thriftiness:" Robert M. Hamilton, *Canadian Quotations and Phrases*, Toronto, 1952, p. 29.

Trunk Pacific, *Get There Perhaps;* Halifax and South Western, *Hellish Slow and Weary;* Kingston and Pembroke, *Kick and Push;* Lake Erie and Northern, *Late Every Night;* Napanee, Tamworth and Quinte, *None Too Quick;* Niagara, St. Catherines and Toronto, *Never Starts on Time;* Sidney and Louisburg, *Slow and Lazy;* and Temiscaming and Northern Ontario (now Ontario Northern), *Time No Object.*

The discomforts and hazards of railway locomotion are recalled by such nicknames as that of Algoma Central and Hudson Bay, *All Curves, Hills and Bridges;* Atlantic, Quebec and Western, *All Queer and Wobbly;* Duluth, Winnipeg and Pacific, *Derailments, Wrecks and Profanity;* Minnesota and Manitoba, *Murder all Manitobans;* Pontiac, Pacific Junction Railway, *Push, Pull, Jump and Run;* and Toronto, Hamilton and Buffalo, *To Hell and Back*, with the variants, *Tramp, Hobo and Bum* and *Tried Hard and Busted.*

The economic side of early railroading appeared in Brockville, Westport and Sault Ste. Marie, *Bad Wages and Seldom See Money;* Canadian National Railway, *Collects No Revenue;* Canadian Pacific Railway, *Can't Pay Rent* or *Can't Promise Returns;*[1] Ottawa, Arnprior and Parry Sound, *Only Abuse and Poor Salary;* and Port Arthur, Duluth and Western, *Poverty, Agony, Distress and Want.* Finally, the language barrier was broken by the Quebec, Montreal and Southern with *Quel Maudit Service.*[2]

III   Plant and Animal Names

The white men who discovered and settled North America were faced with the formidable task of naming the many animals, birds, fish and plants with which the new country abounded. The names given by these early voyagers were drawn, as W. F. Ganong long

[1] Also called, in its early days, *The Chinese Pacific* from the large numbers of Orientals used during construction of the transcontinental line.

[2] These railway nicknames are garnered from Robert M. Hamilton, *Canadian Quotations and Phrases*, Toronto, 1952, pp. 193-195.

ago pointed out, from four main sources.[1] Among the oldest were the native names, taken over by the first hunters, fishermen and settlers who made contact with the Indian tribes. These terms related to creatures new to European experience and for which no other names existed even by analogy, such as *chicamin, moose, pounamon*. Many may be found in several forms thanks to the untrained ears of early observers and the difficulties of accurate transliteration from the Indian tongues into English. Thus *caribou* produced such variants as *caribouck* and *cariboux* (1682–1683), *caribee* (1744), *kerraboo* (1793), *carriboux* (1808), *carriboo* (1820), *caraboo* (1829), *cariborea* (*circa* 1830) and *carraboo* (1846).[2] *Pemmican* or *pemican* has an equally complicated past. C. J. Lovell reported its first traced use in 1743 as *pimmegan*, but later travellers recorded the word variously as *pimmacon, pimmeecon, pimican, pimmecan* and *pimmicum*. Paul Kane in *Wanderings of an Artist* (1859) called it *pemmi-kon*.

The second category consisted of the generic names of forms familiar to Europeans, which were extended to forms within the same genus existing in the New World. The names of most of our plants came into being in this way, as did those of many common animals: *fox, wolf, otter, bear,* or in French *renard, loup, loutre, ours*.

Third were the names of familiar European forms which had no exact correspondence in North America, but were transferred to similar forms, often by reason of a resemblance in cry, habit, appearance, utility or some other salient feature. Sometimes, as Ganong pointed out, the result of this process was to confer a European name upon a North American plant or animal scientifically very different, as when the name *cranberry* was applied to a different species from the one so called in England, or *wintergreen* was used in the New World to describe the plant variously called *Canada tea, deerberry, groundberry, mountain tea, pilberry, spiceberry* and

[1] "The Identity of the Animals and Plants Mentioned by the Early Voyagers to Eastern Canada and Newfoundland," *Transactions of the Royal Society of Canada*, 1909, Ser. II, pp. 197–242.

[2] These spellings and the dates of their appearance are taken from C. J. Lovell, "A Sampling of Materials for a Dictionary of Canadian English Based on Historical Principles," *J.C.L.A.*, 1958, pp. 7–33.

teaberry.[1] In the same way, early settlers gave the name of the English *robin* to a species of thrush, the name *chimney-swallow* to a swift, the name *partridge* to our grouse, and the name *nighthawk* to a bird which is not a hawk. Exactly the same thing happened in French Canada where the red-breasted thrush was called *merle* and the Canada goose *outarde*, while our song-sparrow was christened *rossignol*.

In a fourth class, new names emerged as a result of some peculiarity and, passed along by the early traders and settlers, have persisted down to modern times. Ganong gives as examples *esterlet, gode, marionette, marmette*. He listed some 377 names of animals and plants, including the following of apparently Canadian origin: *caribou*, first used in English in 1676, having been "early adopted from the Micmacs by the French and from the French by New Englanders visiting Acadia;" [2] *lucifee*, a corruption of *loup cervier*, an old French name for the European lynx, transferred to the American species; *siffleur*, alike the white-throated sparrow and the Canadian marmot or woodchuck; and *suisse*, applied by the Acadians to the chipmunk "in allusion to its stripes, which apparently suggested those of the uniform of the Swiss soldiery."

Very little research has yet been done into the onomastics of Canadian avifauna. W. L. McAtee in recording amusing or satirical names applied to North American birds has included a few Canadian examples.[3] Sometimes, he points out, the appellation is derisive, "attaching the name of some race to a bird deemed inferior as food or game," as when in British Columbia the name *siwash duck* is applied to scoters and old squaw, and *siwash goose* to the western grebe. Other facetious names indicate toughness, as when the American bittern and old squaw are called *pine knot* in Nova Scotia, or general worthlessness for food, as when the name *trash duck* is applied to the gadwall in Saskatchewan and to the shoveler in Manitoba.

Not all bird names are derogatory, although many are intentionally humorous. Thus the tiny phalarope, a shore bird no more

[1] G. H. McKnight, *English Words and Their Background*, New York, 1923, p. 28.
[2] See A. F. Chamberlain, *American Anthropologist*, 1901, Vol. III, p. 587.
[3] "Facetious Monickers for American Birds," *American Speech*, 1956, pp. 180–187.

than eight or ten inches long, is called *sea goose* from Newfoundland to New Jersey, *mackerel goose* along the Gulf of St. Lawrence
and *Jersey goose* in Nova Scotia. Other names relate to appearance,
as when Newfoundlanders call the very plump ruddy turnstone
fat oxen. Sometimes the name is sheer fancy: thus the nickname
flying sheep is applied to the whooping crane in Alberta and Manitoba; and the pileated woodpecker is in Saskatchewan called
crow-with-the-hard-face, perhaps, says McAtee, because it "must
have a hard face to dig into trees as it so actively does." Akin to
these are the terms *snippit* for a small shore bird in British
Columbia, and *foolish godwit* for the Hudsonian godwit in
Manitoba.[1]

McAtee has also discussed the effect of folk etymology on bird
names, tracing the mutations of such names as *cape race*, the red-
throated loon, through the gamut of *cape-racer* (New Brunswick,
Nova Scotia), *cape drake* (Nova Scotia), *scapegrace* (Labrador, New
Brunswick, Nova Scotia), *capderace* (Newfoundland), *carbreast*
(Quebec), *corbrace* (Newfoundland, Labrador, Nova Scotia) and
corbrus (Newfoundland, Labrador).[2] In the same vein, *bec scie* for
mergansers has become *Betsy* in Quebec.

The range of folk names for Canadian birds is surprisingly
large. Thus the white-throated sparrow enjoys no fewer than
twenty-eight different names in English and French. Perhaps the
commonest is *Canada bird* from its well-known song which strikes
many hearers as "Sweet, sweet, Canada, Canada, Canada," at
least in New Brunswick, Ontario and Manitoba. But in Manitoba
it is also called the *hard-time Canada bird* from another rendering
of its song as "Hard times, Canada, Canada, Canada." [3] Other
variants are without economic overtones, as when Nova Scotians
hear its song as "Poor, poor Kennedy, Kennedy, Kennedy,"
whence its local name of *kennedy bird.* Yet another version of the

[1] The last two are from W. L. McAtee, " 'Stint' as a Bird Name," *American Speech*,
1956, p. 299.

[2] "Folk Etymology in North American Bird Names," *American Speech*, 1951, pp.
90–95. The author defines folk etymology as "the transformation of a form under the
influence of some other word with which it has an apparent or fancied connection,"
as when asparagus becomes sparrowgrass.

[3] Theodore H. Rand, Nova Scotian poet and educator rendered the song as
"I – love – dear – Canada, Canada, Canada" (*The Whitethroat*, 1900).

same song in Nova Scotia is "Old Sam Peabody, Peabody, Peabody," and the bird is consequently known as *Old Sam Peabody*, or, in Quebec and New Brunswick, *Old Tom Peabody*. *Peabody bird* is an old New England name that is found throughout central and eastern Canada, sometimes as *Peabiddy bird*. To French Canadian ears, the song's key word sounds like an anapaest rather than a dactyl, and the bird is dubbed *Frédéric* or *p'tit Frédéric*, not to mention *linotte* (linnet), *rossignol* (nightingale) and *siffleur* (whistler).

Such variety, though impressive, is exceeded by the yellow-shafted flicker which can boast thirty-one different names in English, French and Gaelic, and the grey jay with thirty-two. The American bittern tops the list with no less than thirty-five names, of which the most prevalent, *stake driver*, is common to the North American range of the bird because "at a distance," writes McAtee, "the notes of the bird suggest resonant pounding." [1]

B. W. A. Massey in the course of an exhaustive study of Canadian fish names found that the names of no less than twenty-nine fresh-water fish originated in the territory now called Canada, among them *ouananiche*, the oldest (*circa* 1640); *whitefish* (1748) also called *tittymeg*; *namaycush* (1787); *masquinonge* (1794), abbreviated to *lunge* (1904); *cisco* (1848); *inconnu* (1823) corrupted to *connie* (1922); *sockeye* (1887); and *coho* (1889).[2] He found *whitefish* to be the first English name to have originated in Canada for a prevalently Canadian fresh-water fish, probably suggested by the French *poisson blanc*. The imaginative Indian name for this fresh-water herring, *adikumaig*, "the reindeer of the waters," was rendered by the white men as the meaningless *tittymeg*, an example of the perversion of native names deplored by Vilhjalmur Stefansson in *Hunters of the Great North*.[3] "It is," he wrote, "the general habit of whites who come into contact with Eskimos or Indians to pronounce any words they hear, and especially . . .

---

[1] W. L. McAtee, *Folk Names of Canadian Birds*, published under the imprimatur of the Minister of Northern Affairs and National Resources, Ottawa, 1958. The author served with the Biological Survey of the United States Department of Agriculture from 1904 to 1941.

[2] " 'OED' and 'DAE:' Some Comparisons," *Notes and Queries*, 1954, pp. 127–129, 522–525; "Canadian Fish-Names in the OED and DAE," *Notes and Queries*, 1955, pp. 435–455; 1956, pp. 41–44, 125–130; 1957, pp. 79–83, 173–177, 203–208.

[3] New York, 1922, pp. 162–163.

names, so as to resemble more or less closely some word of the white man's language."

This difficulty of representing Indian sounds in English or French is well illustrated by the many names applied to the fresh-water salmon (*salmo salar*) of Lake St. John and Labrador waters. The name *ouananiche*, found in the writings of an early Jesuit missionary, Père Masse, about 1640, came from a Cree dialect spoken in central and northern Quebec; after being borrowed by the French settlers from the Indians, it was re-borrowed by the English as the only name for this variety of land-locked salmon. As long ago as 1896, E. T. D. Chambers pleaded for the spelling *ouananiche* on the ground of strict priority of appearance, although he admitted that there had been many contenders.[1] Among those which he documented were *8ananiche* (the symbol *8* being used by the early French missionaries to reproduce the Indian speech sound represented in French by *oui* or *ou*). *Ou* is the usual French fore-runner of *w*, as when the early cartographers wrote *Ouabasche* and *Ouisconsine*. Notwithstanding all prior claims, when the word first appeared in Webster's *Dictionary* in 1892 the spelling adopted was *winninish*, although Chambers' plea has been largely heeded in Canada.

As might be expected, many fish names were borrowed from the Indian tongues. One such is *cisco*, probably a corruption and contraction of *siscowit*, "cooks itself," the fish being described by Bartlett in 1848 as abundant in Lake Ontario, although its range is from Vermont to the Great Lakes and as far north as Hudson Bay and Labrador. The *DC*'s earliest citation is 1917. The *DAE* calls *cisco* "American Indian, probably Algonkin," but Massey feels that the name may, like *namaycush*, the lake trout (*cristivomer namaycush*), have first been borrowed from south of the Ottawa River in what is now Algonquin Park. To the same class belongs *sockeye*, the blueback or nerka salmon of the Northwest, whose name rendered variously as "suk-kegh," "saw-quai" or "suck-eye"

[1] "The Philology of the Ouananiche: A Plea for the Recognition of Priority of Nomenclature," *Royal Society of Canada, Proceedings and Transactions*, 1896, 2nd Ser., Vol. 2, p. 131.

derives by folk etymology from the Salish Indian *suk-kegh*, "red fish," its native name on the Fraser River.

Equally well known to game fishermen is the *muskellunge*, a large pike found in and about the Great Lakes and known by many names, among them *maskinonge*, *masquinonge*, *maskinouge*, *mascalonge*, *muskelunge*, *maskalonge*, and popularly, *lunge* (1904), *longe* and *musky* (1894), not to mention the French versions which include *masquinongé* and *maskinongé*.[1] A. F. Chamberlain derived them all from the Ojibway *maskinonje*, "ugly fish,"[2] as does the *SOED*, although both the *DC* and *DA* translate the name less pejoratively as "great pike." Of probably Canadian French origin is the *connie* (*stenodus mackenzii*), called by the Eskimos *sit*, which Stefansson described as the largest variety of fish in the Mackenzie River and which he supposed to be a corruption of the French *inconnu*.[3]

IV Fabulous Beasts

Canadian folklore shows a comparative dearth of those fascinating, if mythical, animals to which American folk humorists of the last century were so addicted: to name but a few, the *guyascutus*, the *whangdoodle*, the *swamp-gahoon*, the *sidehill dodger* and the *squonk*.[4] It may be that similar creatures also existed in Canada but they have largely eluded observation, and accordingly little

---

[1] Also, in its earliest appearance, *masquenongez* (1789), not to mention *muskinunge*, *muschilongoe* and *muscalinga*. Longfellow recorded two more alternatives in *Hiawatha*, viii, 61–62:

> And he said to the Kenozha,
> To the pike, the Maskenozha ...

[2] "Algonkian Words in American English," *Journal of American Folklore*, 1902, p. 240.

[3] This derivation is confirmed by the *DC* which gives the alternative spelling *conny*.

[4] The genus, and it is a large one, is discussed at considerable length in Mencken, *The American Language, Supplement 1*, pp. 245–252. The *guyascutus* and the *sidehill dodger* (or *bowger*, or *gouger*, or *badger* or *sauger*) were quadrupeds whose legs grew longer on one side than the other, enabling them to graze on steep hillsides. The *whangdoodle* and the *squonk* passed their lives in endless lamentation, and the *swamp-gahoon* is extinct and forgotten in all but name.

is known of their ecology. One recorded specimen is the *kickle snifter* of New Brunswick, concerning which it has been said: "They live in old men's beards and in circular lakes. They bore a hole in the center. They laugh at you. You take them in the scow." [1]

British Columbia, which is the nearest thing to Texas that Canada has been able to muster, seems to be the last home of our apocryphal beasts. There may be found the dread *Sasquatch* of Indian and white legend, a tribe of hairy giants whose existence was first reported by a Hudson's Bay Company trader near Harrison Lake in 1850. The *Sasquatch*, which has been glimpsed periodically since then in remote parts of British Columbia and Alberta, has hitherto successfully defied capture. The following description has, however, been compiled: "He is eight foot tall and hairy, with footprints 22 inches long and seven inches wide. He lives on huckleberries and can hypnotize birds out of the air. He kidnaps Indian maidens and steals fish from housewives' larders. He hurls rocks at prospectors and kills deer with a club." [2] One highly implausible theory posits that the *Sasquatch* originally lived somewhere between Galveston and Corpus Christi, Texas, until obliged by the inroads of civilization to seek refuge in the vastnesses of British Columbia, but the weight of evidence to support this theory is lacking.

The same area also harbours *Whishpoosh*, the giant king of all the beavers who dwelt in the headwaters of the Columbia River; and the *Wendigo* or *Windigo*, also written *Outiko*, from the Algonquin *Uindiko*, "a malevolent spirit of cannibalistic propensities," according to the *Encyclopedia Canadiana*. The usual confusion attends *Wendigo*'s outward manifestations. Mencken, paraphrasing A. F. Chamberlain, calls it "a fabulous giant;" another account likens it to an alligator; still other authorities would

---

[1] "Folk-lore Animals," *Dialect Notes*, 1922, p. 188. Mencken, Supplement I, p. 251, records the *hicklesnifter* without, however, any indication of its habitat or morphology. G. P. Krapp, in *The English Language in America*, happily resurrected the *treesqueak*, an animal that makes a sound like trees rubbing together in the wind, and the *plunkus*, whose chief means of defence is a tail about six feet long, at the end of which is "a huge lump of bony gristle as large as an ordinary football." Dr. Krapp added to Mencken's sketchy notes on the *swamp-gahoon* the fact that it makes snowshoe tracks.

[2] Alison Hunt, "The West Coast's Abominable Treeman," *The Globe Magazine*, July 6, 1957. A subsequent note (June 11, 1966) relates a Sasquatch sighting to the amount of alcohol consumed prior to its appearance.

accord to it no fixed shape at all. Sylva Clapin, who preferred the spelling *Outiko*, defined it without either precision or conviction as a "géant, ou monstre fabuleux dans les légendes sauvages." The *DC* traces it to 1830 in the spelling *Weendegoag*.

British Columbia also boasts an extensive tribe of sea serpents, among them the Indians' *Salt-Chuck-Olouk*,[1] no doubt kin to the more sociable *Cadborosaurus*, which has been observed off Vancouver Island by a mixed bag of sea captains, barristers and less reliable witnesses. *Cadborosaurus* derives the first part of his name from Cadboro Bay, where he often disports himself, and to this root has been added the suffix *-saurus* for verisimilitude. His lineaments are as might be expected: "He was about 100 to 110 feet long. His body was about two and a half feet in diameter. His head was as large as a draft horse's, but it looked more like a camel's. He had fangs in his mouth six to eight inches long. His eyes seemed to roll in their sockets, changing from a reddish color to green." [2] *Cadborosaurus* first began to appear widely in the public prints around 1933 at which time his Indian name was given as *Hiachuckaluck* or *Hiaschuckoluck*, alleged to be Chinook for "big gamble." [3] He was soon nicknamed *Caddy* by newspaper writers, however, and when in the course of time a second specimen made its appearance the theory inevitably developed that they were a pair of sea serpents, male and female, called *Caddy* and *Amy* respectively, and much newspaper space was given over to accounts of their alleged amours.[4]

The most renowned Canadian monster of all is of course *Ogopogo*—a name so perfectly suited to a fabulous being that, were it necessary, one might justify his existence on the strength of his cognomen alone. *Ogopogo* is that unique paradox, a freshwater sea serpent, whose four distinct humps rival the more widely famed Loch Ness monster which has never even laid claim

[1] From the Chinook Jargon: *salt chuck*, the ocean, and *olouk* or *oluk*, a snake.

[2] Ray Gardner, "Caddy, King of the Coast," *Maclean's Magazine*, June 15, 1950, p. 24.

[3] A typical example of newspaper or stab-in-the-dark etymology. The name is not Chinook at all, but Chinook Jargon: *Hias-chuck-oluk* means "very large water snake." "Big gamble" in Chinook Jargon would be *Hias-hee-hee-lema*.

[4] The nickname *Caddy* appears first to have been used by the Victoria *Times*, October 17, 1933.

to a proper name, although according to James Thurber it is familiarly known to millions as *Nessie*.[1] *Ogopogo* lives in land-locked Okanagan Lake, and was called by the Indians *N'ha-a-itk* or "Lake Demon." According to the canon,[2] he received his name on a night in 1924 when the strains of an English music-hall song were first heard in the City of Vernon, British Columbia:

> His mother was an earwig;
> His father was a whale;
> A little bit of head
> And hardly any tail—
> And Ogopogo was his name.[3]

Like *Cadborosaurus*, *Ogopogo* also attained notoriety in the '30s when sea serpents were much in vogue at home and abroad. According to the Toronto *Globe* of March 7, 1929, he was seen by one J. L. Logie, a former mayor and Presbyterian minister's son who had never touched a drop of liquor in his life, and many contemporary reports went out of their way to vouch for the sobriety of attesting witnesses. Notwithstanding this precaution, few people have agreed on *Ogopogo*'s appearance; he is said to have a head like an earless bulldog and the face of a sheep, but another report gives him a shaggy head and a face like a camel, while still another speaks almost lyrically of the slim fawn-like head. Most observers credit him with having a heavy snake's body, but accounts of his length are very contradictory, estimates running between 35 and 100 feet. It has also been said that like his name, which is a perfect palindrome, he appears the same when looked at from either end.

Formerly *Ogopogo* was considered vicious, and is credited with having swallowed a whole canoe-load of Indians and, according to the story, a horse, but as time passed he became a vegetarian and even acquired the pet name *Oggy*. Despite this more tolerant attitude, however, when a number of sportsmen announced their

---

[1] "Is There a Loch Ness Monster?" *Holiday*, September, 1957.

[2] David S. Boyer, "British Columbia: Life Begins at 100," *National Geographic Magazine*, August, 1958, p. 153. The existence of *Ogopogo* has been stoutly defended in the Canadian House of Commons: Toronto *Globe and Mail*, July 20, 1956.

[3] A somewhat different version of the song appeared in the Vancouver *Province*, August 24, 1926. According to the *DC* the name was first applied in 1912.

intention of hunting down British Columbia's sea serpents in 1934, the Deputy Attorney General of the province stated firmly that no official protection could be given to *Cadborosaurus*.[1] Fortunately this stand was at least partly reversed in 1949 when the Attorney General himself expressed the opinion that it was illegal to shoot *Ogopogo*,[2] on the grounds that he was protected by a section of the provincial Fisheries Act which provided that "no one shall hurt or kill fish or marine animals of any kind other than porpoises, whales, walrus, sea lions and hair seals by means of rockets, explosive projectiles or shells."

In due course *ogopogo* came to be the generic term in Canada for a sea serpent as other parts of the country began to lay claim to similar creatures, most of them nameless. This trend reached its apogee when the Toronto *Star* of January 3, 1934, in an outburst of chauvinism headlined a story about the Loch Ness monster with the words "Even Staid London Times Excited by Scots Ogopogo." With the return of prosperity, public interest in sea serpents appeared to decline, although reports of mysterious underwater creatures continue to crop up in remoter areas. In 1957, one was reported from a small town 187 miles east of Quebec City, but to date its subject has only been referred to in the newspapers as "the Monster of Lake Pohenegamook," itself no mean appellation.

Not to be outdone, Manitobans for their part have recalled that during the 1940's Indians dwelling around Lake Manitoba told tales of a ferocious monster which overturned a canoe containing an Indian family and made off with the mother, who was never seen again. The ingestion of Indians is part of Canadian monster lore. As reports continued to come in from fish-inspectors, automobile-dealers and others, the beast was christened, with a sad lack of originality, *Manipogo*, and imprecisely described as being ten or twenty or fifty feet long, with a round or square or diamond-shaped head, swimming at fifteen or thirty miles per hour through Lake Manitoba, or possibly Lake Winnipegosis. This changing locale was vigorously denounced by a member of

[1] Toronto *Mail*, February 14, 1934.
[2] Zoe Biegler, "Meet Ogopogo," *Weekend Magazine*, August 2, 1952.

207 NAMESITS NAMES 207

the provincial legislature who protested, to no avail, against the removal of *Manipogo* to another constituency than his own. The authenticity of *Manipogo* has been vouched for by a zoology professor from the University of Manitoba.[1]

As befits Canada's most populous province, Ontario has in recent years laid claim to its own monster, alleged to inhabit the deep waters of Lake Simcoe. First sighted about 1952 by a fishing guide who promptly dubbed it *Igopogo*, Simcoe's monster has proved to be a not unworthy member of the underwater fraternity, being dark grey in colour and described as having a neck like a stovepipe and a face like a boxer dog.[2]

---

[1] "Manitoba Monster Gets Official Stamp," Toronto *Globe and Mail*, August 6, 1960.

[2] "Igopogo, Simcoe Monster, Reported Sighted Again," Toronto *Globe and Mail*, July 1, 1963.

CHAPTER EIGHT

SLANG

In Canada we have enough to do keeping up with two spoken languages without trying to invent slang, so we just go ahead and use English for literature, Scotch for sermons, and American for conversation.

STEPHEN LEACOCK

SLANG

"CANADA," ERIC PARTRIDGE ONCE WROTE WITH A PRECISION rarely attempted in Canadian linguistics, "also has an extensive and picturesque objective slang, but that slang is 80 per cent American, with the remainder rather more English than native-Canadian." Canadian slang, in his view, was "of less importance than it might at first thought appear to be, although it is linguistically unfair to condemn it for being so much indebted to its near and 'pushing' neighbour," and he concluded that "in another fifty years [this was written in 1933] it will be almost as American as the slang of the United States, an Americanization that will affect the general speech almost as much as it does the slang." [1]

Although Partridge quite properly called attention, invoking Mencken as his authority, to the Americanisms which have long been silting up our speechways, he (along with Mencken) gave no weight to the probability that, as we have already seen, American preceded British English in many parts of Canada. Whether or not we accept the Loyalist theory of the origin of Canadian English, it is beyond dispute that the Canadian vulgate has always been made up in large measure of American, continually fortified by fresh borrowings from the "pushing neighbour." It was, therefore, inevitable from the beginning that American slang should come to be the common flower of our fields while British

[1] *Slang To-day and Yesterday*, London, 1933, p. 292.

211

slang, where it existed, was usually a hot-house import fostered a little self-consciously by private schools with English masters and mistresses, or existing in strictly limited enclaves like the navy, but never seriously touching the life of the people generally.

This occupation of the field by American slang did not come about without much rear-guard skirmishing on the part of the linguistic purity league. Thus A. C. Geikie, the great-grandfather of language study in Canada,[1] indulged in some strictures on the subject. "If *chiseling*," he observed sourly, "only means cheating;[2] and *log-rolling*[3] jobbing; and *clearing out*, or *making tracks*[4] running away; then most men of taste will have little hesitation in their choice between the old-fashioned English of Shakespeare, Milton, Swift and Addison, and such modern *enrichments* of the old well of English undefiled." Geikie went on to give this example of early Canadian vernacular:

A Canadian who has enjoyed the advantages of the American vocabulary will thus describe a very simple transaction:—
'I traded my last yorker for a plug of honey dew, and got plaguy chiseled by a loafer whose boss had dickered his lot and betterments for notions to his store.' Which being translated reads: 'I exchanged my last sixpence for a packet of tobacco, and got thoroughly cheated by a disreputable fellow whose employer had bartered a piece of unproved land to obtain small wares for his shop.'

In the hundred years which followed, no appreciable change could be noted in this state of affairs. Morley Ayearst correctly observed in 1939 that although English slang is more prevalent in Canada than in the United States, most Canadian slang is of American origin.[5] The wider use of English slang north of the border he ascribed to "the close association with Great Britain

---

[1] "Canadian English," *The Canadian Journal*, 1857, pp. 344–355.

[2] Traced by the *SOED* to 1808, but with no comment as to national origin.

[3] Long since a naturalized British subject: see Mencken, *The American Language*, New York, 1936, pp. 227–228.

[4] An example of "the national talent for condensing a complex thought . . . into a vivid and arresting image:" Mencken, *The American Language*, New York, 1936, p. 142.

[5] "A Note on Canadian Speech," *American Speech*, 1939, pp. 231–233.

during the [First] World War, and the fact that a great many Canadians served with the Imperial Army."

The lack of a sizable body of home-grown slang cannot be attributed either to our newness or to our relatively small population, for Australia which is no older and has far fewer people boasts a rich and varied lexicon of domestic slang reaching back into the nineteenth century, of which it is sufficient to recall such examples as *larrikin, Fitzroy cocktail, sheila, fossick* and, best of all, *wowser*.[1] There are several reasons for our inadequacy in this field; one is, of course, the overpowering and omnipresent influence and example of the United States, usually cited as the fountainhead of all our national shortcomings. Probably more to the point is the lack of a linguistic exuberance comparable to that of either America or Australia. No Canadian could ever have thrown back his head and announced: "I sound my barbaric yawp over the roofs of the world," or revelled in the neologisms of *The Sentimental Bloke* of C. J. Dennis. We are largely devoid of the verbal *élan* which produced such inspired Americanisms as *bunkum, crook, rubberneck, blurb, belly laugh, burp, racketeer* and *O.K.*, although we have never hesitated to appropriate such terms for our own.

On the other hand, we are pretty much unmoved by British slang, which is, as G. P. Krapp once remarked, "largely merely a matter of the use of queer-sounding words, like *bally* and *swank*, whereas American slang suggests images and pictures."[2] A good example of this is provided by English school and university slang. Like the better part of English slang in general, it sounds both feeble and childish to Canadian ears which are attuned to a more pungent demotic. At Oxford, according to Morris Marples, one

[1] The etymology of *wowser* is unclear. Mencken, *The American Language*, 1936, p. 265n., quotes the following definition supplied by a Tasmanian correspondent: "a fellow who is too niggardly of joy to allow the other fellow any time to do anything but pray." A good informal introduction to Australian slang may be found in Sidney J. Baker, *The Australian Language*, Sydney, 1945, and a word list in Eric Partridge, *Slang, Today and Yesterday*, London, 1933. Despite the native vigour of its speech, however, Australia is falling more and more under the ubiquitous influence of the United States. As early as July 25, 1936, the Sydney *Morning Herald* complained that "the American element in our slang is growing fast and outstripping the original Cockney element," a process much accelerated by the peaceful invasion of Australia by American servicemen during the second world war.

[2] *The English Language in America*, New York, 1925, Vol. 1, p. 114.

H

of the main methods of word formation is to add suffixes in *-er*, *-ers*, *-agger* and *-oggins* to common nouns,[1] producing such results as *Bodder*, the Bodleian Library, *brekker*, breakfast, *Canader*, a Canadian canoe, *congratters*, congratulations, *Deaner*, Dean, *footer*, football, *Queener*, the Queen Street Cinema, and so on, to the point where the Prince of Wales pub becomes *The Pragger Wagger*, the International Brigade in the Spanish Civil War was the *Internagger Brigagger*, a waste-paper basket is a *wagger-pagger-bagger*, and a certain Reverend Talbot Rice, Rector of St. Peter-le-Bailey became (*circa* 1890) *The Tagger Ragger of St. Pagger le Bagger*. All this would fall very flat indeed in Canada, although we have few things of our own to offer in its place.

Very little scientific study has been made of the slang of the armed services, but from available evidence it seems that Canadian army slang tends to follow the pattern of Canadian civilian slang. Both American and British slang expressions, often of ancient vintage, occur freely in all branches of the armed forces. Early in the second world war, a number of slang terms were reported as being in use among Canadian naval men, although with no assertion that they were native products. Most names for officers and crew had a Royal Navy flavour, as when the commandant was referred to as *the bloke;* the captain as *the skipper, the old man* or *the owner;* the surgeon as *pills;* a first lieutenant as *Number One*, or *Jemmy the One;* and midshipmen as *snotties*, the last-named being a reference to the custom ascribed to British naval ratings in the eighteenth century of wiping their noses on their sleeves, the then uniforms providing no place to store a handerchief. The practice is said to have been stopped by attaching metal buttons to the formerly plain cuffs.

Other Canadian naval slang included *to cut no ice*, to fall flat; *clobber*, clothing, an obvious loan from the Australians; *wash-out*, a muddle or failure; *blinking*, a euphemism for bleeding; *funkhole*, a soft Government job well-removed from the danger area; and *to dazzle*, i.e., camouflage, a ship.[2] By the end of the war a substantial body of Canadian naval slang had developed, which one

---

[1] *University Slang*, London, 1950, pp. 26–29, 69–79.

[2] Toronto *Daily Star*, September 20, 1941.

reporter imprecisely described as being "pure Canadiana with a mixture of Australian and Royal Navy slang." [1] Examples given were the *dooey*, any object at all; *a party*, a girl; *stavers*, hopelessly drunk; *carry the cans*, complain; a *wet*, a drink of liquor; *zizz*, a cat-nap; *flakers*, asleep; *to down periscope* or *submerge*, lie down for a nap; *laid on*, arranged; *blow a bine*, smoke a cigarette; *Q-patch*, quarterdeck; *Joe Buggins*, any seaman; *toothie*, dental officer; *schoolie*, the instructor; and *sin bosun*, the chaplain. The last term was a change from *devil-dodger*, reported as being in use earlier in the war.

In *A Dictionary of R.A.F. Slang* (1945), Eric Partridge included several terms which he attributed to Canadian pilots: *hop the twig*, to crash fatally; and *snargasher*, a training aircraft, the latter a corruption of *tarmac-smasher* derived from the clumsy landings of student pilots. But to the Canadian ear these expressions, particularly the first, have a RAF-ish turn which makes one doubt their authenticity. It may well be that they were part of the vocabulary of Canadian pilots serving in England during the late war, but this is a far cry from certifying them as Canadian slang. That the wartime slang of the RCAF clearly derived from the RAF with occasional glimpses of Americanese was demonstrated by an anonymous reporter in the Toronto *Daily Star* of April 11, 1944, who provided the following glossary of RCAF slang: *duff gen*, inaccurate information; *big job*, bomber; *boogie*, unidentified plan; *a good do*, lots of action; *gong*, a decoration; *along for the ride*, no action; *brown job*, or *pongo*, the army; *shark bait*, the navy; *erk*, ground crew; *the boss*, commanding officer; *plumber*, flight engineer; *screened*, taken off operational duties; *clot*, pilot who plays the fool; *shaky do*, a tough flight; *packed up*, engine failure; and *sprogs*, children.

During the war, there was said to be much concern in Canada at the thought that our boys overseas were being infected by English slang.[2] Some Canadians, particularly those having to do with the Royal Air Force, were reported to be actually using such terms as *flicks* for movies, *browned off* for fed up, *bloke* for guy and

[1] Toronto *Daily Star*, June 9, 1945.
[2] Toronto *Daily Star*, March 24, 1943.

push bike for bicycle. The army, being of sterner stuff, was alleged to have resisted such temptations.[1] Not all Canadians who came into contact with the RAF were completely won over, however, and some small attempt at coining their own slang within the larger framework was reported, one modest contribution being *wag* for wireless air gunner.[2]

Eric Partridge in *Slang Today and Yesterday* (London, 1933) compiled a small glossary of terms employed by Canadian soldiers during the first world war. This word-list contained few expressions which, Partridge freely admitted, were not also very dated American slang, and of the remainder fewer still now sound familiar to Canadian ears. Among them are: *buck*, to boast or complain; *cagnes*, a barracks (compare the French *cagna*, a dugout); *Charlie Chaplin's Army Corps*, the Canadian Casualty Assembly Centre at Shorncliffe, Kent; *cow*, milk; *Coxey's army*, a "ragtime," i.e., farcical army; *criq*, brandy, "from the French Canadians;" *dosh*, a "bivvy," i.e., fox-hole; *gat*, a revolver;[3] *honey-bucket*, latrine; *hooch*, spirits, "like *gat* and *buck* it was general among the Americans;"[4] *hooza-ma-kloo*, "equivalent to the Tommy's *ooja*," i.e., thingumajig; *jake*, good, genuine; *java*, tea (surely a slip of the pen for coffee); *mazuma*, money; *mulligan*, camp stew; *outfit*, army unit; *pard*, a pal; *pill*, cigarette; *punk*, bread; *the Ross*, Ross rifle; *sand*, sugar; *side kick*, a chum; *S.O.L.*, "short of luck,"[5] *swipe*, steal; *take*, O.K.;[6] and *toodle-em-buck*, the game of crown and anchor. The strongly, if archaic, American flavour of many of

---

[1] "Flyers Use English Terms, Soldiers Say 'Baloney,' " Toronto *Daily Star*, June 7, 1943.

[2] Toronto *Daily Star*, September 4, 1941.

[3] Probably from gatling gun, according to Mencken, although there are other theories. The gatling gun was an early type of machine gun invented by an American, Richard Jordan Gatling. *The Encyclopaedia Britannica*, 14th ed., reported with a perfectly straight face that "the invention was adopted by almost every civilized nation."

[4] Mencken, *The American Language*, 1936, p. 121, says that *hooch* derives from the United States occupation of Alaska in 1867. The soldiers set up an illicit still, borrowing the native *hoocheno* for the fruit of their labours. By the operation of a familiar process, the word was shortened to *hooch* during the Klondike gold rush of 1897, and *hooch* it has remained ever since.

[5] *S.O.L.* is almost certainly a Canadianism according to Eric Partridge in *A Dictionary of Slang and Unconventional English*, London, 1951. The expanded versions "short of luck" and "slightly out of luck" are both euphemisms.

[6] Partridge suggests that this may be a perversion of *jake*.

these expressions is apparent enough, although Canadians may need a glossary to understand some of Partridge's definitions. According to the *DA*, *buck* in the sense given goes back to 1851; *Coxey's army* was "a group of several hundred unemployed who in 1894, chiefly under the leadership of J. S. Coxey, marched to Washington, D.C., in an effort to secure relief through legislation;" *gat* was first used in 1911, and *java* to signify coffee as long ago as 1850. Similarly *mazuma* and *mulligan* antedate the first world war, both going back to 1907, *punk* is as old as 1891, *swipe* dates back to 1889 and *pard* to 1850.

In the second world war, the Canadian Army showed itself less bound by British convention then either the navy or air force, and by 1941 was reported to be coining a language of its own, the following being a few printable samples: *Joe Pill*, medical officer; *Joe Cash*, paymaster; *Joe Doe*, or *Joe Tooth*, dental officer; and *Moe*, the medical officer. The generic term *Joe* was also used to designate men on the rifle ranges, the Number One man being *Joe Foresight* and the Number Two man *Joe Backsight*.[1] Other terms were: *rompers*, summer shorts; *cronks*, soda crackers; *corn on the cob*, beans; *pea-shooter*, a .22 rifle; *sod-busters*, defaulters who had to work out their sentences; *bingo boys*, permanent staff men; *tea cosies*, winter service hats; *push the boat out*, buy drinks for the crowd. These so-called innovations were stretched by drawing on such first world war reliables as *swinging the lead, working a ticket* and *corn in Egypt*.[2] One quasi-military slang term in widespread use during the second world war was *zombie* to describe a male taken into the army for "limited," i.e., home military service, but who could not be sent overseas on active service. The word comes originally from the voodoo cult, signifying a "dead body made to walk and act and move as if it were alive." Because of its long-standing historical connotations, the word *conscription* could not be used by the then Government, although in the closing days of the

---

[1] *Joe* alone and in combination has had a lengthy history. The military *Joe* perhaps derives immediately from *Joe Doakes*, "a name for a fictitious individual regarded as representing a large class" (*DA*), but there is a long line of slang "Joes," both English and American, going back at least to *Joe Bunker*, an American, traced by the *DA* to 1787.

[2] Toronto *Daily Star*, September 13, 1941.

war something virtually indistinguishable from conscription did in fact exist. Even the American euphemism *selective service* was considered too strong for Canadian sensibilities.

The Canadian troops in Italy during the second world war were reported to talk their own lingo, being a mixture of Canadian and English slang interlarded with scraps of very basic Italian. As with most Canadian military slang, very few examples were permanently recorded, and fewer still appear to have survived the armistice. A contemporary observer listed the following: *vino* or *bingo*, wine; *brew up*, a burned-out tank; *Moaning Minnie*, *Wupping Willie*, or *the Andrews Sisters*, a German mortar; *stove pipe*, a Canadian mortar; *bully*, corned beef; *foo*, forward observation officer; *windy*, an overly nervous soldier; and *shellwacky*, one who is suffering from long exposure to heavy fire.[1]

Some twelve years after hostilities had ended, a newspaperman reviewing Canadian service slang in the second world war for the Toronto *Star* found that almost none of it had survived the ravages of peacetime, only a handful of words having passed into general use.[2] Among the passé terms were listed *grippo* or *gash*, free; *bound rigid*, bored; *bottle* or *rocket*, a severe scolding; *to tear off a strip*, reprimand sharply; and *jankers*, jail.[3] Of service slang which survived, the author listed *flake out*, to rest horizontally; *pusser*, correct; *slops*, stores; *to flog*, to sell service issue goods illegally; and *ropey*, unattractive. In general use as having transcended the boundaries of slang, he included *gnatter*, to talk interminably;[4] *clot*, a tiresome fellow; *flap*, great excitement; and *popsy*, a girl, especially one given to slightly illicit relations. As

[1] Toronto *Daily Star*, February 16, 1944. If these reports are correct, Canadian troops appeared to fancy antique English slang. Thus Eric Partridge in *A Dictionary of Slang and Unconventional English* (4th ed. 1951) traces *swing the lead*, to loaf or malinger, to pre-1920, the phrase being a corruption of *swing the leg* a nautical term *c.* 1860, having the same meaning. *Working a ticket*, more usually *one's* or *the* ticket, "to obtain one's discharge from the Army by having oneself adjudged physically unfit," dates from the 1890's, while *corn in Egypt*, to signify plenty, especially of food, is at least as old as 1830. Partridge dates *bully* to 1883, *windy* to late 1915 and *minnie* to 1915, from the German *Minenwerfer*, literally a mine-thrower.

[2] Scott Young, "Slang Enriches Language," Toronto *Star*, August 7, 1957.

[3] Some of these were still used in army circles, among them *gash*, *rocket* and *to tear off a strip*.

[4] The commoner spelling is *natter*. Partridge suggests that it may be a portmanteau of *nag* and *chatter*.

with earlier compilations, many of these terms have a strongly English flavour, and few if any are certifiably Canadian.

The Canadian national preoccupation with sports appears to have inspired very few slang or jargon terms that have endured; among them one might include *rink rat* and *homer*.[1] Our native sporting vocabulary, in fact, is relatively small. Hockey, despite a Canadian near-monopoly of the game for many years, was in the beginning merely the combination of two foreign pastimes: ice skating borrowed from the Low Countries, and field hockey which had been played in England since the Middle Ages. Not even the name is Canadian, the *SOED* tracing it to 1527 in reference to the iceless game and tentatively suggesting a connection with the Old French *hoquet*, "crook," from the fact that it is played with sticks hooked or curved at one end. The game which North Americans call *hockey* is by Britons referred to as *ice-hockey*.[2] A vaguely related game attained mid-Victorian popularity in England under the name of *bandy*, a solid rubber ball being used in place of a puck, but hockey properly so called seems first to have been played at Kingston, Ontario, on Christmas Day, 1855, although prior honours are claimed for both Halifax and Montreal.

Notwithstanding its foreign ancestry, the modern game of hockey is wholly Canadian, as is much of its vocabulary. The derivation of the word *puck* is obscure, indeed the *SOED* which traces it to 1891 calls its origin unknown, but many hockey terms are almost certainly Canadianisms, among them *faceoff*, *check*, *blue line* and *hockey cushion*, an outdoor boarded rink.[3]

Of certain Canadian origin is *lacrosse*, traced by the *DC* to 1791 and said to be the oldest organized sport in North America. By

[1] A *rink rat* (or *arena rat*) is a boy who spends much of his time at a rink, often doing odd jobs in return for seeing hockey games. The *DC* defines a *homer* as (a) a supporter of the home team, or (b) a referee who favours the home team.
[2] Mencken, *The American Language, Supplement 2*, 1945, p. 471.
[3] The last from J. E. Belliveau, "Do You Speak Good Canadian?" *Star Weekly*, July 20, 1957. *Rink* itself is of very ancient parentage. Like a great many English sporting terms, it was borrowed from Old French, probably from *renc*, a row or rank. The *SOED* traces its earliest use to *c.* 1637 as the expanse of ground within which a joust or race took place. By 1787, it came to mean a stretch of ice marked off for curling, and by 1867 it had acquired its modern meaning of a sheet of ice for skating. The *DC* suggests that *puck* is a British dialect variant of *poke*.

its Indian name, *baggataway*, it was called by the early French settlers *le jeu de la crosse* because of the resemblance between the curved stick and a bishop's crozier (*la crosse*), whence the modern name of the sport.

The game of *football* has had an even more complicated past. The common ancestor of all football games is lost on the playing fields of antiquity, but as the name would suggest it was probably played with the feet only, its modern English version being called variously *association football* or *soccer*. In 1823, a Rugby boy, so the story goes, first conceived the idea of catching the ball and running with it, from which developed the game of *rugby union football*, known and still played in Canada as *English rugby* or *English rugger*. The Canadian version of *rugby union* is officially called *rugby football*, and is commonly if ambiguously referred to by the general public sometimes as *football* and sometimes as *rugby*. Canadian rugby football closely resembles American football in vocabulary and method of play with, however, a few terminological differences. Thus, in the United States, "the *snap*, the *insides*, and the *middles* play under the labels *center*, *guards* and *tackles*, and the *flying wing* has no counterpart at all." [1] Canadian professional rugby football also boasts several slang terms, among them *homebrew* and *import*. [2]

The highly specialized jargon of the underworld has been studied since at least 1567, when one Thomas Harman published a work in England called *A Caveat or Warning for Common Cursetors, Vulgarly called Vagabones* in which were set out a number of terms of criminal argot. It had many successors over the centuries, as virtually every corner of the subject was investigated by enthusiastic students. Among recent works, Frank O'Leary, *A Dictionary*

---

[1] W. S. Avis, "Speech Differences Along the Ontario-United States Border, I, Vocabulary," *J.C.L.A.*, October, 1954, p. 13.

[2] According to Dr. W. S. Avis of Royal Military College, Kingston, a *homebrew* is "a player born in Canada and trained, for the most part, in the Canadian system and, therefore, not affected by the regulations governing the signing of American players." An *import*, as the term implies, is "a player not a citizen of Canada or who has not lived in Canada long enough to qualify as a 'Canadian' in the regulations governing professional leagues." When such a person has played in Canada for a certain number of years he becomes a sort of *ad hoc* Canadian, and may properly be referred to as an *ex-import*. The *DC* notes the use of both *homebrew* and *import* has been extended to baseball and hockey.

of American Underworld Lingo (New York, 1951) and Eric Partridge, *A Dictionary of the Underworld, British and American* (London, 1950), have recorded modern terminology in the United States, England and Australia, the last-named country boasting a rich vein which goes back to convict days. David W. Maurer, one of the leading American authorities on underworld slang, characterizes "its machine-gun staccato, its hard timbre, its rather grim humor, its remarkable compactness" and remarks that "it appears to be well standardized from coast to coast and from the Gulf into Canada." [1]

Little attempt has been made to investigate the lingo of the Canadian underworld. Professor Mario Pei suggests that, as might be expected, Canadian gangster slang is much influenced by the wealth of cant across the border and records that what he calls "the Toronto police glossary" includes such expressions as *hard-rock*, a tough guy, *soup-capers*, safe-blowing, *mousefeet*, rubber-soled shoes, and *bluebeetles*, policemen.[2] There can, however, be few Torontonians who have ever heard any of these terms, none of which sounds authentically Canadian. To them an anonymous reporter in the Toronto *Star* of January 25, 1950, added *sammy*, a hat; *kicks*, shoes; *blowers*, cigarettes; *rawjohn*, a fight; *African soup-bone*, elbow; *greeble*, a no-good girl; *go on the boost*, to commit burglary; and *leather*, a wallet.

Eric Partridge in his compendious *Dictionary of the Underworld* acknowledges in a brief foreword his indebtedness to "the leading newspaper in Toronto," but no great store of Canadian crooks' slang is readily discernible in some eight hundred double-columned pages. To date the main repositories of this specialized language have been the daily newspapers. Thus, the Toronto *Telegram* has compiled a word list of Canadian prison slang, a clearly defined branch of thieves' cant, based on the latter with the addition of some distinctive terms of its own.[3] But the *Telegram's* list is largely made up of American borrowings: *benny*, a coat; *fuzz*, the police; *paper-hanger*, a bad cheque artist; *score*, a robbery; with an assist

[1] "The Argot of the Underworld," *American Speech*, December, 1931, pp. 99–118.
[2] *The Story of English*, Philadelphia, 1952, p. 184. Partridge gives two parallel terms: *soup man*, a safe-blower, and *bluebird*, a police officer in uniform.
[3] Wesseley Hicks, "Talk With a Twist," Toronto *Telegram*, March 13, 1958.

H*

here and there from English rhyming slang: *fleas and ants*, pants; *ones and twos*, shoes; *oscar hocks*, socks; and *twist and twirl*, a girl. As in most areas of Canadian speech, a great deal of research here remains to be done.

The slang of young Canadians is also largely unexplored and unrecorded, although one highly specialized area has received some attention. In 1969, the Addiction Research Foundation published a study of the inhabitants of Yorkville in the City of Toronto,[1] an area comparable to the larger Haight-Ashbury district of San Francisco. The group studied was essentially a youthful, even an adolescent one: the hippies ranged in age from 16 to 22, while other sub-groups, such as the motorcyclists, were somewhat older. The goals of most Villagers boiled down to a general "doing their own thing," which, in the words of the authors, "usually means investigating various drug effects, contemplating eastern religions and engaging in frequent sexual exploits."

A glossary of 188 "Yorkville terms" compiled by the same researchers reflected this analysis to some extent. Thus, the largest group of 99 terms was concerned with drugs and drug-related experiences. The terms for L.S.D. were many: *acid, blue babies, brown acid, orange wafers, pink ozzy, pink wafers, purple ozzy, purple wedge* and *white lightning*. These conform to the general run of North American drug lingo, as did other Yorkville terms for narcotics: thus, marijuana may be called *pot, grass* or *Mary Jane*, and a *joint* is a cigarette (the butt being a *roach*), while heroin is variously *H, smack* or *schmeck*, and hashish is commonly *hash*. A number of terms described the mode of administering narcotics: to take a drug is to *do*, or to *do up* if the drug is psychedelic. The use of *drop* (to take orally) and *mainline* (to inject in a vein) would be understood almost anywhere in North America.

No Yorkville terms were strictly referable to the second goal of "contemplating eastern religions," although the next largest group of expressions related to what can be called mental states: to

---

[1] By its full title, *The Yorkville Subculture: A Study of the Life Styles and Interaction of Hippies and Non-Hippies*, Toronto, 1969. The study was prepared by Reginald G. Smart and David Jackson from the field notes of Gopala Alampur.

blow one's mind ("to break with one's personal reality"); to *groove* ("to be lost in pleasant thoughts"); to be *nowhere* ("to be completely lost to reality"); to *put through changes* ("to alter another person's perspective; to 'blow his mind' "); to *wig out* ("to have a psychotic experience"). Other expressions describe the result of such processes, progressing from *high* ("a pleasant exhilarated mood") through *scattered* ("driven out of one's mind, distracted") and *wiped out* ("a strong high") to the finality of *zonked* ("unconscious").

Sexual terms constituted about 6 per cent of the glossary, most of them drawn from the general bag of somewhat dated North American slang: to *shack up* ("to live with a girlfriend or boyfriend"); to *ball* ("to have sexual intercourse"); *butch* ("a lesbian who plays the male role") and *gear-box* ("a homosexual male"). Nor were police terms either new or confined to the Yorkville context: *busted* ("caught by the law") and the many words to describe a policeman: *cop, fuzz, man, speeds and narcs* ("officer in the Narcotics Department of the police"). Some originality appeared in *horsemen,* the R.C.M.P.

Yorkville slang thus partakes of the characteristics of Canadian slang in general: its idiom is largely American, and much of it is far from new. For example, *snow* as a term for cocaine is dated back to about 1920 by Partridge[1] and *coke* to about 1910. Other Yorkville expressions go back to the nineteenth century: *mark,* a gullible person; *dope,* a generic term for any drug (1889); to *put on* in the sense of to mislead, from *put-on,* a deception (about 1860); a *cop* (1859) derived from *copper* (about 1850), i.e., one who "cops" or arrests.[2] Other Yorkville terms were even older: *nest,* to signify "the female genitalia" is traced by Partridge to the eighteenth century, while *clap* for gonorrhea is as old as 1587 according to the *S.O.E.D.* which calls the term "now vulgar" and qualifies its dating with the notation "[?]". Partridge is no more precise as to the date of first use, but appends as an example which can only be called respectable a line from Samuel Johnson's satirical poem *London:*

---

[1] *A Dictionary of Slang and Unconventional English,* 1951, from which the dates of the following terms are taken.

[2] To *cop* in the sense of to catch or capture is traced by the *S.O.E.D.* to 1704.

> They sing, they dance, clean shoes,
> or cure a clap.

Given the dearth of Canadian English studies, one should not be surprised to find that Canadian slang has shared in the general neglect.[1] The fact seems to be, however, that Canada has made a small but genuine contribution to this field of linguistics and one looks forward to a more scientific investigation of the subject than has hitherto been attempted.

---

[1] For a brief introduction to cursing and swearing in English Canada see the author's *Speaking Canadian French*, Toronto, 1967, pp. 60–62.

CHAPTER NINE

THE FUTURE OF CANADIAN ENGLISH

— But do you know what a nation means? says John Wyse.
— Yes, says Bloom.
— What is it? says John Wyse.
*— A nation? says Bloom. A nation is the same people living in
the same place.*
*— By God, then, says Ned laughing, if that's so I'm a nation
for I'm living in the same place for the past five years.*
*So of course everyone had a laugh at Bloom and says he, trying
to muck out of it:*
— Or also living in different places.
— That covers my case, says Joe.

JAMES JOYCE

THE FUTURE OF CANADIAN ENGLISH

IF THE FUTURE OF THE ENGLISH LANGUAGE SEEMS TODAY LESS assured than it did in, say, 1900 when the British Empire was at its apogee, English nevertheless remains the most widely diffused of the languages of mankind, past or present. It is spoken as a native tongue by about 150,000,000 Americans, 55,000,000 inhabitants of the British Isles including Eire, more than 10,000,000 Canadians, and about 30,000,000 citizens of the other Commonwealth countries and colonies. In addition, English is spoken as a second or auxiliary language by from 50,000,000 to 125,000,000 people, making a grand total of perhaps 300 or 325 million English speakers or about one-seventh of the population of the globe. Numerically these figures are surpassed only by Chinese and the Indic languages, but since each of these is divided into a number of mutually unintelligible dialects it is customary to consider them as groups of languages; and in any case, neither can equal the geographical distribution of English. Even Russian, despite its greatly enhanced importance in the past generation, is probably spoken by no more than 170,000,000 citizens of the U.S.S.R., and by relatively few people outside the Soviet Union in their daily lives. English, on the other hand, may be heard around the globe; more people speak English than Russian, German, French and Italian combined, and it seems probable that English will continue to hold this dominant position, and even expand through-out the world at a greater rate than any other language.

The dialects of English are many and varied, most of them being readily intelligible to other English speakers. Great Britain alone accounts for some forty-odd dialects, including the English of Scotland, which in many ways has closer affinities with spoken Canadian than Received Standard English, although the Scots pronunciation of words like *book, cute* and *cat* clearly sets it apart from Canadian. Each of the Dominions speaks its distinctive variety of English, as do most of the colonies, but overshadowing all of them is the American dialect of English, which, although it may lack the prestige of Received Standard, began long ago to overtake its influence. "When I first became interested in the subject," Mencken observed in his preface to the fourth edition of *The American Language* (1936) "and began writing about it (in the Baltimore *Evening Sun* in 1910), the American form of the English language was plainly departing from the parent stem, and it seemed at least likely that the differences between American and English would go on increasing. That is what I argued in my first three editions. But since 1923 the pull of American has become so powerful that it has begun to drag English with it, and in con-sequence some of the differences once visible have tended to disappear . . . . But the Englishman, of late, has yielded so much to American example, in vocabulary, in idiom, in spelling and even in pronunciation, that what he speaks promises to become, on some not too remote tomorrow, a kind of dialect of American, just as the language spoken by the American was once a dialect of English."

If, making due allowance for Mencken's hyperbole, something of the sort has been going on for the past forty years between England and America, separated as they are by the detergent waters of the Atlantic Ocean, one should not be surprised to find that a similar development in more acute form has taken place between Canada and the United States, which have never had more than an imaginary line to keep them apart. From the very beginning, there had been an intimate mingling of peoples from both sides of what was not until 1828 finally defined as the international boundary.[1] Long before the Revolutionary War, however, or the fall of Quebec, New Englanders had colonized much of Nova Scotia, and a steady influx of population from the south has continued ever since, two of the most significant groups being, as we have seen, the Loyalists in the eighteenth century and the Americans who helped settle the Canadian west in the nineteenth. Much that is American about Canadian speech can doubtless be attributed to this source, although it is not always easy to distinguish the area of its influence.

Of even greater importance and obscuring what might be called the ethnic penetration is the cultural dependence of Canada on the United States. Although always resented and resisted, this has for a hundred years and more been instrumental in introducing contemporary American idiom into Canadian English. As long ago as 1902, a writer in the *Saturday Review* of London was complaining that all cabled news printed in Canadian journals passed through American channels and, to quote a member of the House of Commons, got "considerably muddier in the process." [2] Muddy or not, the influence of American films, magazines and books, and latterly radio and television, has quite overwhelmed Canadian English, and as M. W. Bloomfield puts it, not perhaps without some irony, "has kept Canadian English 'up-to-date.' " [3]

Linguistically Canada had a confused and difficult upbringing. The early British and American settlers filled the towns and clearings with their dialects, ruling out all possibility of a standard speech for many generations. With little native literature and less self-assertiveness, Canadians were slow to develop or recognize that theirs was in any way a distinctive speech. When the dust of the contending dialects had begun to settle, say by the close of the nineteenth century, it appeared that what was being spoken across

---

[1] For a general account of this osmotic process, see J. B. Brebner and M. L. Hanson, *The Mingling of the Canadian and American Peoples*, New Haven, 1940.

[2] "Canada and the Americanizing of News," *Saturday Review of Politics, Literature, Science and Art*, London, January, 1902, pp. 39–40. It is true that Canadian news associations have existed in one form or another since 1907, but their idiom is for the most part indistinguishable from that of the American press.

[3] "Canadian English and Its Relation to 18th Century American Speech," *Journal of English and Germanic Philology*, 1948, pp. 59–67.

230 SPEAKING CANADIAN ENGLISH

the land was very akin to the American dialect of English. To many of the early observers what was not British about Canadian English was American, and this view is still widely held, although the existence of "a distinctive Canadian speech and tone throughout the Dominion" has long been admitted.[1] More recently one school of Canadian linguists has been bent on furthering the latter belief. Thus M. H. Scargill insists with some heat that Canadians do speak Canadian. Who, he asks rhetorically, discovered *insulin* and named it from the Latin;[2] who named the *splake*—and what do Americans and British know of *Clear Grits*, *Digby chickens*, *Socreds*, *Land of the Little Sticks*, *separate schools*, *nitchies* and *Manitoba waves*?

A similar view has been put forward by F. E. L. Priestley writing in *British and American English Since 1900*.[3] Setting out to establish that "Canadian speech has tended to preserve a national identity," Priestley sees the enormous American influence on our speech habits as being kept in check "by growing national self-confidence in Canada." In his view, "the industrial power and the importance in world trade achieved by Canada in the last quarter of a century have given Canadians a calm conviction that they need be neither English nor American, but Canadian. This conviction acts as a persistent and effective limit to that wholesale imitation of American modes of thought and speech which one might expect or fear." His general conclusion is that "the half-century has . . . brought about the emergence of a distinct Canadian national character, and a distinct Canadian language," and he cites the Canadian Broadcasting Corporation as both an illustration of and a model for what he has in mind. In Priestley's opinion, "The maturing of the C.B.C. drama and of C.B.C. commentaries has brought with it some tendency to establish a national standard of speech; and anyone wishing to know what Canadian English is like when purged of individual peculiarities and accidentals would be well advised to listen to the best C.B.C. announcers and to

---

[1] Sir Robert Falconer, *The United States As a Neighbour*, Cambridge, 1925, p. 203.

[2] In fact, the nominator of *insulin* was neither Sir Frederic Banting (who called it *isletin*) nor a Canadian.

[3] Eric Partridge and John W. Clarke, eds., London, 1951.

C.B.C. drama. These offer something which is not a copy of British English, nor yet of American English."

Yet one may seriously question whether CBC English does in fact foreshadow the Canadian language of the future, or whether it is little more than an artificial standard imposed neither consistently nor successfully on a largely impervious public. Although CBC English is a controlled speech, governed by official edict, its effect on Canadian English at large seems slight. We have noted that the CBC habit of pronouncing *schedule* as "shed-yule," *à l'anglaise*, has been imitated by some Ontario speakers, although exactly twice as many of the speakers tested preferred the American "sked-yule;" [1] and despite a conscious effort by the CBC to replace some of the bad old speechways by a more hygienic standard, recent samplings do not indicate any very widespread response. Moreover, Priestley's choice of CBC English as the Canadian standard will seem something less than felicitous to many native sons whose sensibilities are periodically inflamed by the number of genuine and spurious English accents to be heard over the Canadian airwaves.

It is true that Priestley's thesis, confirmed by Eric Partridge in the same work, has at least the merit of plumping for a distinctive Canadian speech which, the authors predict, will become increasingly Canadian with our continually growing population and greater economic self-sufficiency. But unfortunately this view, however flattering it may be to the national ego, is not supported by any adequate evidence, and none is forthcoming elsewhere.[2] Canadians may well have "a calm conviction that they need be neither English nor American," but language is the product of social, ethnic and historical factors, and it is only in the light of these that any valid appraisal of Canadian English can be attempted. Part of the difficulty lies in the conflicting claims made on behalf of British and American English respectively to be the only lawful progenitor of Canadian English. Throughout Canada's

[1] W. S. Avis, "Speech Differences Along the Ontario-United States Border: III, Pronunciation," *J.C.L.A.*, 1956, pp. 53–54.

[2] The same theme has been developed by W. S. Avis in "Canadian English Merits a Dictionary," *Culture*, 1957, pp. 245–256, and is repeated by Raven I. McDavid, Jr., in his abridgement of *The American Language*, New York, 1963, p. 470.

history a great many Canadians have always felt closer in sentiment and outlook to England than to the United States, and as a corollary there has been a long-standing antipathy towards the United States going back to the invasions of 1776 and 1812–1814, and the early fears of annexation which were not finally laid to rest until Lincoln's presidency. These feelings have inevitably found their reflection in the English language spoken in Canada and in the attitudes of the Canadian people towards that language.

Yet it remains very much to be seen whether, at this stage of the game, the CBC or any artificial standard can successfully prevail against the steadily growing approximation to American English. Although many Canadians still regard American speech with dislike or even contempt, and the schoolmarm has waged unceasing warfare against it, except for pockets of resistance in such relatively inaccessible terrain as Newfoundland and the Ottawa Valley, American English has penetrated to every corner of the country. Samplings demonstrate clearly the predominance in both southern Ontario and Montreal of a speech much resembling General American, albeit with "enough unusual linguistic features to prevent it being classed as purely Northern American." [1]

Nor is this similarity to American English to be explained on historical grounds only, for the process is a continuing and, in all probability, an accelerating one. In Alberta, Scargill found that of some six hundred English speakers tested, almost two-thirds had a pronunciation which was predominantly American, the remainder using a "free" pronunciation, i.e., British or American, with neither showing any particular predominance, a trend which follows the southern Ontario and Montreal pattern. [2] "It seems likely," he concluded, "that a full survey of the speech of these same Albertans ten or twenty years from now will show the disappearance of 'free' pronunciation and the establishment of a predominantly American pronunciation throughout the province."

[1] Walter S. Avis, "Speech Differences Along the Ontario-United States Border," *J.C.L.A.*, October, 1954, pp. 13-17; March, 1955, pp. 14-19; October, 1956, pp. 41-59. D. E. Hamilton, "Notes on Montreal English," *J.C.L.A.*, Fall, 1958, pp. 70–79.
[2] "Canadian English and Canadian Culture in Alberta," *J.C.L.A.*, March, 1955, pp. 26–29.

If the determinism of this outlook seems bleak and unpromising, there are many who would agree that it is historically as well as statistically valid. And yet the stubborn fact remains that Canadian English is *not* the same as General American, and one may seriously question whether it ever will be. For despite the ever-growing influence of the United States, this country has somehow managed to maintain a separate identity, and the hope is perhaps not vain that she will continue to do so. It speaks well for her people that Canada could have passed her entire history in the shadow of a great nation without being eclipsed. And this is seen to be even more of an achievement given the quality of unconcern which, at the beginning of this study, we noted that most English-speaking Canadians have habitually displayed towards their own language. With the renewed flowering of Canadian letters in the last twenty-five years, one may perhaps see this indifference give way to a greater awareness of the origins of Canadian English and its resources, to which the printed word has yet to do justice. For it is a speech which still has as much power to charm the ear of an appreciative listener as when, on the eve of the first world war, it moved Rupert Brooke to note in his travel diaries that "what Ottawa leaves in the mind is . . . the rather lovely sound of the soft Canadian accent in the streets." [1]

---

[1] *Letters from America*, London, 1917, p. 57.

LIST OF WORDS AND PHRASES

discust, 150
Disraeli, 188
distil, 147
distill, 147
district attorney, 86
dived, 153
divide, 33
division, 81
dly, 108
do, to, 222
Dobrovodu, 178
docile, 117, 124, 134
dock, n., 24
doctrinal, 124
dodtrel, 96
dogs, 85
dolve, 24
dominion, 81
Dominion, 161, 161n
Dominion of Canada, The, 161
Don, 169
donated, 10
donation, 10
donation-meeting, 10
dooey, 215
dope, 223
Dorchester County, 166
Dorchester Crossing, 166
Dorchester Port, 166
Dorchester Station, 166
Dorchester Street, 166
Dorchester, Town of, 166
Dorchester Township, 166
dosh, 216
dotterel, 96
Douai, 169
Doukhobor, 66
dour, 15
Douro, 169
do up, to, 222
dout, 96
dove, 153
Dovercourt, 187
down periscope, to, 215
down town, 23
doxey, 102
do you have, 155, 156
do you have any matches, 155

draft, 102
drains, 71
drake, 67
drama, 132
drank, 153, 154, 154n
draw, 33
draw (a load), 77
Dresden, 169
dresh, 96
dressing gown, 74, 75
drieth, 102
drily, 148
dripping, 32
drive (of logs), 25
driveadh, 94
driver, 79n
droke, 33, 96
drop, to, 222
drought, 136
drouth, 136
drug-store, 72, 79
Drumheller, 183
Drumhellerite, 184
drung, 96
drunk, 154, 154n
drunk, has, 154
dry diet, 100
dry farming, 33
dry-goods, 24
dry-goods clerk, 24
dryly, 148
Dubuque, 177
duckish, 98
dude ranch, 66
due, 137
due to, 154
Dufferin, 167
duff gen, 215
duke, 117, 137
Duluth, Winnipeg and Pacific, 196
Dumfries, 169
dummy, 105
dunch, 98
duplex, v., 67
Durham boat, 69
dust-bin, 71
dust-cart, 71
duster, 33
dustman, 71
duty, 117
dwoll, 96
dwy, 98
dynamo, 80

do you have the time, 155
dynasty, 122

ean, 102
ease, 127, 127n
East Coast, the, 186
Eastern Townships, 66
economic, 122
Ecossais Sauvages, les, 193
editorial, 70, 80
Edmontonian, 184
Edward, 188
Edwardsburg, 167
eelworm, 31
Effingham, 166
Efisga, 159
ego, 133
egotism, 133
eh?, 77
either, 117, 128, 129
elastic band, 77
Eldon, 167
electoral district, 81
Electric City, the, 183
elevator, 44, 66
Elizabeth, 188
Elizabethtown, 167
Elmira, 169
Embarras, 177
empt, 102
Empty Basket, 179
end of steel, 68
endorsation, 67
engine driver, 80
engineer, 80
English rugby, 220
English rugger, 220
Enniskillen, 169
envelope, 122
Epagwit, 173
epinette, 69
epoch, 133
erect, 139
Erie, 171
Erin, 169
erk, 215
Ernestown, 167
escrod, 98
esker, 33
Eskimo, 92
Espanola, 169
Espinosa, 176

J

panelled, 147
paper-hanger, 221
paradise apple, 105
parcel, 71
parceling, 147
parcelling, 147
pard, 216, 217
pariah, 124
Paris, 169
parka, 93
parliament, 81
parlor, 75
parlour-car, 79
parry, 134
partridge, 198
party, 215
pass, 130
passage, 75
Passamaquoddy, 170
Passiooks, 108
past, 131
pasture, 32
patent, 117, 124
path, 130, 131
Paticake Brook, 179
patio, 141
patriot, 124
patriotes, 84
pavement, 66, 75
paw, 140
P.C., 83
Peabiddy bird, 200
Peabody bird, 200
peace, order and good
  government, 81
Pearl Button, 191
pea-shooter, 217
pea-soup, 192
pea-souper, 192
pecan, 88
pedal, 128
peddle, 98
peddler, 147
pedlar, 147
peh-pah, 108
P.E.I., 186
P.E.I. potatoes, 186
pekan, 88
pékané, 88
pelm, 97
pembina, 88
pembina buggy, 88
pembina cart, 88
pemican, 197

pemmican, 7, 66, 68,
  197
pemmi-kon, 197
Penetang, 176
Penetanguishene, 171,
  176
People of the North,
  16n
perambulator, 44
perm, 74n
permanent, 74n
permanent way, 80
Perry, 134
Perth, 169
perticular, 56
Peshkiv, 178
petal, 128
Peterboors, 195
Peterborough, 182, 183
petrol, 66, 70, 80
Petrolia, 178
petrol pump, 80
pharisee, 85
pharty, 94
pickerel, 73, 74
Picket-wire River, 177
Pictonian, 185
piddle, 98
Piebiter Creek, 176
piggery, 32
piggin, 101
pig-pen, 32
pig-stable, 32
Pig Street, 187
pigsty, 32
pike, 73, 74
pike-pole, 25
pilberry, 197
pill, 216
pills, 214
pimican, 197
pimmacon, 197
pimmecan, 197
pimmeecon, 197
pimmegan, 7, 197
pimmicum, 197
pine knot, 198
pink ozzy, 222
pink wafers, 222
Pipestone River, 174
pitcher, 71
Pittsburg of Canada,
  182n
piu-piu, 108

placate, 24, 123n
placer, 66
Plains City, the, 182
plains provisions, 67
platelayers, 80
plawmosh, 101
plebiscite, 122
plenary, 123n
plenty, 142
plough, 147
plow, 147
plumber, 215
plunkus, 203n
Plympton, 169
pocalogan, 33
podaydoes, 141
pogey, 69
poh, 108
Poison, 176
poisson blanc, 200
Pokesudie, 190
Poletica, 178
political union, 17
polonais, boire comme
  un, 193
Poltava, 178
pongo, 215
Pontiac, Pacific Junc-
  tion Railway, 196
poo, 108
pook, 96
pool, 127
pool train, 69
poorly, 15
poplar bluff, 33
popsy, 218
porch, 73, 77
Porcupine, 178
pore, 140
Porkopolis, 181
porridge, 15, 70, 71
Port, The, 183
Portage, 183
Portage la Prairie, 183
Portager, 185
Port Arthur, Duluth
  and Western, 196
Port Credit, 183
Port Dalhousie, 189
porterhouse, 72
Port Mouton, 189
Port Royal, 173

scrouge, 101
scrumpshy, 103
sculp, 99n
Seaforth, 169
sea goose, 199
seal, 126
season-ticket holders, 79
Seaway City, the, 183
Sebastopol, 170
SEC, 82
secretary, 129
sedan, 80
seesaw, 31
seigniory, 66, 68
Seine, 169
selective service, 218
Selkirk Cape, 167
Selkirk, Port, 167
semi-, 135
semis, 135
senate, 81
senator, 81
senile, 122, 133, 134
sense, 142
sensual, 140
sentaichan, 94
separate school, 67, 230
serenade, 31
serviette, 73, 76
session, 81
set the table, 32
setting hen, 32, 77
seudair, 94
sewerage, 71
sewer rat, 84
shack up, to, 223
shades, 70, 76, 77
shaganappi, 66
shaky do, 215
Shannoc River, 171
shan't, I, 153
shanty, 17
shark bait, 215
sharooshed, 100
Shattagee, 181
sheaf, 77
sheila, 213
shellwacky, 218
shem, 108
Sheniong, Lake, 172
Sheptetski, 178
Shickshock, 171
shimmel, 105

shimmick, 97
shin-plaster, 105
shivaree, 31
shock, 77
shoe, 73, 74
shone, 117
shoneen, 101
shop, 79
shoppe, 79
shore crap, 101
shores, 97
should, 8
shoulder, 80
Shubenacadie, 170
shunting, 80
shut, 108
Shyde, 192
sicheturms, 102
sick at the stomach, 153
sick in the stomach, 153
sick of the stomach, 153
sick to the stomach, 153
sidehill badger, 202n
sidehill bowger, 202n
sidehill dodger, 202, 202n
sidehill gouger, 202n
sidehill sauger, 202n
side kick, 216
side, putting on, 73
sidewalk, 24, 66, 75
Sidney and Louisburg, 196
siffleur, 198, 200
silencer, 70, 80
silk (corn), 77
sill, 126
Silver City, the, 182
silver thaw, 33, 98
Simcoe, 167
Simcoe, Lake, 172
simultaneous, 122
sin-bosun, 215
single ticket, 79
Sioux, 177
sirloin, 71
sirup, 151
siscowit, 201
sish, 100
sit, 202
sitting-room, 75
Siwash, 108
siwash duck, 198
siwash goose, 198

six foot of, 15
Skedaddle Ridge, 59
skedaddlers, 59
Skedaddlers' Reach, 59n
skiff, 99
skimmelton, 31
skookum, 89
skipper, the, 214
skirr, 102
Slave Harbour, 179
Slawa, 178
slay, n., 68
sled, 73
slee, 68
sleek, 134
sleepers, 80
sleigh, 68, 73
Slickman, 192
slide, 96
Slide-Out, 176
slip one's gallows, 98
slob, 33, 98
slops, 218
slough, 136
Slow and Lazy, 196
slurp, 104
smack, 222
Smack Cover, 177
Smackover, 177
Smalley, 192
smart, 25
smear cheese, 105
smelt storm, 33
smike, 17
Smith, 191
smoochin, 97
smoulder, 151
Snake's Bight, 179
snap, 220
snap-apple night, 98
snargasher, 215
snippit, 199
snotties, 214
snow, 223
snow apple, 69
snow shed, 33
soccer, 220
sockeye, 200, 201
sockeye salmon, 66
sock-suspenders, 72
Socred, 66, 69
Socreds, 228
sod, 127

Williamsburg, 167
willigiggin, 97
will you go with?, 104
Wilson, 142
Windigo, 203
wind-screen, 80
windshield, 80
Windsorite, 184
windy, 218, 218n
wine, 99
winey friend, my, 84
wing, 80
winninish, 201
Winnipeg, 174
Winnipeg couch, 19n
Winnipeger, 184, 184n
winter, 142
wintergreen, 197
Winterland, 179
wiped out, 223
wisketjan, 68
witch, 118
wiyaskimowok, 92
wolf, 197
won't, I, 153

Woodstock, 183
Woodstonian, 185
wootch, wootch,
  wootch, 104
woots, woots, woots,
  104
wop, 193
working a ticket, 217,
  218
worm, 31
worry, 116
worshiped, 147
would, 8
wowser, 213, 213n
wrench, 75
wristbands, 37
Wupping Willie, 218

yaffle, 97
yard, 73
Yarmolynci, 178
Yarmouth, 169
Yarmouthian, 184
yarry, 98
Yoho, 179

York, 167, 169, 172
York boat, 67, 69
York Harbour, 180
Youbel, 192
Youghall, 190
Young, 191
younker, 102
Your Honour, 86
Your Lordship, 86
Your Worship, 86
Y.T., 66, 187
Yuk., 187
Yukon, 170
Yukoner, 66
Yurick, 192

Zbaraz, 178
zebra, 133
zed, 73, 74
zee, 73
zizz, 215
zombie, 217
zonked, 223
Zorro, 177

BIBLIOGRAPHY

Ahrend, Evelyn R., "Ontario Speech," *American Speech*, 1934, pp. 136-139.

Alexander, Henry, "American English," *Queen's Quarterly*, 1937, pp. 169-175.

——————————, "The English Language in Canada," *Royal Commission Studies, A Selection of Essays Prepared for The Royal Commission on National Development in the Arts, Letters and Sciences*, Ottawa, 1951, pp. 13-24.

——————————, "Is there an American Language?" *Queen's Quarterly*, 1926, pp. 191-202.

——————————, "Is There a Canadian Language?" *CBC Times*, February 27, 1955, pp. 2-3.

——————————, "Linguistic Geography," *Queen's Quarterly*, 1940, pp. 38-47.

——————————, *The Story of Our Language*, Toronto, 1940.

Allen, Harold B., "Canadian American Speech Differences Along the Middle Border," *Journal of The Canadian Linguistic Association*, 1959, pp. 17-24.

Anon. "Canada," *Encyclopedia Canadiana*, Ottawa, 1957, Vol. 2, p. 182.

——————————, "Canada and The Americanizing of News," *Saturday Review of Politics, Literature, Science and Art*, London, January, 1902, pp. 39-40.

——————————, "Canada Gets Own Dictionary," *Toronto Daily Star*, December 21, 1959.

——————————, "Canuck or Kanuck," *Encyclopedia Canadiana*, Ottawa, 1957, Vol. 2, p. 230.

——————————, "C.B.C. Uses Two Dictionaries, Can't Go Wrong, Critics Told," *Toronto Daily Star*, January 13, 1949.

——————————, "Clear Grits," *Encyclopedia Canadiana*, Ottawa, 1957, Vol. 5, p. 44.

——————————, "Copycat Canadians" (G.H.M.), *Toronto Daily Star*, March 18, 1957.

——————————, "Flyers Use English Terms, Soldiers Say 'Baloney'," *Toronto Daily Star*, June 7, 1943.

——————————, "Folklore Animals," *Dialect Notes*, 1922, p. 188.

——————————, "Igopogo, Simcoe Monster Reported Sighted Again," *Globe and Mail*, July 1, 1963.

——————————, "Manitoba Monster Gets Official Stamp," *Globe and Mail*, August 6, 1960.

——————————, "Mr. Hoover and the Microphone," Ottawa *Journal*, August 13, 1932.

——————————, "Parliament Goes to Hollywood," Ottawa *Journal*, April 7, 1934.

——————————, "Say it in Canadian," *Toronto Daily Star*, February 9, 1957.

——————————, *The United States and Canada as Seen by Two Brothers in 1858 and 1861*, London, 1862.

Armstrong, G. H., *The Origin and Meaning of Place Names in Canada*, Toronto, 1930.

Avis, Walter S., *A Bibliography of Writings on Canadian English (1857-1965)*, Toronto, 1965.

——————————, "Canadian English Merits a Dictionary," *Culture*, 1959, pp. 245-256.

Avis, Walter, S., *"Darn* in *The Clockmaker,"* *American Speech*, 1951, pp. 302-303.
——————, "The Past Participle 'Drank' in Standard American Usage," *American Speech*, 1953, pp. 106-111.
——————, "Speech Differences Along the Ontario-United States Border, I: Vocabulary," *Journal of the Canadian Linguistic Association*, 1954, pp. 13-18.
——————, "Speech Differences Along the Ontario–United States Border, II: Grammar and Syntax," *Journal of the Canadian Linguistic Association*, 1955, pp. 14-19.
——————, "Speech Differences Along the Ontario–United States Border, III: Pronunciation," *Journal of The Canadian Linguistic Association*, 1956, pp. 41-59.
Ayearst, Morley, "A Note on Canadian Speech," *American Speech*, 1939, pp. 231-233.

Baker, Sidney J., *The Australian Language*, Sydney, 1945.
Baugh, Albert C., *A History of The English Language*, 1st ed., New York, 1935.
——————, *A History of The English Language*, 2nd ed., New York, 1957.
Beauchesne, Arthur, *Rules and Forms of The House of Commons of Canada with Annotations, Comments and Precedents: A Compendium of Canadian Parliamentary Practice for The Use of Members of Parliament*, 4th ed., Toronto, 1958.
Belliveau, J. E., "Do You Speak Good Canadian?" *Star Weekly*, July 20, 1957.
Bengtsson, Elna, *The Language and Vocabulary of Sam Slick*, Uppsala, 1956.
Berton, Pierre, "Explaining and Expanding Our Own Canadian Glossary," *Toronto Daily Star*, October 31, 1962, p. 37.
——————, "A Glossary of Distinctive Canadian Terms," *Toronto Daily Star*, October 23, 1962, p. 37.
Biegler, Zoe, "Meet Ogopogo," *Weekend Magazine*, August 2, 1952.
Bishop, Isabella (Bird), *The English Woman in America*, London, 1856.
Black, Mary J. L., "Fort William Streets," *Thunder Bay Historical Society*, *Annual Report*, 1924-1926, pp. 22-25.
Blish, Helen, Note in *American Speech*, 1930, p. 78.
Bloomfield, Morton W., "Canadian English and Its Relation to Eighteenth-Century American Speech," *Journal of English and Germanic Philology*, 1948, pp. 59-67.
Bourinot, J. G., "Canadian Historical Names," *The Canadian Monthly*, 1875, pp. 289-300.
——————, *The Intellectual Development of the Canadian People*, 1881.
——————, "The Ottawa Valley: Its History and Resources," *The Canadian Monthly*, 1875, pp. 41-55.
Boyer, David S., "British Columbia: Life Begins at 100," *National Geographic Magazine*, August, 1958, p. 153.
Bradley, A. G., *The United Empire Loyalists, Founders of British Canada*, London, 1932.
Brebner, J. B. and M. L. Hanson, *The Mingling of The Canadian and American Peoples*, New Haven, 1940.
Bremner, Benjamin, *Tales of Abegweit*, Charlottetown, 1936.
Bridges, Robert, *On English Homophones*, Oxford, 1919.
Bristed, Charles Astor, "The English Language in America," in *Cambridge Essays*, London, 1855.
Brooke, Rupert, *Letters from America*, London, 1917.
——————, *The Prose of Rupert Brooke*, ed. Christopher Hassall, London, 1956.
Brown, Harrison, *Admirals, Adventurers and Able Seamen*, Vancouver, 1956.

Buchanan, M. A., "Notes on Portuguese Place Names in North-Eastern America," in *Estudios Hispanicos Homenaje a Archer M. Huntingdon*, Wellesley, Mass., 1952, pp. 99-104.

Campbell, J. L., "Scottish Gaelic in Canada," Edinburgh *Scotsman*, January 30' 1933.

——————————, "Scottish Gaelic in Canada," *American Speech*, |1936, pp. 581-583.

Canada, *Decennial Census*, Ottawa, 1961.

Canadian Broadcasting Corporation, *A Guide to the Pronunciation of Canadian Place Names*, Toronto, 1959.

——————————, *Handbook for Announcers*, Toronto, 1946.

Canadian Conference on Education, *Some Arguments for and against Reformed English Spelling. A Report Prepared for The Canadian Conference on Education by a Committee Representing the Canadian Linguistic Association and The Association of Canadian University Teachers of English*, Kingston, 1962.

The Canadian Dictionary, Montreal, 1962.

Canfield, Mrs., E. J. *Street Names of Woodstock*, Woodstock, 1932.

Canniff, William, *History of the Early Settlement of Upper Canada*, 1869.

Carriere, J. M., "Indian and Creole *Barboka*, American *Barbecue*," *Language*, 1957, pp. 148-150.

Cartwright, George, *A Journal of Transactions and Events During a Residence of Nearly Sixteen Years on the Coast of Labrador*, Newark, 1792, ed. Charles Wendell Townsend, London, 1911.

Chamberlain, Alexander F., "Algonkian Words in American English," *Journal of American Folklore*, 1902, pp. 240-267.

——————————, "Dialect Research in Canada," *Dialect Notes*, 1890, pp. 45-56.

——————————, "Memorials of the Indians," *Journal of American Folklore*, 1902, pp. 107-116.

——————————, Note in *American Anthropologist*, 1901, Vol. III, p. 587.

Chambers, E. T. D., "The Philology of the Ouananiche: A Plea for the Recognition of Priority of Nomenclature," *Royal Society of Canada, Proceedings and Transactions*, 1896, 2nd Ser., Vol. 2, p. 131.

Clapin, Sylva, *A Dictionary of Americanisms*, New York, 1902.

Clark, John W., see Vallins, G. H.

Cowan, Helen I., *British Emigration to British North America; the First Hundred Years*, Toronto, 1961.

Craig, Gerald M., *Early Travellers in the Canadas, 1791-1867*, Toronto, 1955.

Craigie, Sir William, *The Study of English*, Society for Pure English, Tract No. XXVII, 1927, pp. 199-200.

Creighton, H., *Folklore of Lunenburg County*, Ottawa, 1950.

Crone, Kennedy, *British Spelling of English as the Canadian National Standard*, Montreal, N.D. [*c*. 1931].

Daviault, Pierre, "The Evolution of the English and French Languages in Canada," *Transactions of the Royal Society of Canada*, 1959, Ser. 3, pp. 63-72.

Davidson, Alexander, *The Canadian Spelling Book Intended as an Introduction to the English Language*, Toronto [*c*. 1840].

Day, Samuel Phillips, *English America, or Pictures of Canadian Places and People*, London, 1864.

Dean, Christopher, "Is There a Literary Canadian English," *American Speech*, 1963, pp. 278-282.

A Dictionary of American English, Chicago, 1944.

A Dictionary of Americanisms on Historical Principles, Chicago, 1956.

Dictionary of Canadian English Series:

————————, *The Beginning Dictionary*, Toronto, 1962.

————————, *The Intermediate Dictionary*, Toronto, 1963.

————————, *The Senior Dictionary*, Toronto, 1967.

A Dictionary of Canadianisms on Historical Principles, Toronto, 1967.

Doering, John Frederick and Eileen Elita Doering, "Some Western Ontario Folk Beliefs and Practices," *Journal of American Folklore*, 1938, pp. 60-68.

Douglass, William, *A Summary Historical and Political of The First Planting, Progressive Improvements and the Present State of the British Settlements in North America*, London, 1755.

Dowd, Eric, "What's in a Name?" *Globe and Mail*, January 22, 1960.

Duff, Louis Blake, *The Romance of Our Place Names*, Fort Erie, N.D. [1934].

Dulong, Gaston, *Bibliographie linguistique du Canada français*, Quebec, Paris, 1966.

————————, "Le mot sauvage en franco-canadien," *Journal of the Canadian Linguistic Association*, 1961, pp. 161-163.

Duncan, John M., *Travels Through Part of the United States and Canada in 1818 and 1819*, Glasgow, 1823.

Eames, Frank, *Gananoque: The Name and Its Origin*, Aouan Island, 1942.

Elliott, A. Marshall, "Origin of the Name 'Canada'," *Modern Language Notes*, 1888, pp. 327-345.

Emeneau, M. B., "The Dialect of Lunenburg, Nova Scotia," *Language*, 1935, pp. 140-147; 1940, pp. 214-215.

England, G. A., "Newfoundland Dialect Items," *Dialect Notes*, 1925, pp. 322-346.

Evans, Mary S., "Terms from the Labrador Coast," *American Speech*, 1930, pp. 56-58.

Falconer, Robert A., *The United States as a Neighbour*, Cambridge, 1925.

Fidler, Isaac, *Observations on Professions, Literature, Manners and Emigration in the United States and Canada made during a Residence There in 1832*, London, 1833.

The Fonetic Herald, Port Hope, Toronto, January, 1885–May, 1889.

Fowler, H. W., *A Dictionary of Modern English Usage*, Oxford, 1937; 2nd ed., revised by Sir Ernest Gowers, Oxford, 1965.

Fraser, Simon, *The Letters and Journal of Simon Fraser, 1806-1808*, Toronto, 1960.

Ganong, W. F., "The Identity of The Animals and Plants Mentioned by the Early Voyagers to Eastern Canada and Newfoundland," *Transactions of The Royal Society of Canada*, 1909, Ser. 2, pp. 197-242.

————————, "A Monograph of the Place-Nomenclature of the Province of New Brunswick," *Royal Society of Canada, Proceedings and Transactions*, 1896, Ser. 2, Vol. II, pp. 125-289.

Gardiner, Herbert F., *Nothing But Names*, Toronto, 1899.

Gardner, Ray, "Caddy, King of the Coast," *Maclean's Magazine*, June 15, 1950, p. 24.

Geddes, James, and Rivard, Adjutor, *Bibliographie du parler français au Canada*, Paris, Quebec, 1906.

Gickie, A. C., "Canadian English," *The Canadian Journal*, 1857, pp. 344-355.

Gill, J. K., *Dictionary of the Chinook Jargon*, Portland, Ore., 1909.

Godley, John Robert, *Letters from America*, London, 1844.

Goodchild, Fred H., *British Columbia, Its History, People and Industry*, London, 1951.

Graham, Robert Somerville, "The Anglicization of German Family Names in Western Canada," *American Speech*, 1955, pp. 260-264.

——————, "The Transition from German to English in the German Settlements of Saskatchewan," *Journal of the Canadian Linguistic Association*, 1957, pp. 9-13.

Greenleaf, Elizabeth B., "Newfoundland Words," *American Speech*, 1931, p. 306.

Gregg, R. J., "Notes on the Pronunciation of Canadian English as Spoken in Vancouver," *Journal of The Canadian Linguistic Association*, 1957, pp. 20-26.

Greig, J. Y. T., *Breaking Priscian's Head*, London, 1929.

Haliburton, Thomas C., *The Clockmaker, or Sayings and Doings of Samuel Slick of Slickville*, 1836.

——————, *The Old Judge; or Life in a Colony*, 1849.

Hamilton, Donald E., "Notes on Montreal English," *Journal of The Canadian Linguistic Association*, 1958, pp. 70-79.

Hamilton, Robert M., *Canadian Quotations and Phrases*, Toronto, 1952.

Hanley, M. N., "Serenade in New England," *American Speech*, April, 1933, pp. 24-26.

Hanson, M. L., "A Resume of The History of Canadian and American Population Relations," *Conference on Canadian-American Affairs*, Boston, 1937.

——————, see Brebner, J. B. and M. L. Hanson.

Haugen, Einar, "Bilingualism in the Americas," *26 Proceedings of the American Dialect Society*, November, 1956.

Hazlett, William Carew, *British Columbia and Vancouver Island*, London, 1858, pp. 241-243.

Hicks, Wesseley, "Talk with a Twist," Toronto *Telegram*, March 13, 1958.

Hill, George Wm., "Nomenclature of The Streets of Halifax," *Nova Scotia Historical Society, Collections*, 1911, Vol. 15, p. 3.

Hislop, Mary, *The Streets of Winnipeg*, Winnipeg, 1912.

Hodgins, J. G., *Documentary History of Education in Upper Canada*, Toronto, 1895, quoted in H. F. Angus, *Canada and Her Great Neighbour*, Toronto, 1938.

Hogg, F. D., "Words and Terms for Court Proceedings," *Globe and Mail*, December 7, 1957.

Horwill, H. W., *American Variations*, Society for Pure English, Tract No. XLV, 1936, p. 175.

——————, *A Dictionary of Modern American Usage*, Oxford, 1935.

Howison, John, *Sketches of Upper Canada, Domestic, Local and Characteristic*, London, 1821.

Hunt, Alison, "The West Coast's Abominable Treeman," *The Globe Magazine*, July 6, 1957.

Hutchinson, Bruce, *The Unknown Country*, New York, 1962.

Jackson, David, see Smart, Reginald J. and David Jackson.

Jacobs, Melville, "Notes on the Structure of Chinook Jargon," *Language*, 1932, pp. 27-50.

James, Henry, *A Question of Our Speech*, Boston, 1905.

Jameson, Anna, *Winter Studies and Summer Rambles in Canada*, 1839.

Johnson, George, "Place Names of Canada: The Carletons," *The Canadian Magazine*, 1898, pp. 287-295.

——————, "Place Names of Canada: Selkirk," *The Canadian Magazine*, 1899, pp. 295-406.

Jones, C. Meredith, "Indian and Pseudo-Indian Place Names in The Canadian West," Winnipeg, 1955 (*Onomastica*), No. 12.

Jones, Daniel, *English Pronouncing Dictionary*, 1924.

————, *The Phoneme, Its Nature and Use*, Cambridge, 1950.

Jones, Joseph, "Hail Fredonia!" *American Speech*, 1934, p. 12.

Joos, Martin, "A Phonological Dilemma in Canadian English," *Language*, 1942, pp. 141-144.

Keenleyside, H. L., "Place Names of Newfoundland," *Canadian Geographical Journal*, 1944, pp. 255-263.

Kennedy, A. G., *A Bibliography of Writings on the English Language (to 1922)*, Cambridge and New Haven, 1927.

————, *Current English*, Boston, 1935.

Kenyon, John S., "Some Notes on American R," *American Speech*, 1926, p. 333.

Kirkconnell, Watson, *Canadian Toponymy and the Cultural Stratification of Canada*, Winnipeg, 1954.

Kirwin, William, "Labrador, St. John's and Newfoundland: Some Pronunciations," *Journal of The Canadian Linguistic Association*, 1960, pp. 115-116.

Krapp, George Philip, *The English Language in America*, New York, 1925, 2 vols.

————, *The Pronunciation of Standard English in America*, New York, 1919.

Kurath, Hans, "New England Words for the Seesaw," *American Speech*, April 1933, pp. 14-18.

Lambert, Eloise and Mario Pei, *The Book of Place Names*, New York, 1959.

Lambert, John, *Travels Through Canada and the United States of America in the Years 1806, 1807 and 1808*, 3rd ed. London, 1816.

Lampman, Archibald, The Toronto *Globe*, February 27, 1892.

Langevin, H. L., *Report by the Hon. H. L. Langevin, C.B., Minister of Public Works*, Ottawa, 1872.

Langton, John, "On the Early Discoveries of the French in North America," *Canadian Journal* (N.S.), 1857, pp. 393-406.

Lardner, John, "Languages Here and There," *The New Yorker*, September 26, 1959, pp. 171-174.

Larsen, Thorlief and Francis C. Walker, *Pronunciation: A Practical Guide to Spoken English in Canada and the United States*, Toronto, Oxford, 1930.

Laundy, Philip, see Wilding, Norman W. and Philip Laundy.

Lawrence, D. H., *Pansies*, 1929.

Leechman, Douglas, "The Chinook Jargon," *American Speech*, 1926, pp. 531-534.

Lehmann, Heinz, *Zur Geschichte des Deutschtums in Kanada*, Vol. 1, Stuttgart, 1931, Vol. 2, Berlin, 1939.

Lighthall, W. D., "Canadian English," *The Week* (Toronto), August 16, 1889, pp. 581-583.

Lovell, Charles J., "A Sampling of Materials for a Dictionary of Canadian English Based on Historical Principles," *Journal of The Canadian Linguistic Association*, 1958, pp. 7-33.

————, "Whys and Hows of Collecting for the Dictionary nf Canadian English—I, Scope and Source Material," *Journal of the Canadiao Linguistic Association*, 1955, pp. 5-8.

Lower, A. R. M., *Canadians In the Making*, Toronto, 1958.

McAtee, W. L., "Facetious Monickers for American Birds," *American Speech*, 1959, pp. 180-187.

McAtee, W. L., "Folk Etymology in North American Bird Names," *American Speech*, 1951, pp. 90-95.

——————, *Folk Names of Canadian Birds*, Ottawa, 1958.

——————, " 'Stint' as a Bird Name," *American Speech*, 1956, p. 299.

McDavid, Raven I., Jr., "*H* before Semi-Vowels in the United States," *Language*, 1952, pp. 41-62.

——————, "Linguistic Geography in Canada: An Introduction," *Journal of The Canadian Linguistic Association*, October, 1964, pp. 3-8.

——————, "Midland and Canadian Words in Upstate New York," *American Speech*, 1951, pp. 248-256.

——————, "The Second Round in Dialectology of North American English," *Journal of The Canadian Linguistic Association*, 1960, pp. 108-115.

——————, "Shivaree: An Example of Cultural Diffusion," *American Speech*, 1949, pp. 49-55.

——————, "Why Do We Talk That Way?" *CBC Times*, February 11-17, 1951, pp. 2, 8.

McFall, William Alexander, *Relation of Wars of Europe to the Place Names of Ontario*, Toronto, N.D. [*c*. 1945].

McGee, Thomas D'Arcy, *Confederation Debates*, February 9, 1865.

McKnight, G. H., *English Words and Their Background*, New York, 1923.

McLay, W. S. W., "A Note on Canadian English," *American Speech*, 1930, pp. 328-329.

McLean, John, *The Indians, Their Manners and Customs*, Toronto, 1889.

MacDonagh, Michael, "Unparliamentary Language," *The Nineteenth Century*, 1935, pp. 359-366.

MacKendrick, John N., "Local History in The Street Names of Galt," *Waterloo Historical Society, Annual Report*, 1919, pp. 67-72.

MacLaren, D. H., "British Naval Officers of a Century Ago; Barrie and its Streets, A History of Their Names," *Ontario Historical Society, Papers and Records*, 1919, Vol. 17, pp. 106-112.

Marckwardt, Albert H., *American English*, 1958.

Marples, Morris, *University Slang*, London, 1950.

Massey, B. W. A., "Canadian Fish-Names in the *OED* and *DAE*," *Notes and Queries*, 1955, pp. 435-455; 1956, pp. 41-44, 125-130; 1957, pp. 79-83, 173-177, 203-208.

——————, "*OED* and *DAE*: Some Comparisons," *Notes and Queries*, 1954, pp. 127-129, 522-525.

Mathews, M. M., *The Beginnings of American English*, Chicago, 1931.

Maurer, David W., "The Argot of The Underworld," *American Speech*, December, 1931, pp. 99-118.

Mavor, William, *The English Spelling Book, Accompanied by a Progressive Series of Easy and Familiar Lessons; Intended as an Introduction to The Reading and Spelling of The English Language*, Kingston, 1831.

May, Sir Thomas, *A Treatise on the Law, Privileges, Proceedings and Usage of Parliament*, 15th ed., London, 1950.

Mencken, H. L., *The American Language*, 4th ed., New York, 1936.

——————, *The American Language, Supplement I*, New York, 1945.

——————, *The American Language, Supplement II*, New York, 1948.

——————, *The American Language*, abridged ed. by Raven I. McDavid, Jr., and David W. Maurer, New York, 1963.

——————, "Names of Americans," *American Speech*, 1947, p. 248.

——————, "Some Opprobrious Nicknames," *American Speech*, 1949, pp. 25-30.

Meredith, Mamie, "Language Mixture in American Place Names," *American Speech*, 1930, pp. 224-227.

——————————, "Notes on American Weather Terms," *American Speech*, 1931, p. 466.

Miffin, R. J., "Some French Place Names of Newfoundland," *American Speech*, 1956, pp. 79-80.

Moore, W. F., *Indian Place Names in the Province of Ontario*, Toronto, 1930.

Munroe, Helen C., "Montreal English," *American Speech*, 1929, p. 21.

——————————, " 'Raise' or 'Rise'?" *American Speech*, 1931, pp. 407-410.

Nicholson, Brian, "Pure B.B.C. Accent is Handicap Here, English Girl Finds," Toronto *Telegram*, July 22, 1953.

——————————, "Why It Hurts—To Have an English Accent," Toronto *Telegram*, July 23, 1953.

Nicholson, Margaret, *A Dictionary of American-English Usage, Based on Fowler's Modern English Usage*, Oxford, 1957.

Nicollet, Joseph, *Report Intended to Illustrate a Map of the Hydrographical Basin of the Upper Mississippi*, Washington, 1843.

O'Leary, Frank, *A Dictionary of American Underworld Lingo*, New York, 1951.

Orkin, Mark M., *Speaking Canadian French*, Toronto, 1967.

Palmer, H. E., J. V. Martin and F. G. Blandford, *Dictionary of English Pronunciation with American Variants*, Cambridge, 1926.

Partridge, Eric, *British and American English Since 1900*, London, 1951.

——————————, *A Dictionary of R.A.F. Slang*, London, 1945.

——————————, *A Dictionary of the Underworld, British and American*, London, 1950.

——————————, *Slang To-day and Yesterday*, London, 1933.

——————————, *Usage and Abusage*, 5th ed., London, 1957.

Patterson, George, "Notes on the Dialect of the People of Newfoundland," *Journal of American Folklore*, 1895, pp. 27-40; 1896, pp. 19-37; 1897, pp. 203-213. These contributions are summarized under the same title in *Proceedings and Transactions of the Nova Scotia Institute of Science, N.S.*, Vol. 2, 1894-1898, pp. 44-77.

Pei, Mario, *Language for Everybody*, New York, 1956.

——————————, *The Story of English*, Philadelphia, 1952.

——————————, see Lambert, Eloise and Mario Pei.

Phillips, Charles E. P., *The Development of Education in Canada*, Toronto, 1957.

Pilling, J. C., *A Bibliography of The Chinookan Languages*, Washington, 1893.

Poirier, Pascal, "Des vocables algonquines, caraïbes, etc., qui sont entrés dans la langue," *Transactions of The Royal Society of Canada*, 1916, Ser. 3, p. 339.

Porter, B. H., "A Newfoundland Vocabulary," *American Speech*, 1963, pp. 297-301.

Pound, Louise, "On the Pronunciation of 'Either' and 'Neither'," *American Speech*, 1932, pp. 371-376.

Priestley, F. E. L., "Canadian English," in *British and American English Since 1900*, ed. by Eric Partridge, London, 1951, pp. 72-79.

Read, Allen Walker, "British Recognition of American Speech in the Eighteenth Century," *Dialect Notes*, 1933, pp. 313-334.

Reed, T. A., "The Historic Value of Street Names," *Ontario Historical Society, Papers and Records*, 1929, Vol. 25, pp. 385-387.

Report of the Historiographer of The Education Department of The Province of Ontario for the Year 1908, "What We Owe to the United Empire Loyalists in the Matter of Education," Toronto, 1909.

Rivard, Adjutor, *Etudes sur les parlers de France au Canada,* Quebec, 1914.

Robertson, Stuart, *The Development of Modern English,* New York, 1954.

Ross, Alan S. C., "U and Non-U: An Essay in Sociological Linguistics," in *Noblesse Oblige,* ed. Nancy Mitford, London, 1956, p. 11-36.

Rudnyckyj, J. B., *Canadian Place Names of Ukrainian Origin,* Winnipeg, 1957.

Sandilands, John, *Western Canadian Dictionary and Phrase-Book,* Winnipeg, 1912.

Scaife, Walter Bell, *America's Geographical History,* 1492-1892, Baltimore, 1892.

Scargill, M. H., "Canadian English and Canadian Culture in Alberta, *Journal of the Canadian Linguistic Association,* 1955, pp. 26-29.

——————, "Canadians Speak Canadian," *Saturday Night,* December 8, 1956, pp. 16-18.

——————, "Eighteenth Century English in Nova Scotia," *Journal of The Canadian Linguistic Association,* 1956, p. 3.

——————, "The Growth of Canadian English," in *Literary History of Canada,* ed. by C. F. Klinck, Toronto, 1965, pp. 251-259.

——————, "A Pilot Study of Alberta Speech: Vocabulary," *Journal of The Canadian Linguistic Association,* October, 1954, pp. 21-22.

——————, "Sources of Canadian English," *Journal of English and Germanic Philology,* 1957, pp. 610-614.

Seary, E. R., "The French Element in Newfoundland Place Names," *Journal of The Canadian Linguistic Association,* 1958, pp. 63-69.

The Shorter Oxford English Dictionary, London, 1950.

Skelton, Isabel, "The Name 'Canada'," *The Canadian Magazine of Politics, Art and Literature,* 1921, pp. 312-314.

Smart, Reginald G., and David Jackson, *The Yorkville Subculture; A Study of the Life Styles and Interaction of Hippies and Non-Hippies,* The Addiction Research Foundation, Toronto, 1969.

Smith, George H., "The Street Names of Port Colborne," *Welland County Historical Society, Papers and Records,* 1938, Vol. 5, pp. 192-198.

Smith, Michael, *A Geographical View of The Province of Upper Canada, and Promiscuous Remarks Upon The Government,* 1813,

Stefansson, Vilhjalmur, *Hunters of The Great North,* New York, 1922.

Story, G. M., "Newfoundland English Usage," *Encyclopedia Canadiana,* Ottawa 1957, Vol. 7, pp. 321-322.

——————, "Research in the Language and Place Names of Newfoundland," *Journal of The Canadian Linguistic Association,* 1957, pp. 47-55.

Strong, William Duncan, "More Labrador Survivals," *American Speech,* 1931, pp. 290-291.

Tait, George, "Street and Place Names and Early Reminiscences of Bridgeburg," *Welland County Historical Society Publications,* 1927, Vol. 3, pp. 104-113.

Thomas, Edward Harper, "The Chinook Jargon," *American Speech,* 1927, pp. 377-384.

——————, *Chinook: A History and Dictionary,* Portland, Ore., 1935.

Thurber, James, "Is There a Loch Ness Monster?" *Holiday,* September, 1957.

Todd, Henry Cook, *Notes upon Canada and The United States from 1832 to 1840,* Toronto, 1840.

Tomkinson, Grace, "Shakespeare in Newfoundland," *Dalhousie Review,* 1940, pp. 60-70.

Trueblood, Thomas C. "Spoken English," *Quarterly Journal of Speech*, 1933, pp. 513-521.

Tweedie, W. M., New Brunswick, Nova Scotia, and Newfoundland," *Dialect Notes*, 1894, pp. 377-381.

Vallins, G. H., *Spelling*, London, 1954.

Velyhors'kyj, Ivan, *The Name and Term 'Canada'*, Winnipeg, 1955.

Walker, Francis C., see Larsen, Thorlief and Francis C. Walker.

Wallace, W. S., "Political History," *Encyclopedia Canadiana*, Ottawa, 1957, Vol. 8, p. 229.

——————, "United Empire Loyalists," *Encyclopedia Canadiana*, Ottawa, 1957, Vol. 10, pp. 184-185.

Webster, Noah, *An American Dictionary of the English Language*, 1828.

——————, *Dissertations on the English Language*, Boston, 1789.

Weld, Isaac, *Travels Through the States of America, and The Provinces of Upper and Lower Canada During the Years 1795, 1796 and 1797*, London, 1799.

White, James, "Place Names in Quebec," in *Ninth Report of the Geographical Board of Canada*, Ottawa, 1910, Part II.

——————, "Place Names in The Rocky Mountains between the 49th Parallel and The Athabasca River," *Proceedings and Transactions of The Royal Society of Canada*, 1916, Ser. 3, Vol. 10, pp. 501-535.

Wilding, Norman W. and Philip Laundy, *An Encyclopedia of Parliament*, London, 1958.

Willet, John, "Epitomized History of St. John, N.B.," *New Brunswick Historical Society, Collections*, 1927, Vol. 4, No. 11, pp. 143-205.

Wilson, Harold, " 'Crosshanded' and 'Sad'," *American Speech*, 1938, p. 236.

Winks, Robin W., *Canada and The United States: The Civil War Years*, Baltimore, 1960.

Wintemberg, W. J., "The Crimean War and Some Place Names of Canada," *Royal Society of Canada, Proceedings and Transactions*, 1927, Ser. 3, pp. 71-79.

——————, "Early Names of the Ottawa River," *Transactions of the Royal Society of Canada*, 1938, Ser. 3, Sect. 2, pp. 97-105.

——————, Note in *Journal of American Folklore*, 1903, p. 128.

Wyld, H. C., *The Best English*, Society for Pure English, Tract No. XXXIX, 1934.

——————, *A History of Modern Colloquial English*, London, 1921.

Young, Scott, "Slang Enriches Language," *Toronto Daily Star*, August 7, 1957.

INDEX

a, broad, 47; flat, 47
Acadian French, 14; expulsion of, 51, 55
Acadie, 51
Accent, American, 11; British, 57, 120; Ottawa, 231; Scottish, 57
Acthronyms, 192n
Addiction Research Foundation, 222
Agricultural terms, 32
Ahrend, Evelyn R., 25n, 27
Alampur, Gopala, 222n
Alberta, 32; fabulous beasts of, 203; settlement of, 58; speech, 125ff, 230
Alexander, Henry, 26, 29n, 31n, 32, 64n, 70, 94, 104, 115n, 116n, 130
Algonquin terms, 88ff
Allen, Harold B., 32n, 76, 118n, 133n, 138n, 155n
American Anthropologist, 198n
American English, 56; compared with British, 64ff, 71ff; compared with Canadian, 23, 25; expressions, 7ff, 9, 16, 23ff, 63ff; General, 26, 41, 45, 65, 115ff; in New England, 115; Standard, 115ff; study of, 18; vernacular, 69–70
American influence, 8ff, 44; on Canadian English, 125ff, 211; on news, 229
American Language, The, 7n, 18n, 26n, 27n, 30n, 31n, 36n, 37n, 72n, 73n, 78n, 92n, 93n, 100n, 107n, 109n, 140n, 154n, 155n, 159n, 177n, 180n, 191n, 195n, 198n, 199n, 200n, 212n, 218n, 221n
American newspapers, 9
American Revolution, Canada at time of, 50
Americans, settlement in Canada, 58
Angus, H. F., 9
Animals, calls of, 95, 104; names of, 69, 88ff, 197ff; of folklore, 202ff
Annexation, fears of, 232; linguistic, 24

Antigonish County, settlement of, 52
Armstrong, G. H., 170n, 171n, 173n
Australia, early settlers of, 55
Australian English, 18; accent, 55; slang, 213
Avis, W. S., 4, 18n, 26, 28, 31n, 36n, 42n, 50n, 58n, 69n, 74n, 75n, 118, 123, 123n, 127n, 131, 138n, 152n, 154n, 220n, 231n, 232n
Ayearst, Morley, 26, 100n, 212

Baker, Sidney J., 18n, 213n
Banting, Sir Frederick, 230n
Barrie street names, 188
Baugh, Albert C., 43, 44
Beauchesne, Arthur, 85
Beauharnois County, 15
Belliveau, J. E., 219n
Bengtsson, Elna, 36n
Bennett, J. A. W., 18n
Berton, Pierre, 69n
Bibliography of Canadian English, 4
Bibliography of Canadian French, 4
Biegler, Zoe, 206n
Birds, names of, 69, 198ff
Bishop, Isabella (Bird), 34
Black, Mary J. L., 188n
Blandford, Martin and Palmer, 25n, 130
Blish, Helen, 177n
Bloomfield, M. W., 5, 26, 45n, 47, 47n, 48, 49n, 57, 229
Bluenose, 13
Bourinot, J. G., 36n, 162n, 163n, 167n, 172n, 173n
Boyer, David S., 205n
Bradley, A. G., 49n, 51n, 54n, 55n
Brebner, J. B. and Hanson, M. L., 51n, 52n, 53, 55n, 59n, 229n
Bremner, Benjamin, 173n
Bridges, Robert, 114, 140n
Bristed, Charles Astor, 6n
British Columbia, 43n; early population of, 107; fabulous beasts of, 203; place names of, 176; speech, 132

Toronto *Globe and Mail*, 37n, 46n,
86n, 140n, 190n, 205, 205n, 206n,
207n
Toronto *Globe Magazine*, 203n
Toronto street names, 187
Toronto *Telegram*, 120n, 221, 221n
Tories, 49n
Trade language, 107n
Trade union terms, 80
Trading posts, early, 53
Tree names, 88ff
Trueblood, Thomas C., 55
Tweedie, W. M., 98

Ukrainian communities, 178
United Empire Loyalists, 48ff, 49,
49n
University of Victoria Lexicographical Centre, 19n

Vallins, G. H., 145, 146, 146n
Vancouver, nicknames for, 182n;
Province, 205n; speech, 126, 132,
134, 138, 141, 142
Velyhors'kyj, Ivan, 160n, 163
Vernacular, American, 69–70
Victoria, B. C., 43; *Times*, 204n
Vinay, Jean-Paul, 42
Vocabulary, 44; classification of, 65;
distinctive, 27

Wacousta, 36
Walker, Francis C. and Larsen,
Thorleif, 116n, 130, 135
Waterloo County, settlement of, 54
Weather terms, 33
Webster, Noah, 64, 65, 145
Weekend Magazine, 206n
Week, The (Toronto), 4n, 12n, 24n,
164n
Weld, Isaac, 54
Welland County, settlement of, 54
Western Canada, personal names of,
191; settlement of, 58; speech, 16,
30, 58
White, James, 174n
Whitman, Walt, 165, 165n
Wilding, Norman W. and Laundy,
Philip, 84
Willet, John, 187n
Wilson, Harold, 100n
Winks, Robin W., 59n
Winnipeg, street names, 188
Wintemberg, W. J., 170n, 173n, 194n
Wright, Philemon, 54
Wyld, H. C., 114, 130, 139

Yorkville, 222ff
Young, Scott, 218n